Fredrik Barth

Anthropology, Culture and Society

Series Editors:
Professor Vered Amit, Concordia University
and
Professor Christina Garsten, Stockholm University

Recent titles:

Fredrik Barth

An Intellectual Biography

Thomas Hylland Eriksen

PlutoPress
www.plutobooks.com

First published in Norwegian 2013.
First English language edition published 2015 by Pluto Press
345 Archway Road, London N6 5AA

www.plutobooks.com

Copyright © Universitetsforlaget 2013
English translation © Thomas Hylland Eriksen 2015

The right of Thomas Hylland Eriksen to be identified as the author of
this work has been asserted by him in accordance with the Copyright,
Designs and Patents Act 1988.

British Library Cataloguing in Publication Data
A catalogue record for this book is available from the British Library

ISBN   978 0 7453 3536 0   Hardback
ISBN   978 0 7453 3535 3   Paperback
ISBN   978 1 7837 1305 9   PDF eBook
ISBN   978 1 7837 1307 3   Kindle eBook
ISBN   978 1 7837 1306 6   EPUB eBook

10   9   8   7   6   5   4   3   2   1

Typeset by Stanford DTP Services, Northampton, England
Text design by Melanie Patrick
Simultaneously printed by CPI Antony Rowe, Chippenham, UK
and Edwards Bros in the United States of America

Contents

List of Illustrations

Series Preface

Anthropology is a discipline based upon in-depth ethnographic works that deal with wider theoretical issues in the context of particular, local conditions – to paraphrase an important volume from the series: *large issues* explored in *small places*. This series has a particular mission: to publish work that moves away from an old-style descriptive ethnography that is strongly area-studies oriented, and offer genuine theoretical arguments that are of interest to a much wider readership, but which are nevertheless located and grounded in solid ethnographic research. If anthropology is to argue itself a place in the contemporary intellectual world, then it must surely be through such research.

We start from the question: 'What can this ethnographic material tell us about the bigger theoretical issues that concern the social sciences?' rather than 'What can these theoretical ideas tell us about the ethnographic context?' Put this way round, such work becomes *about* large issues, *set in* a (relatively) small place, rather than detailed description of a small place for its own sake. As Clifford Geertz once said, 'Anthropologists don't study villages; they study *in* villages.'

By place, we mean not only geographical locale, but also other types of 'place' – within political, economic, religious or other social systems. We therefore publish work based on ethnography within political and religious movements, occupational or class groups, among youth, development agencies, and nationalist movements; but also work that is more thematically based – on kinship, landscape, the state, violence, corruption, the self. The series publishes four kinds of volume: ethnographic monographs; comparative texts; edited collections; and shorter, polemical essays.

We publish work from all traditions of anthropology, and all parts of the world, which combines theoretical debate with empirical evidence to demonstrate anthropology's unique position in contemporary scholarship and the contemporary world.

Professor Vered Amit
Professor Christina Garsten

Preface

I was meant to get to Iraq on my own. There, [Professor Robert] Braidwood would feed me and equip me with the gear I needed, as well as giving me a bit of money that I could use to continue doing fieldwork on my own. Braathens S.A.F.E. flew to Hong Kong once a week, and I thought that I might have a chance there. So I went to Mr Braathen and said, 'Would you have room for a young Norwegian researcher who is going out with an American expedition?' He said yes, he was keen on supporting Norwegian research, so he could give me a discount. He usually gave a 25 per cent reduction on the ticket – would that be sufficient? No, I had to confess that I hadn't even checked the price. So he told me and asked whether it would help. I had to admit that it did not help sufficiently – and he then gave me a fifty per cent discount. And sent me off.[1]

This is how Fredrik Barth recounts the prelude to his first remote fieldwork, in Iraqi Kurdistan in 1951. This fieldwork did not lead to a string of important publications, and would indeed nearly result in his early demise as an academic; but his early work in Kurdistan marked the beginning of a life's work which is remarkably original, comprehensive and consistent. That work is the subject of this book.

Even if you did not previously know who Barth was, you felt the aura when he entered the room. When he entered the rostrum in the 1980s, we saw a tall, slim man with sharp features, a grey moustache, a hairline which seemed to recede slightly every year, long fingers and an aristocratic bearing. He never raised his voice, and frequently indulged in humorous anecdotes from the field, accompanied by a boyish grin. The content of his lectures might seem simple and easy to comprehend, but we would later understand that this was because they were carefully structured and followed a strict logical development. A lecture with Barth gave the audience the feeling of being present at a special event.

This is not a conventional biography of the 'life and times' kind, where the life of the protagonist is described in minute detail, with sideways glances to the social network and the zeitgeist. Rather, this book should be read as intermediate between a long dialogue and a history of ideas. The main character is Fredrik Barth (b. 1928), one of the towering figures of twentieth-century social anthropology, but his achievements and ideas must inevitably be related to broader tendencies both in anthropology and more generally. The approach is biographical, historical and dialogical. I am not a disinterested observer in this respect, but participate in the intellectual world to which Barth has made such important contributions. Since I began to study social anthropology at the University of Oslo in 1982, Barth has been a constant presence as a discussion partner, mainly by means of intellectual shadow boxing, but occasionally these jousts have taken on a physical form as well. At the time, Barth was professor at the Ethnographic Museum in downtown Oslo, while we studied at the Department of Social Anthropology at the Blindern campus of the University of Oslo a couple of kilometres up the hill. His relationship to the department was fraught and complicated, but whenever the students asked if he would come and give a lecture, he obliged if he was able to. Barth never used a script, and rarely wrote on the blackboard; yet, his occasional lectures were among the most condensed and lucid we had experienced. Since I have myself later done research on ethnicity and nationalism, many foreign colleagues have, over the years, assumed that Barth had been my mentor and supervisor. This was not the case, as the above should make clear, but his charisma was still of such a magnitude that he tended to have a spiritual presence in the auditorium at Blindern, even if he was physically located eight stops away by tram.

Outside anthropology, Barth is scarcely known, and if at all, then chiefly through his 'Introduction' to the influential book *Ethnic Groups and Boundaries* (1969). He is something of the anthropologist's anthropologist, however, having done more fieldwork than most and adamant that the magic of anthropology springs from the minutiae of detailed, experience-near ethnography. My main intention in this book is to give a critical assessment of the significance of Barth's work in anthropology, and to discuss its broader significance for cultural self-reflection. In principle, anthropology, being a discipline which has human life as its subject matter, is of limited value unless it can shed light on our self-understanding as human beings.

In order to achieve this objective, it is nevertheless necessary to place Barth's intellectual itinerary in a wider context, and I intend to use his own method to account for his choices, positioning and priorities. In his research, Barth is primarily concerned to understand social processes as they are being instigated by people who do their best to make the most of their situation, given the constraints and opportunities offered by their environment. The broader intellectual world within which Barth's research often developed, whether organically or by dialectical negation, included theoretical tendencies such as structuralism, Marxism and system theory, as well as specialised anthropological contributions such as cultural materialism, structural-functionalism and cultural hermeneutics. Barth's consistent focus on actors and tangible social processes has, retrospectively, proved to be more robust than many of the intellectual fashions influencing social thought in the postwar period, but I shall eventually argue that there is a point, evident in Barth's own itinerary as a scholar, where the limitations of his methodology become apparent.

This book is no hagiography or uncritical celebration of an admired scholar. Rather, it is a critical examination of a unique and innovative thinker, and just as Barth's own texts have often been written with a polemical aim, I present his ideas without trying to conceal possible objections. This approach is fully in keeping with Barth's spirit. He never belonged to a particular school or nurtured a wish to produce loyal disciples himself; instead, he has tried to live in accordance with the naturalist Niko Tinbergen's maxim, 'watching and wondering', revising one's notions when proven mistaken.

During the work on this book, I have received much assistance from colleagues at home and abroad. The list of Barth's published work at the back of this book, produced by university librarians Astrid Anderson and Frøydis Haugane at the University of Oslo, reproduced with their permission and lightly edited, has been very helpful. I am also deeply grateful to Professor Edvard Hviding, University of Bergen, for allowing me to peruse and quote a large body of interview transcripts based on a series of conversations between Barth and Hviding in 1995. A remarkable gift, this act of generosity should serve as a reminder that reciprocity remains not only a fundamental category in social anthropology, but also in life itself. Moreover, I have benefited greatly from conversations with and comments from colleagues and other academics, and in this context I would like to mention in particular Michael Banton, Theo Barth (no relation), Jan Petter Blom, Ottar Brox, Nils Christie, Gunnar Haaland (spelt Håland in Norwegian), Gudmund Hernes, Richard Jenkins, Arne Martin Klausen, Adam Kuper, Iver B. Neumann, Gunnar Sørbø, Tian Sørhaug, Arve Sørum and Richard A. Wilson. Barth's youngest son Kim Wikan Barth went out of his way to tell me about a very unusual childhood and adolescence. I should like to thank Unni Wikan especially, for having encouraged and supported this project, and for having sharing her valuable comments and perspectives throughout the process of writing.

This book is a translated and revised version of the eponymous book published in Norwegian by Universitetsforlaget in 2013. I have tinkered a bit with it while translating, but it remains, essentially, the same book. I would, in this context, like to thank the series editors Christina Garsten and Vered Amit for their encouragement, Anne Beech at Pluto Press for continued support of my work, and a clutch of colleagues and reviewers in the press for providing valuable input and suggestions in the year between submission of the Norwegian manuscript and the completion of the English version.

I am also grateful to Unni Wikan and Fredrik Barth for graciously having allowed me to use photographs from their personal archives.

I am grateful to Fredrik Barth himself for his support and incisive comments, and for a series of good conversations from the period after he 'left home'. These meetings made me understand, belatedly, that the most important thing I have learnt from Barth, ever since I saw the TV series *Other People's Lives and Our Own* as a teenager in 1979, is that most of what we take for granted could have been different. That the cultural diversity of the world deserves to be explored without prejudice. And, last but not least, that there is no reason to believe that you stand to lose your own values by being interested in other people's.

Oslo, August 2014

Part 1

A Man of Action

1

Watching and Wandering

As so frequently in social anthropological description, our task is to find out what kind of things there are to know about this society, rather than to attempt a rigorous recording of answers to questions that are already in principle known to the investigator.[1]

The first Barth on Norwegian soil was a mining engineer from Saxony, brought to the then Danish province by the king to assist in the excavation of silver from the mines in Kongsberg. As Fredrik Barth expresses it, he came to the country as a development expert. One of his descendants, Thomas (Tom) Fredrik Weybye Barth (1899–1971), also saw value in rocks. He became a geologist, took his doctoral degree at the age of 27, and travelled to Germany on a scholarship in 1927. During his academic sojourn in Leipzig, his first and only son was born on 22 December 1928, four years after his sister Tone. In accordance with family tradition, the son was christened Thomas Fredrik Weybye Barth like his father, but – presumably to avoid confusion – the tradition also specified that every second male heir should be called Tom and Fredrik, respectively, on an everyday basis.

Fredrik Barth's mother Randi (née Thomassen, 1902–1980) had no academic career, but she had considerable artistic interests. Fredrik was very close to his mother. Throughout his life, he has spoken Norwegian with a mildly rolling 'r', which was at the time usually associated with having been brought up by a governess from the southern coast, but in Fredrik's case it came from a mother and maternal aunts from Kristiansand.

The family did not remain in Germany. Tom Barth soon obtained a new scholarship and later a position at the Carnegie Institution in Washington, and Fredrik was barely six months old when the family moved there, where they remained until he was seven and ready to start school. At the time, his parents wished to return to Norway, so when an academic job opportunity appeared in Oslo, they moved home. Tom Barth became professor of geology the following year. His career was broken off during the Second

*Fredrik
Barth,
universitets-
stipendiat.*

1.   Barth as research fellow, by Gösta Hammarlund (photo
     reproduced by permission of Gösta Hammarlund).

World War, when he took part in the resistance movement. After the
war, Tom Barth spent three years in Chicago as visiting professor, before
returning to the Mineralogical-Geological Museum in Oslo, where he
would remain as professor and head until his retirement in 1966.

Tom Barth was a charismatic man with considerable personal authority.
He was also known for his extreme self-discipline. Even on nights when
the family returned late from a party, he would often go to his study and
make corrections to a manuscript he was working on. He came across as
powerful rather than severe, and would have been a natural role model for
his son.

Fredrik Barth explains that the family at first rented a flat near
Holmenkollen in western Oslo, which was confiscated by the Luftwaffe in

April 1940. They were evicted on 20 April and moved to another location in western Oslo, where Fredrik spent his formative years.

In spite of its location in a famously egalitarian society, Oslo is deeply divided by class along an east–west axis. Fredrik Barth grew up, and would later live, in the leafy western parts of the city, in an area inhabited by educated and moderately wealthy people. Finishing primary school at Tåsen, his upper secondary school years were spent at Blindern, where the main university campus is now located. Barth seems to have enjoyed school; he excelled in all subjects and was generally 'outstanding', according to his old schoolmate, the renowned criminologist Nils Christie. Among other things, he was an unusually skilled draughtsman.

With the hindsight of more than half a century, Barth recalls the time of the occupation – he was 16 when it ended in 1945 – as a 'strangely good situation', where 'you could be on the side of the majority, on the one hand, and at the same time oppose the powers that be. A time when there was no temptation to join a protest group railing against society, since the excitement was in fighting for that which was legitimate!'

It nevertheless appears that Barth had a rebellious streak. Along with Christie and another schoolmate, Sven Knudsen, Barth founded an extra-curricular study group at his home and an anti-religious student association. In its very formal and ceremoniously signed budget, the latter organisation had an entry, estimated at the value of 3 kroner (a modest sum), described as 'Confirmation condolences'. The Lutheran confirmation was a rite of passage almost universally participated in by adolescent boys and girls at the time.

Among the most significant of Barth's experiences during the occupation were the periods when he was sent off to the country, to live with small farmers in Engerdal, in a remote part of southern Norway near the Swedish border. He helped with the collection of lichen and moss for cattle fodder, moving from summer pastures in the hills to autumn pastures in the lowlands. Rural life was still quite traditional, with few mechanical implements, and as a teenager Barth got a taste for it. Only a few years later, he would carry out a minor field study in the same area.

Towards the end of his school years, Barth also spent a short period as an apprentice with the sculptor Stinius Fredriksen, who taught him clay modelling. He remarks, not without a certain pride, that he has contributed the right shoe of Fredriksen's statue of the painter Lars Hertevig, still on public display in Stavanger. At the time, it was by no means obvious to Barth that he should commit his life to research, and he has retained a passion for art throughout his life, although this interest is scarcely discernable in his writings.

When, in 1946, Tom Barth was offered a chair at the University of Chicago, his son was given the option of joining him, and seized the opportunity. To use his own term, a change in his opportunity situation seemed to have been decisive for the early choice of the path his life would follow. Had Chicago not emerged as an option, Barth might conceivably have become a sculptor rather than a social anthropologist. However, unlike what might have been expected, given his family background, he did not opt for the natural sciences, but for human sciences with a major in anthropology.

Father and son left for the USA, almost as two bachelors, his mother opting to stay in Oslo. Fredrik's sister Tone married the chemist Terkel Rosenqvist in 1945, and the couple moved to Trondheim, where Rosenqvist got a post at the Norwegian Institute of Technology.[2] The University of Chicago was, then as now, among the finest academic institutions in the country. In the years following the Second World War, American universities were infused with a surplus of vitality, since a whole generation of GIs, who had been obliged to interrupt or postpone their studies in order to do military service, returned with state grants. Thus it came to pass that the young Barth entered into academic life as a precocious teenager, along with students who were years older than himself. In retrospect, he says that becoming an anthropology student at Chicago entailed 'the realization of my highest wish'.[3] Like many curious boys, he had been fascinated by zoology and evolution, and he had followed lectures by the palaeontologist Anatol Heinz on human origins, but shortly after the end of the war he discovered that it was possible to study cultural and social anthropology. This was partly the result of a brief meeting with the American anthropologist Conrad Arensberg, who was travelling through Oslo in May 1945, still in uniform.

Barth was not yet 18 when he began his studies, and by the time he turned 21 he had succeeded in finishing his Master's degree and marrying his fellow student Mary 'Molly' Allee (1926–1998), the daughter of zoology professor Warder Clyde Allee. There are good reasons to believe that Barth's father-in-law, who had devoted much of his career to research on group dynamics in animals, exerted a certain influence on Barth, who would soon go on to develop his own analytical strategies concerning humans in groups. The student from Norway must have made an impression on his teachers, since the archaeology professor Robert Braidwood hired him, in spite of his young age, as a field assistant on his planned expedition in Iraqi Kurdistan. Barth's plan was to remain in Kurdistan after the departure of the archaeologists, in order to do ethnographic fieldwork.

In the academically dominant countries, anthropology as a discipline grew rapidly in the years following the Second World War. The exception was Germany, where the discipline was in disarray. Many German anthropologists, among them a fair number of Jews, had succeeded in leaving the country in time, while others not only stayed on but compromised themselves by collaborating with the Nazis before and during the war. A number of senior German anthropologists were indeed themselves active Nazis and party members.[4] This is not entirely coincidental. There was no clearly established and universally recognised distinction between biological and cultural explanations in anthropology before the war, and there were many anthropologists, not least in Germany and Central Europe, who viewed cultural variation in relation to assumed racial differences. Besides, many anthropologists shared with the Nazi ideologists a concern about cultural mixing and its possible degenerative effects. The dominant anthropological concept of culture shared its origins with the concept of culture informing nationalist ideology, which developed into an extreme and racist vein by the Nazis. This concept of culture is often traced to the philosopher and theologian Johann Gottfried Herder (1744–1803), in his youth a radical thinker who emphasised that all peoples had their unique *Volksgeist*, or 'folk soul', associated with language, place and custom.[5] Nationalists and cultural relativists have for 200 years built on an understanding of culture rooted in Herder's ideas, emphasising outward boundaries and inward similarities. Transferred from the otherworldly serenity of academic discourse to the political domain, such a concept of culture can easily inspire fighters for purity and fervent border guards. The South African ideology of apartheid was largely developed in the interwar years by the German-born anthropologist Werner Eiselen, professor at the University of Stellenbosch.[6] One justification for the enforced 'apartness' (*apartheid*) of the peoples was that exaggerated contact would be harmful and weaken their vital force, sense of identity and social cohesion. According to this view, cultural mixing would make South Africans of various origins uprooted and alienated.

Several leading anthropologists in the German-speaking world were familiar with and sympathetic to such ideas, and in what has later been described as a major scandal,[7] several kept their academic positions after the war, although their international influence was by now zero. Moreover, none of these tendencies were taught to Barth. Racial explanations of cultural diversity were out of fashion in the USA when he came into the discipline.

In the remaining areas of global academic influence, the situation was very different from that in Germany. In France, a vibrant intellectual milieu had developed in the interwar years around the seminars conducted by Marcel Mauss (1872–1950), and many in Mauss's circle had field experiences outside Europe. Soon, Claude Lévi-Strauss (1908–2009) would set a new agenda for kinship studies with his new theory, structuralism, when he published his monumental comparative study of kinship, *Les structures élémentaires de la parenté* in 1949.[8] When Barth began his studies at Chicago, Lévi-Strauss, 18 years his senior, had just left the library of the New School of Social Research in New York, where he had been working on his big book. However, French anthropology would never be particularly influential on Barth, not even when structuralism became a major intellectual trend a couple of decades later.

British anthropology, meanwhile, positively flourished after the war, and was about to establish itself, for the time being, as theoretically dominant. While the rival founders of twentieth-century British social anthropology, Bronislaw Malinowski (1884–1942) and A.R. Radcliffe-Brown (1881–1955), were no longer physically present – Malinowski died in the USA during the war, and Radcliffe-Brown retired in 1946 – their students and successors formulated ambitious theoretical programmes, with the aim of turning social anthropology into a fully fledged science. The emphasis was frequently on kinship and politics in small-scale societies. Barth would soon begin to relate himself actively to this tradition, and is often – partly accurately – considered part of it. He was particularly attracted to the practical, tangible approach to social processes which was typical of the British School.

However, no other country came close to the USA as regards the number of anthropologists in the country and the sheer scope of the research they carried out. The discipline had a different history, and a rather different structure, in the USA than in Britain and France. In Europe, anthropology traced its roots to sociology and law (thus the label *social* anthropology). Especially in Great Britain, the main focus of the discipline was social structure, power and politics. American anthropology had a different history. The first American anthropologist of significance was Lewis Henry Morgan (1818–1881), who – among other things – carried out field studies among the Iroquois in the north-eastern forests near the Canadian border. Morgan was an unsentimental materialist and systematiser who developed theories about cultural evolution and technological change which would influence Marx's and Engels's late writings about pre-capitalist societies. However, Morgan's intellectual legacy had been dormant, gathering momentum and building compound interest, for almost a century before a group of young researchers finally reclaimed it in the 1950s, by proclaiming an interest in material culture and evolution. The explanation for this massively delayed reception of Morgan's evolutionist materialism can be summarised in one name: Franz Boas.

Boas (1858–1942) was German-born, Jewish and an immigrant, and presided over the anthropology department at Columbia University from 1899 until his death. His own field research took place primarily among Inuit and indigenous peoples on the US north-west coast, and he was the de facto leader of American anthropology for 40 years. He taught several generations of students, from Alfred Kroeber and Edward Sapir to Margaret Mead and Ruth Benedict, who would define mainstream American anthropology until decades into the postwar era, with repercussions that are acutely felt even today.

It is possible to argue that Boas created modern American anthropology as a German *Geisteswissenschaft* – human, or spiritual, science – in the tradition of Herder, Wilhelm von Humboldt and Wilhelm Dilthey, by contrast to the earthy and pragmatic materialism of a Morgan, who was a native Yankee. From Herder, Boas had inherited a concept of culture which could be used comparatively; the university model developed by Humboldt in the early decades of the nineteenth century emphasised general knowledge accompanied by personal development (*Bildung*) rather than exaggerated specialisation, and the philosopher Dilthey's theory of interpretation offered methodological cues as to how one could study the symbolic universes of other peoples. In the Boasian version, the study of symbols and their significance, that is *cultural* anthropology, became a central preoccupation for the discipline.

Boas is widely considered to be the originator of the cultural relativist method, according to which each culture should be understood on its own terms and not within a pre-ordained evolutionary scheme. However, he also insisted that anthropology had to be taught and learned in its full breadth, which meant in practice that it should encompass four fields, all of which had to be studied: physical anthropology (including human evolution), archaeology, anthropological linguistics and, finally, socio-cultural anthropology. The four-field approach is less influential today, but most American anthropology majors still have to take basic courses in human evolution and archaeology.

The department at Chicago where Barth enrolled as a student was based on the Boasian four-field model, but in other respects it was the least Boas-influenced unit among the leading departments in American anthropology. There are two immediate explanations for this anomaly. First, the University of Chicago had a lively and intellectually innovative department of sociology, where ethnographic field methods were actively used. Under the leadership of Robert Park, the Chicago sociologists had been producing pioneering work in the burgeoning area of research on ethnic relations ever since the end of the First World War; and they also developed new methodological devices for research into group relations in complex societies.[9] Interestingly enough, Barth – who would later have a huge influence on research on ethnicity – had no contact with this group during his studies. On the other hand, he did make the acquaintance of Erving Goffman (1922–1982). Goffman would in the ensuing years become a sociologist whose work on individual agency and role theory had a decisive influence on Barth's work in the 1960s, and who in turn admired Barth's deft analyses of social situations. At the time they were unlikely to have suspected that they would both carve out such illustrious careers.

In addition to the exuberance of the Chicago sociologists, Radcliffe-Brown also played a part in removing the department somewhat from the Boasian mainstream. Radcliffe-Brown, an adherent of Durkheim's sociology and widely considered the leading theorist in British social anthropology, had spent six years as professor of anthropology at Chicago from 1931 to 1937. Several of Barth's teachers had been students of Radcliffe-Brown, and they had learnt that the study of social relations and social structure was far more fundamental than the study of symbolic meaning.

The year 1946 was one full of promise. The world was slowly shaking off the dust, sweat and despair from six years of dreadful war, energetically building new palaces on the ruins of the old, determined to leave the sins of the past behind and enter the second half of the century with an optimism that can at least partly be attributed to the awareness that evil had been defeated, at least for now. In Paris, Sartre and de Beauvoir smoked unfiltered cigarettes and drank coffee at their regular Montparnasse café while watching passers-by, writing literature, polemicising angrily against the hegemons, and philosophising about the 'waiter–ness' of the waiter. In Harlem, the African-American renaissance would develop the most sophisticated and technically dazzling popular music to see the light of day since Mozart. The United Nations was founded amid widespread feelings of cosmopolitan bliss, and an international committee was busy at work drafting the International Declaration of Human Rights (despite the protests of the American Anthropological Association, where a committee under the leadership of Boas's student Melville Herskovits criticised it for not incorporating cultural differences in its assessment of human rights). Indians and Indonesians were preparing for independence, and the winds of decolonisation would soon blow across Africa and the Caribbean as well. It was a new world, a new era, and there was no doubt that the precocious teenager Fredrik Barth was, in 1946, the right man in the right place.

Anthropology in Chicago was equally oriented to the natural sciences and to the humanities. In his undergraduate studies, Barth learnt about mathematical models for genetic research, anatomy and physiology; in physical anthropology, his main teacher was the outstanding primatologist Sherwood 'Sherry' Washburn, and his teacher in archaeology was the Mesopotamia expert Robert Braidwood. In cultural and social anthropology, Barth's teachers included Robert Redfield, known for his village studies in Mexico and India, as well as Radcliffe-Brown's students Fred Eggan and Lloyd Warner. Redfield had an interest in scale and comparison, and argued for the need to incorporate the study of 'great traditions' when an anthropologist did research in a small place, or into a 'little tradition'. Barth would inherit Redfield's interest in scale, but only belatedly his passion for the great traditions of the world.

In spite of his intensive studies, Barth found time to take part in a small archaeological excavation in Colorado during the summer of 1947, and when the dig was done he decided to hitch-hike westwards to the Pacific coast. This endeavour was initially unsuccessful. Following weeks in a dusty pit, he must have resembled a seasoned vagrant. Things nevertheless improved immediately when he became acquainted with a hobo who taught him the art of jumping onto freight trains without being found out.[10] In this way, Barth got a month's worth of free train rides in the western USA, from the deserts of Nevada to California's beaches.[11]

This is a typical Barth anecdote. His entire life, he has been driven by curiosity, and when the world finally lay at his feet, he had no intention of letting it remain undisturbed. He has always been adept at seizing opportunities, at just the right moment, when they offer themselves. On this particular occasion, this ability took him around remote parts of the USA, but it would later benefit him in more tangible and productive ways.

The natural science approach which Barth both brought with him from home and learnt in his interdisciplinary anthropology studies at Chicago doubtless contributed to shaping his methodology and theoretical views. Throughout his life, he has been strongly averse to speculation, flimsy generalisations and over-interpretation. He has insisted on observation as the most significant source of knowledge, and has always been reticent as regards wide-ranging generalisations.

The Chicago years were formative both at a professional and a personal level for Barth. Well into his eighties, he still speaks English with an audible American accent, and although he would later be more deeply attached to British social anthropology, he has retained a strong relationship to American anthropology throughout his life. The last academic position Barth held was as a part-time professor at Boston University until he finally retired in 2008.

The offer from Braidwood mentioned at the start of the Preface came Barth's way before his Master's dissertation had been submitted. An important component of Braidwood's project consisted of dating the domestication of wild sheep and wild goat, and perhaps other animals as well, so Braidwood needed an osteologist capable of classifying animal bones. With Barth's limited but extant background in palaeontology, Braidwood felt that he was the right man for the job. It is not entirely unthinkable that Tom Barth, the geology professor at Chicago, whispered a few words in Braidwood's ear as well. Be this as it may, Braidwood was from the beginning aware that Barth's real motivation for travelling to Iraqi Kurdistan consisted in a desire to carry out anthropological fieldwork there. The plan was, as mentioned in the quoted passage that opens the Preface, to stay on in the Kurdish mountains after the archaeologists had gone home.

The excavations in Iraq were to start only in 1951, and in the meantime Barth went home to Oslo. In the autumn of 1949 he was 20 years old, with a degree in anthropology, just married and out of work. It was around this time that he became acquainted with the 'attic group' at the Ethnographic Museum in Oslo, a handful of young men who studied anthropology with Professor Gutorm Gjessing (1906–1979), and who would later leave their mark on Norwegian and Scandinavian anthropology, albeit somewhat in the shadow of Barth. This group is interesting beyond the local setting in so far as it embodies a shift from an earlier, chiefly Germanic anthropology to a largely Anglo-Saxon anthropology, a shift that took place in Norway during the 1950s, but which has parallels in similar developments elsewhere, mostly later, in countries influenced by German anthropology.

The Ethnographic Museum occupied the second and third floors of the Historical Museum in central Oslo. Modest in scale and ambition by international standards, the museum nevertheless contained a research department and was, at the time, the only institution in Norway where social and cultural anthropology of any kind was taught. On the upper floors of the museum, Barth would meet Axel Sommerfelt, son of the famous linguist Alf Sommerfelt, a pipe-smoking young man who was already conversant with the main tendencies in contemporary anthropology, especially the British School. The analytically sharp Jan Petter Blom, later a familiar sight at the University of Bergen with his beret and bow tie, would become a dominant figure in Bergen anthropology after the departure of Barth. Henning Siverts was also in place upstairs at the museum, a witty and original researcher who would later experiment with punch cards and computer technology in his analysis of village life in Mexico. Later, others would join the tiny club of anthropology students, and nearly everybody in the pioneering 'attic group' would work as teachers and researchers at the universities of Oslo and Bergen from around 1960 until around the turn of the millennium.

Whether or not Barth ever became a fully fledged member of the 'attic group' is an open question. He 'came into the attic like a whirlwind', as one of his colleagues from this period expresses it, before leaving on fieldwork or to Cambridge. It has been said that life in the museum attic was – like life in many museums, one assumes – characterised by a slow and thoughtful rhythm, except in the short periods when Barth was there. He brought with him a vitality, an intensity and a charismatic presence which must have been noticeable already in 1949.

As the son of Professor Barth, Fredrik had several contacts in academic life. He nevertheless never warmed to Gutorm Gjessing, and the feeling was mutual. According to the young lions in the attic, Gjessing's anthropology was somewhat antediluvian. He wished to study 'Man' in all his breadth, including his ecology, economy, politics, rituals, history, art, religion, evolution and not least archaeology – and, if at all possible, he preferred to do all of this at once. There was a kinship between Gjessing's anthropology and the American four-field variety, a main difference being that the Americans studied the four fields separately. Gjessing, trained as an archaeologist, was also a museum enthusiast, and held that decent and interesting research could perfectly well be carried out on the museum's collection of objects. However, his students had discovered British social anthropology, and were of the conviction that the subject ought to concentrate on the study of actual social life rather than dead objects. This conflict probably never became clearer than at the meeting where Barth, as the students' delegate, proposed, slightly tongue in cheek, that the museum could sell off its collections to fund fieldwork. He definitely did not become one of Professor Gjessing's favourites.

Instead, Barth was connected, at this time, to a project directed by the sociologist Sverre Holm about Norwegian rural communities, and he received a small grant to carry out a study in Sollia, near Engerdal, where he had spent a summer during the war. The aim was to create a kind of ecological description of human adaptation, which would indicate how Norwegian mountain farms made use of their often meagre resources. In addition, an American sociologist interested in marriage practices was visiting the country at the time. Barth could provide him with some material as well.

To Barth, the short project in Sollia was important since it functioned as a practical test in anthropological fieldwork. The degree in Chicago had been taught with no practical exercises resembling fieldwork. As a rule, ethnographic research method is difficult to teach, and it is best learnt in practice. No two ethnographic experiences are identical, and although there are a number of standard procedures, it is always necessary to improvise.

A great deal of social research uses interviews – formal or informal, qualitative or quantitative – as their main source material. It is often said that the quantitative method, whether based on statistical material or questionnaires with standardised response options, produces a little knowledge about many respondents. With the qualitative method, where in-depth interviews are the main data source, the situation tends to be the opposite: the researcher speaks with relatively few respondents, but as a compensation, they get to know a great deal about those who have been interviewed in depth. Anthropology transcends this basic distinction by positing a third research method: participant observation. This method is neither capital intensive nor labour intensive. It is fairly inexpensive to send an anthropologist on fieldwork; it costs little more than a return ticket, sufficient funds for sustenance and perhaps money to pay an assistant. Although it may in its way be exhausting, fieldwork is not really characterised by hard work. Much of the time in the field tends to be spent on waiting or routine activities while the anthropologist chats with those present about topics in which they are interested. Observation is just as important as conversation.

Having said this, it needs to be emphasised that fieldwork is very *time intensive*. Since the anthropologist in the field ideally does not ask leading questions, but waits for informants themselves to raise interesting issues, speeding up data collection is not recommended. When the ethnographer speaks with their informants, they try to have an ordinary conversation with them, and the informants may well ask as many questions as the anthropologist. They, too, may be interested in understanding another culture. Fieldwork, therefore, can be tiring. Barth, who has been one of the most active fieldworkers in twentieth-century anthropology, readily admits that he is often exhausted by being in the field, longing for a few hours of peaceful contemplation after having socialised with informants for a full day. As an ethnographic fieldworker, you use your whole self as a research instrument, and one may therefore conclude that if it does not make you feel exhausted sometimes, you are doing something wrong.

In addition, anthropologists do not assume that listening to what people have to say is enough. They also need to see what people actually do. Generally, therefore, there are two kinds of data in ethnographic fieldwork: interview data based on conversations between ethnographer and informant; and observational data, including informal conversations between informants. Regrettably, contemporary anthropological research is increasingly dominated by interview data, which can quickly be collected through conversations, and which can relatively easily be edited and written out – unlike social interaction and other kinds of observational data, which must be understood, contextualised and, not least, translated into language. This shift towards interview data is probably largely a result of time constraints and the mounting pressure to publish fast and in large quantities.

Barth's anthropology is, perhaps more than anything else, a demonstration of the importance of making observations. Although he occasionally makes himself visible in his own texts, there is no hint of self-indulgence, and he tends to focus more on what people do than on what they say. Barth's approach, especially in his earlier work, has sometimes been labelled 'methodological individualism', a designation for which he himself has limited enthusiasm. This perspective assumes that all social phenomena can be understood through individual persons and their actions. Barth takes exception to this view, but there is no doubt that he has, throughout his long career, consistently represented an actor-oriented anthropology, where tangible social processes – rather than structures or cultures – are at the forefront.

Participant observation as a main method in ethnographic data collecting was first practised systematically by Malinowski during his fieldwork in the Trobriand Islands off New Guinea in the periods 1915/16 and 1917/18. Many had done fieldwork before Malinowski, but without an explicit methodology, and without making a clear distinction between interview and observation. Franz Boas, for example, mainly used interviews (often carried out by excellent research assistants such as George Hunt, himself a member of the Tlingit people), and this was also the case with Malinowski's contemporary and rival, Radcliffe-Brown, who was arguably more accomplished as a theorist than he was as an ethnographer. To Malinowski, it was of the utmost importance that the anthropologist relinquishes the comforts of the missionary's veranda, pitches his tent on the beach and lives among the natives. For scientific reasons, he had to stay in the village long enough for the residents to begin to ignore his presence and for the ethnographer to identify regularities in social life. The field situation, in a word, had to approach normality as closely as possible.

In order to succeed in this kind of field research, it is necessary to use your entire self as a research instrument. You are obliged to take social initiatives, talk to people, listen to them, tag along as they carry out their everyday chores, make observations and small talk, all the while without being perceived as an intruder or a spy. Barth soon became an exceptionally skilled fieldworker, with a unique capability of seeing quickly what was at stake for people and what a given social situation means. A younger colleague explains how he learned to view the world in a new way during a lecture given by Barth in the early 1990s.[12] Barth drew up four elliptical shapes on the blackboard, explaining that they represented animal tracks he had seen in his snow-covered garden a few days earlier. The question was what kind of information could be gleaned from these meagre data. A student (with a possible background in scouting) suggested that they belonged to a squirrel and a hare. When Barth asked about the direction in which they moved, one of the more zoologically trained students answered that they seemed to move in opposing directions, although the tracks were virtually identical. Barth, then in his mid sixties, proceeded to jump back and forth on the podium, first as a hare, then as a squirrel, in order to demonstrate why the student was right.[13] The point is that identical physical expressions do not necessarily refer to identical content or meaning. The skill of observation does not merely concern seeing, but also understanding what it is that one is seeing.

Upon completing his study of mountain farms in Sollia, Barth travelled on his discounted ticket with Braathens S.A.F.E. (today a long defunct airline) in order to join Braidwood's expedition. When the archaeologists had gone home, he stayed behind, drawing on a network of Kurdish workers whose acquaintance he had made during the excavations. With the courteous assistance of the Kurdish leader Baba Ali Shaikh Mahmoud, he received his research permission, and the Baba even invited him to study his tenant farmers outside the town of Suleimaniyya. As Barth said later, his situation in Kurdistan could scarcely have been luckier.[14]

In the anthropology of earlier times, a researcher might perhaps be able to get away with not having formulated a clear research question. If you had only spent a certain time in a suitably exotic place, anything you discovered might come across as interesting. Anthropologists returning from the field in the 1930s and even the 1940s could still justify their fieldwork by referring to general curiosity and a desire to contribute ethnographic descriptions of a remote people. This was no longer the case by the 1950s, and Barth's research question in Kurdistan was both pointed and ambitious. He wished to study variation in social organisation among Kurdish tribes and groups which were culturally similar, and ultimately hoped to be able to explain the causes of this variation.

The monograph that came out of this early fieldwork, *Principles of Social Organization in Southern Kurdistan*, begins as follows:

> Scattered over the South Kurdish countryside are a great number of small, compact villages, essentially similar in their physical aspects, yet highly variegated with respect to their composition and organization, ranging from extended lineage organizations to fully developed feudal organization.[15]

The culture is, generally speaking, uniform across the region, but there is great diversity with respect to social organisation. The main explanation is that the possibilities for autonomous local political organisations based on kinship are far better in the Zagros mountains than on the Mesopotamian plains, and that Kurds were thus incorporated into centralised political entities when migrating into the floodplains. Having formerly been autonomous, they gradually became tenant farmers.

The central question in the book, however, does not concern the origin of this variation, but how the shared social categories, or roles, function in relation to the different social forms. This is a clear-cut comparative project, the closest anthropology comes to the experimental method of the natural sciences. Certain variables are kept constant (in this case culture and social roles), while some vary, that is, the social form, including hierarchies, division of labour and political power.

Without knowing it, on the first page of his first ethnographic work, Barth defined an intellectual project that would keep him occupied for decades, concerning the interrelationship between societal forms, the articulation of the level of action with that of symbolic meaning, which options actors have under different regimes of incentives and constraints, and how they go about exploiting their opportunities. Barth often speaks of his kind of anthropology as being process-oriented. Rather than concentrating on the internal logic and structure of a local community, he has been far more interested in exploring what people do in a given situation and why they do it. The constraints are there, and it is necessary to know them. It is sometimes said that social scientists either have their focus on the forest (structure) or on the trees (individuals). Barth's method, one could argue, consists in looking for the forest in the trees.

Barth was not yet 23 when he returned from Kurdistan in the autumn of 1951, but he had set out a course for himself and even deviated from a couple of conventions in the main currents of the anthropology of the day. At this time, anthropologists tended to study single societies, while Barth had done short stints of fieldwork in several villages with a view to discerning variation and producing comparative analyses. Additionally, he had an interest in individuals and their strategies, which was unfashionable on both sides of the Atlantic, for slightly different reasons.

In the early 1950s, British social anthropology was dominated by structural-functionalism, an approach developed by Radcliffe-Brown in anthropology (the sociologists and others had their own champions of structural-functionalism) and inspired by the great French sociologist Emile Durkheim (1858–1917). This theory tried to show how different parts of a society were connected and integrated, how the elements or institutions of a society strengthened each other mutually and contributed to the maintenance of the totality of the social system. Structural-function-alism has since been much criticised, sometimes unfairly, for introducing teleological explanations in social science – that is, the idea that the cause of a phenomenon can appear after the effect. Neither Radcliffe-Brown nor his students held such a patently absurd view, but they assumed that a selective process took place where institutions, practices and customs which were functional in contributing to the maintenance of a society would survive, while dysfunctional phenomena would tend to be shunted to the side by the ongoing reproductive process of society.

Structural-functionalist anthropology placed a great emphasis on the study of norms and rules, and sifted, refined, simplified and distilled empirical data in order to end up ultimately with an abstract, general description of the social structure. Barth was never attracted to this theoretical programme. Already in *Principles*, he regarded social life as being dynamic, improvised and governed as much by individual decisions as by societal norms. When, a few years later, he oriented himself towards British anthropology, he would therefore associate himself with Malinowski's students rather than those of Radcliffe-Brown, although he had come under the influence of Radcliffe-Brown's ideas as a student at Chicago.

In terms of theory, Malinowski was a more straightforward functionalist than Radcliffe-Brown. He held that social institutions of various kinds (family, economy, politics etc.) were as a matter of fact upheld *because* they satisfied some human need or other, a view few others have defended subsequently. However, in his field method, Malinowski wished to come as close as possible to individuals, their motivations and their actions, seeing the understanding of tangible social processes as a main objective in ethnographic work. Malinowski's general scepticism of wide-ranging generalisations and model building of the Radcliffe-Brownian type also made perfect sense to the young Barth. Malinowski's student Raymond Firth had, in 1951, proposed the term 'social organisation' as a supplement to, and perhaps a replacement for, 'social structure', in order to emphasise the dynamic, improvised aspect of social life.[16] Already in *Principles*, Barth speaks of organisation rather than structure. Social life was already seen by him as shifting and marked by improvisation, just as much as it was by rule abiding.

During his fieldwork in Iraqi Kurdistan, Barth collected wide-ranging material about, among other things, soil quality, climate, agricultural techniques and the relationship between farmers and herders. He studied marriage patterns, comparing the practice known as FBD preference (parallel cousin marriage, i.e. a male ego marries, if possible, their father's brother's daughter) with the underlying logic in situations where unrelated men swap sisters. In the central analytical chapter of the book, he compares Jaf, a large, kinship-based, nomadic group, with Hamawand, which is also kinship based, but consists of sedentary farmers, contrasting both with villages which do not have kinship at the base of their social organisation at all, but are incorporated into larger, feudal units.

Kurds who descend from the mountains are easily incorporated into larger political units when they move into the plains, where there is a higher population density and intensive irrigation for agriculture. The explanation, according to Barth, is their political vulnerability. FBD marriage strengthens the lineage system, but weakens the ability to build alliances across the kin group. The predicament is fundamental in societies where kin ties are the most important principle of political loyalty, and this is today visible in politically fragmented countries such as Palestine and Somalia, not to mention Kurdistan itself. 'No supra-lineage political authority is developed, and no interaction between a lineage and other groups is necessary, except for a certain minimum of trade', Barth concludes.[17]

Principles of Social Organization in Southern Kurdistan is an interesting work, not least because it points towards Barth's mature work. His interest in power and authority, as well as the relationship between religious and secular power, is already evident here; but he also describes the relationship between different kinds of religious power. Among the Kurds, the learned *mullah* or *haji* enjoyed great formal authority. A *haji* (someone who has undertaken the *haj*, the pilgrimage to Mecca) was by definition high in rank and could not be a tenant farmer or a labourer. The dervish, on the other hand, was low ranking and could not be a feudal landowner. The dervish, or *sayyid*, belonged to the mystical Sufi tradition of Islam. He had no formal position in society, but could nevertheless wield considerable informal power by virtue of his personal qualities. The distinction between the *haji* and the dervish discussed briefly in *Principles* is, incidentally, reminiscent of the distinction between the guru and the conjurer, which Barth would develop decades later, in a comparison between knowledge transmission practices in Bali and New Guinea.[18]

Upon his return from Kurdistan, Barth applied for Norwegian research money in order to spend a year at the London School of Economics (LSE), where he planned to write up the material with a doctoral dissertation in mind. He was drawn to the LSE by Raymond Firth in particular, but the Department of Social Anthropology there, developed by Malinowski in the interwar years, was one of the best in the country, along with Oxford, where Radcliffe-Brown's former student E.E. Evans-Pritchard now held the chair.

When Barth arrived at the LSE early in 1952, however, it turned out that Firth had left for fieldwork in Tikopia. Instead, Barth met and became acquainted with the unknown, but bright and incisive, Edmund Leach, who would become an important source of inspiration and an intellectual sparring partner for many years. Barth has never concealed the fact that Leach is the anthropologist from whom he has learnt the most, although Leach would eventually move in a different direction from his Norwegian colleague.

Edmund R. Leach (1910–1989) already had a background in engineering when he began to attend Malinowski's seminars at the LSE in the 1930s.[19] During the war, he was stationed in Burma, and took the opportunity to do fieldwork among the Kachin, a hill people in the northern part of the country, which has received much international attention more recently in connection with the opium trade, ethnic discrimination and unrest. Leach would soon become widely respected, but also feared, for his brilliant, often arrogant form, and especially his first monograph, *Political Systems of Highland Burma*,[20] which has enjoyed a sustained influence on anthropological thinking about the relationship between kinship, politics and myth. It belongs to a select handful of monographs with which every anthropologist, at least in Europe, needs to be familiar.

Leach had been to Kurdistan and understood Barth's project. For his own part, he had just written an article, 'Structural Implications of Matrilateral Cross-cousin Marriage',[21] using both his own Burmese material and the sensational French book about kinship that had just been published (Lévi-Strauss's *Structures élémentaires de la parenté*), and he was keen to exchange materials and ideas with the gifted student from Norway.

Leach and Barth were an odd pair. From the end of the 1950s, Barth began to work with game-theoretical models in order to analyse individual strategies for maximisation, while Leach became increasingly engrossed in structuralism, exploring the possibilities of studying cultural universes as systems of signs based on meaningful contrasts.[22] By then they had been moving in opposite directions for a few years. In the early 1950s, they were nevertheless perfectly compatible in their orientations, sharing an interest in discovering mechanisms that could engender transformations of dynamic social systems. Leach's analysis of the Kachin showed both how Kachin could become Shan, that is change their ethnic identity; and how their own political system shifted between the egalitarian *gumlao* and the hierarchical *gumsa* varieties. Barth's analysis of the Kurds in northern Iraq had a similar aim, namely to study the mechanisms behind and the implications of change and variation. When Barth later organised a symposium about ethnicity, which would lead to his most frequently quoted article, Leach's analysis of the relationship between Kachin and Shan constituted one of the central terms of reference.

By now, Barth was on a roll. In the midst of writing up his Kurdish material, he nevertheless spent the summer holiday of 1952 doing fieldwork in Solør near the Swedish border north-east of the Oslo region, where the Romani people, a hybridised category of Gypsies established across Scandinavia, were numerous. He rode his bike from locality to locality, conducted interviews and made observations, and wrote an article, 'The Social Organization of a Pariah Group in Norway',[23] on the basis of this short field trip. He seemed to be driven by an insatiable curiosity for that which was culturally different, but he was also efficient in transforming his insights into analytical texts. But the summer came to an end, and he returned to London, later coming home to Oslo before Christmas.

Barth submitted *Principles* as a doctoral dissertation in Oslo in January 1953; Leach would publish his book on the Kachin the following year. Leach's *Political Systems* became an instant classic, while Barth's *Principles* was judged and found wanting.

The doctoral committee in Oslo, whose task it was to evaluate and write a report on the dissertation, consisted of Gjessing, Holm and the ethnologist Knut Kolsrud. Eventually, the linguist Georg Morgenstierne also joined the committee. Looking back, Barth suspects that the committee thought it something of a scandal that such a young man should take the prestigious Doctor Philosophiae degree, which – unlike the Ph.D., which was introduced later in Norway – tended to be taken by scholars at the height of their powers.

> They dithered for a while, and at the end, they found the solution: They consulted Evans-Pritchard and asked him whether this dissertation would have been accepted at Oxford. And Evans-Pritchard could confirm that it would not, since they required at least a year of fieldwork. And that [criterion] was not fulfilled. The committee then concluded that it had been told that it would not pass in Oxford. Thus there was no reason why it should be accepted in Oslo either.[24]

An interpretation which may be just as credible as Barth's own is that the committee lacked the necessary competence to evaluate his Kurdish work. None of the committee members were social anthropologists, and they must have had difficulty in evaluating the meticulously collected data and tables concerning kinship, marriage patterns and lineage organisation. Today, it might be objected that the dissertation was too short (containing 140 pages) to pass as a monograph, but at the level of analytical sophistication and data quality, there is little doubt that it met the requirements of a doctoral dissertation in 1953, notwithstanding the brevity of the fieldwork.

Barth would in the end not publish much from his Kurdish fieldwork. Apart from the unambitiously published book (which appeared in the occasional papers series of the Ethnographic Museum), much of the material would remain unused until the writing of the theoretical essay *Models of Social Organization*, where the variation in social organisation among Kurds in northern Iraq became a main case in his development of generative models.[25]

At this particular juncture, Barth found himself in a difficult situation. His eldest son, Thomas Fredrik Weybye Barth (Tom) was born in 1951, while Barth himself was in Kurdistan. Since Molly had settled for a role as a housewife, Fredrik was the sole breadwinner, but he lacked work, and, as it happened, he also lacked the degree that might have admitted him to an academic career. It is true that his contemporaries at the Ethnographic Museum were far from possessing anything resembling a higher degree, but on the other hand they shared neither Barth's level of ambition nor his family responsibilities.

In the end, it was Georg Morgenstierne who came to Barth's rescue. Bad conscience over the debatable rejection of Barth's doctoral dissertation may have played a part; be this as it may, Morgenstierne helped Barth to obtain a five-year university fellowship, from 1954 to 1958. Barth would use these years very efficiently. He knew that if you took a glance at an ethnographic map of the world at that time, there was a large area, from Kurdistan to north-western India, which was an almost unexplored area in social anthropology, a subject which had so far shifted between North America, the Pacific and Africa as its key regions. He decided to carry out research in a Pashto speaking area in north-western Pakistan.

2

The Power and the Glory

Khyber Pakhtunkhwa, formerly known as North-Western Province, in Pakistan occasionally makes international news in ways which indicate that this mountainous and remote region is even today only partly under the control of the state. The area is wedged between the borders to Afghanistan and Kashmir, and in cultural terms the Pashto speakers of Swat, Pathans or Pakthuns, have more in common with many Afghans than with most Pakistanis. The language belongs to a different branch of the Indo-European tree than Punjabi and Sindhi, the largest language communities in Pakistan; and most Taliban leaders are Pashto speakers..

Although Pakistan gained independence in 1947, it was only in 1969 that the north-western region was formally incorporated into the country, having shifted for centuries between being an independent princely state, a conglomerate of stateless areas and a mixture of both. Formal inclusion into the state has, nevertheless, scarcely dampened the local enthusiasm for freedom, and scepticism about remote, centralised power. Neither American nor Pakistani soldiers have succeeded in achieving long-term control of the area.

In this area, Barth saw opportunities to explore political processes in a society which was politically complex without being part of a modern state. The Pakhtuns had large-scale irrigated farms, they lived in large villages and towns, and they had a complex division of labour involving feudal relations and many kinds of specialists. They were participants in the world religion of Islam, and maintained a political organisation which had developed over a long period as a result of local processes and regional challenges.

Georg von Munthe af Morgenstierne (1892–1978) was a linguist of international stature. He had begun his field research soon after the First World War, and his main area was Indo-Iranian languages. Morgenstierne was considered the Western world's main authority on Pashto. When Barth received his fellowship in 1954, he began to study Pashto with Morgenstierne, about whom it is said that he was pleased to finally have a

2. With Kashmali in Swat, 1954 (photo reproduced by permission of Fredrik Barth and Unni Wikan).

student; apparently, it had been years since he last had one. Eventually, the lectures took place in Morgenstierne's home, and the professor lectured as if he spoke for a full auditorium, although there was only one student present. When he had achieved a certain fluency in Pashto, Barth went to Pakistan. Again, Mr Braathen gave him a 50 per cent discount on the flight to Karachi.

As is the case today, it was virtually impossible at the time to obtain a research permit without being physically present during the processing of the application. Showing up at the local administrative office in question, demonstrating deference by waiting for hours in the corridor without complaining, and perhaps presenting a small token gift from one's remote European home country were symbolic acts that could well facilitate the process. However, getting permission to live and do research in an area over which the young Pakistani state did not even have political control turned out to be even more complicated than it might otherwise have been. In the end, the Pakistani authorities accepted that Barth could travel to the small princely state in Swat, surrounded by stateless areas. Provided the *wali* (ruler) agreed, Barth was allowed to do his research there.

The *wali* accepted Barth's presence in his domain and gave him a free hand with his research, not only in Swat Valley itself, but also in the surrounding areas which could be reached without entering Pakistan proper.

Known for its great natural beauty, Swat Valley is sometimes described as Pakistan's Switzerland. Surrounded by green hills and snow-clad mountains, the Swat River runs through a fertile valley, which lies at an altitude between 1000 and 1500 metres above sea level and is blessed with an almost perfect climate for agriculture. In periods when it has been considered safe for Westerners, the valley has been a popular destination for adventurous tourists. The total population of Swat was about 400,000 in 1954. (Sixty years later, it had trebled.) This is where Fredrik Barth arrived in late winter 1955, at the mercy of the *wali*. His fieldwork in Swat, by many considered his most important, lasted until November 1955. This is where he would collect the data that not only led to his doctoral degree at Cambridge and his first properly published monograph, but also two of his most important articles and, 15 years later, material that was utilised in the path-breaking volume *Ethnic Groups and Boundaries*.[1] He would return to Swat on shorter visits in 1961, 1964, 1974 and 1977.

Upon arriving in the valley, Barth established contact with a small college that the *wali* had created. This would be an early impulse for many anthropologists. When arriving in the field, without knowing anybody, your first instinct is to make contact with anything that resembles something you are familiar with. In this way, he immediately made the acquaintance of Aurangzeb Khan, who was not only the history teacher at the school, but also one of the most powerful chiefs in the valley. Barth explains that Aurangzeb had just

taken a new, young, somewhat prettier wife, and so he had difficulties at home – and his old bodyguard and servant, Kashmali, sided wholeheartedly with his first wife. So it was inconvenient for Aurangzeb to have him around. The two of them were master and servant, and it had been like that since they were both children, so there was an intimate and close relationship which had just now turned very uncomfortable and was really about to be severed. And so Aurangzeb Khan solved this problem by telling me: 'Look here, I've got a very trusted fellow, my servant Kashmali. You can have him while you are here. My pleasure!'[2]

Kashmali would become a key informant and organiser throughout Barth's fieldwork. As the servant of a prominent chief, he was familiar with the local caste system and social relationships among the elite, and had a good overview of current conflicts and gossip. Being Barth's trusted manservant, he also accompanied the anthropologist everywhere during his fieldwork. In the preface to *Political Leadership among Swat Pathans*, Kashmali's efforts are duly acknowledged:

> I should particularly mention my servant Kashmali. To defend his own and his master's prestige, he carefully coached me in etiquette, explained the labyrinth of friendship and enmity between the persons I met, and thus contributed greatly to my success with others and to my knowledge of the area.[3]

Kashmali is featured prominently in Barth's retrospective texts, mostly written in Norwegian in his later years, but he is not visible in the ethnography and analyses from Swat Valley, although he must have been present in most of the situations described. At that time, anthropologists rarely gave an account of the broader context of their data collecting. Native servants and interpreters were scarcely worthy of a footnote, but the anthropologist himself also tended to remain in the background of the text. This was, after all, the mid 1950s, a time when young men of good class rarely appeared in public without a tie and a briefcase (unless they were anthropologists on fieldwork), when polite form reigned and women wore high heels and expansive hats. It was only with the breakthrough of feminism and student radicalism from the late 1960s onwards that concepts such as 'reflexivity' and 'subject position' entered the methodological vocabulary. Owing to the efforts of feminist and later postcolonial anthropologists, what had formerly been seen as unseemly immodesty and irrelevant chit-chat, namely anthropological analyses depicting the researcher as an active participant in the field, was turned into a virtue and, for some, a necessity. In the 1950s, however, the disinterested, allegedly neutral scientific gaze was what guaranteed prestige and credibility.

Raising questions concerning power and authority in stateless societies was not a novelty in British social anthropology, which Barth had now become affiliated with. Quite the opposite: it was one of the most important issues at the time, especially at Oxford. The problem is obvious: What are the mechanisms, or principles, enabling societies to remain relatively stable, coherent and peaceful in the absence of a central authority, monopoly of violence, police, courts of justice and prisons? Why is it that in so many societies the general situation is not a Hobbesian 'war of all against all' but instead one in which life is relatively stable and peaceful?

In the introduction to the influential edited volume *African Political Systems*, Evans-Pritchard and Meyer Fortes offered a short answer.[4] In their view, there were three main types of African political systems: the band, which was exclusively based on kinship (prototypically the Bushmen of Southern Africa); the traditional state (like the Luganda kingdom in British East Africa, now Uganda); and the segmentary, lineage-based society, which was the most common form. Segmentary societies could be hierarchical, in the sense that clans and lineages were ranked, but on an everyday basis they functioned in an egalitarian way, so that each person was comparable to – and structurally equal to – any other person in their generation or age group. The groups expanded and contracted according to circumstances. In his monograph *The Nuer*, Evans-Pritchard had described the political logic of segmentary societies lucidly. If the conflict was a minor one, concerning, for example, the division of an inheritance, brothers or cousins came into conflict with each other. In the case of conflicts involving more people, for example concerning cattle theft, murder or disputes about grazing or water rights, the alliances grew on both sides. In such cases, entire lineages, who might consist of a dozen warriors or more, would align themselves against opposing lineages. The basic logic, described by Evans-Pritchard and many others before and after him, can be summarised thus: It is I against my brother, my brother and me against our cousins; my brother, our cousins and me against our more distant agnates, and so on.[5]

Segmentary systems are flexible since the operative group expands and contracts as required. At the same time, they are vulnerable since they are incapable of producing long-term stability. The divide-and-rule logic governing alliances within segmentary systems can easily be exploited by outsiders wishing to obtain sovereignty over the entire region. Such a strategy was far from unknown in the age of imperialism in Africa, where the British in particular were notorious for the practice of divide and rule. But in postcolonial societies, the fragility of segmentary alliances is no less evident than in the past. The new state of South Sudan is an obvious example, where the Nuer are one of the dominant groups, along with their old enemies, the Dinka. While they were still fighting their common enemy, the Arabic-speaking Muslims of northern Sudan, they usually managed to join forces through an uneasy truce, but after independence in

2011, divisions have multiplied and deepened. Comparable developments have characterised Afghanistan following the Soviet departure in 1989, in the very cultural region where Barth arrived just before the rainy season in 1954.

Barth had read Evans-Pritchard and Fortes, and he engaged actively with lineage theory and the segmentary models of the Oxford anthropologists. At the same time, he was attracted by a social science where the main objective did not consist in explaining how societies function, but accounting for what it is that makes people do what they do. Among the recent ancestors of social anthropological theory, he had a far stronger affinity with Max Weber than with Emile Durkheim. Weber developed theories of action, while Durkheim was more interested in the integration of societies than individual agency.

Swat was, as the foregoing sketch indicates, a fairly complex society with elements of feudalism and rudimentary statehood; it was more stratified and unequal than Evans-Pritchard's Nuer, but among the landowners competing for popular support and land, a segmentary logic clearly applied. The valley had been inhabited by Muslims speaking an Indo-European language for about a thousand years, but intensive irrigated agriculture went much further back. The Pathans were a border people, who had settled, probably deliberately, in an area which was difficult to control from the outside, framed by high mountains and with narrow passes as well as many places suitable for staging an ambush; in brief, a perfect site for guerrilla resistance against a numerically superior state power.

The valley itself, however, was topographically straightforward and easy to oversee. It is located outside the central trade routes connecting China, Iran and India (the famous Khyber Pass is further north), and contact with the outside world was limited. Tea was actually introduced into Swat only 30 to 40 years before Barth's fieldwork. Since the sixteenth century, the Yusufzai clan had been politically dominant, and they ran an efficient feudal agricultural society with a main emphasis on cereals, but they also had livestock and grew some rice. As Barth says, 'There was no state control in Wittfogel's sense, but it was really a fairly large-scale and intensive irrigated agriculture'.[6] Karl Wittfogel's theory about hydraulic despotism described societies based on irrigation through rivers and canals, where those who commanded the higher reaches of the river had an effective grip on the rest of the people, since they could at any time turn off the tap.[7]

Swat was intermediate. The system offered good opportunities for ambitious people to improve their lot, but it necessarily happened at someone else's expense, since practically all arable land was already cultivated, and nobody had considered using the land for anything but agriculture. The actual work was, naturally, carried out by poor tenant farmers and labourers; the actual landowning caste comprised a small minority, perhaps as little as 1 per cent. A tenant farmer was allowed to keep 40 per cent of the harvest on unirrigated land, but only 20 per cent on irrigated land. In other words, the landowners demanded rent not only for the land, but also for the river water gushing forth from the Hindu Kush. Although Swat lies on the extreme north-western margin of the Indian cultural area, the caste system is operative and regulates the division of labour and access to resources.

As in many traditional societies, land could not be sold and purchased in Swat. It could only be transferred through inheritance or conquest. It was also possible to give land to holy men. In order to achieve and retain political power, the land owners had to make certain that their tenants were kept contented. They would otherwise risk losing their support, playing into the hands of their competitors. For this reason, it was important to be generous and hospitable in the men's houses. This was where the workers met in their free time, and they expected their squire to offer food and drink. If, as a landlord, you failed to meet your obligations in this domain, you risked losing the loyalty of your tenants. If they began to frequent another man's house, they might later claim that they were working for him and not for you, and he would eventually receive the surplus of their production.

Seen from a bird's-eye perspective, politics in Swat might seem relatively stable. A structural-functionalist anthropologist would, without too much effort, be able to describe 'the political system' and the mechanisms contributing to its reproduction, without paying much attention to individual actors. It was a segmentary system with horizontal alliance formations and vertical patron–client relationships, which had much in common with both the Nuer, as described by Evans-Pritchard, and the Tallensi of Ghana, studied by Fortes. There was nevertheless an important difference: the alliances in Swat were governed by aims which might be intrinsically conflictual. I have already mentioned that clients, or tenants, could change their loyalty on strategic grounds. If their employer did not look after their needs in the men's house, they might switch to another landowner and become his tenant instead. Moreover, there was no unambiguous set of rules governing the formation of alliances among the landowners. In fact, Barth would soon discover, remote kinsmen would align themselves against their closer kinsmen. Brothers, who rarely entered into open conflict, were an exception.

The explanation is as simple and logical as the functional explanation of FBD marriage. If my brother and I each have a son and a daughter, and ensure that they marry each other, we avoid a fragmentation of the family's property. The Pathans practise sibling equivalence, which means that all sons inherit equally. When it comes to competition for land, which is obtained through inheritance or conquest, the fields are generally closer to each other the closer their owners are related. My fields would typically border on my brothers' and first cousins' fields. If I, as a good, ambitious Pathan chief, wish to extend my property, my gaze is drawn to the nearest fields first. I would much rather move my border posts a few hundred yards outwards than become responsible for remote fields which are not contiguous with mine. This is why I would tend to find allies among my remote relatives, or even people with whom I am not related at all. They would find themselves in a similar situation where they live, and thus we help each other in out-competing our nearer agnatic relatives by attracting as many of their tenants as possible.

In such a system, it cannot be predicted exactly how a given individual will act in a particular situation. People make strategic decisions under a regime of well-defined incentives and constraints, but the decisions they make are genuinely unpredictable, since they depend on a complex balancing act in which the differing consequences of any course of action are weighed against each other. In his monograph from Swat, Barth recalls the Chicago anthropologist Ralph Linton's distinction between ascribed and achieved statuses, concluding that 'patrilineal descent defines the only principle of ascription of status or rights',[8] that is to say that your kinship relations on your father's side determine your place in the caste hierarchy, and also provide unequivocal leads for your professional life. But everything else is being defined either through contractual agreements between individuals, or through open conflict. This means that there is a considerable open space allowing for individual strategic thinking, manipulation, covert alliance building and maximisation. Although FBD marriage is meant to reduce the potential of conflict between cousins, it does not always work out like this in practice. Even if I should be married to my uncle's daughter, who is my cousin's sister, it is far from unthinkable that I could end up in a protracted and bitter conflict with my cousin, provided the promised gain is sufficiently tempting.

Such dilemmas were hugely fascinating to Barth, and the political dynamics resulting from strategic choices would become the central theme of his monograph, as well as several of the articles from his Swat research. However, he also pursued another couple of themes, namely ecology and the relationship between different forms of political leadership. Indeed, his initial plan was to concentrate on the latter topic in his doctoral dissertation, to be written in Cambridge after his return.

A limitation in Barth's fieldwork in Swat was his lack of access to women as informants. The Pathans practise strict gender segregation, and it was completely impossible for Barth, as an unrelated man, to get close to women. When, many years later, he wrote the biography of the *wali*, the prince remarked, with some exasperation, that although he was the ruler of the entire valley, he had to go abroad to be able to eat lunch with his wife.[9] Malala Yousufzai, the now world-famous Nobel Peace Prize winner and victim of attempted murder when she was shot by a militant Muslim in the autumn of 2012 for campaigning for girls' right to an education, belongs – as the name suggests – to the politically dominant Yusufzai clan, and lived in Mingora, the largest town in Swat Valley. Gender equality neither was nor is widely considered part of the common cultural stock of the region.

Religious puritanism has for many years enjoyed strong support in Swat, and the Afghan Talibans are popular. Representing a kind of leadership which follows different principles to those of the landowners, it was discernable and influential in the 1950s as well. Saints, that is men of holy descent, generally own some land, but only a few of them are large landowners. Their source of power and influence lies elsewhere, namely in their privileged access to the sacred and their assumed superior faculty of judgement. As Barth describes the saints, they seem more reminiscent of holy men in Hindu India (*sadhu*s) than of Muslim leaders elsewhere: 'Truly "Saintly" behaviour implies moderation, piety, indifference to physical pleasure, and withdrawal from the petty and sordid aspects of common life; and also wisdom, knowledge, and the control of mystical forces'.[10] Culturally, Swat Valley must be considered part of the Indian subcontinent, although it has been Muslim for a thousand years.

The relationship between saints and landowners is treated at length in Barth's monograph. They represent distinct forms of power, but can benefit from aligning with each other. A saint needs military protection to maintain his influence in a region, while landowners depend on the goodwill of the saint when they need a broker in a conflict situation.

The other sub-theme, which would yield great benefits from a modest investment (as a strategically inclined Pathan might have put it), concerned ecology and ethnicity. Having spent some months in the field, Barth took a break. It was at the height of summer, and the valley was heating up. The cooler mountain air further up felt tempting, and Barth has always been fond of walking – indeed, his preferred way of doing fieldwork consists in walking with informants while chatting. However, the mountains were partly uncharted, outside the jurisdiction of the *wali*, and could be dangerous for visitors. If Swat presented itself as a backwater in the British Empire and the Indian subcontinent, later as a remote and inaccessible part of Pakistan, then the mountains in the north appeared to be wild and lawless, even to the Pathans. Barth would be the first European to have passed through the area he planned to visit, as he made certain to follow a different route from the British land surveyor Aurel Stein, who had been through the same mountains previously.

The trek into the mountains, only a few days' walk due north from Swat Valley, brought Barth across the cultural boundary between the subcontinent and Central Asia. This boundary, interestingly, corresponds roughly with a geological one, since the Eurasian continental plate meets the Indian one precisely in the Hindu Kush. The mountain peoples spoke different languages and respected neither saints nor castes. They had no feudal organisation, were attracted by nomadism, and were in many ways culturally closer to Uzbeks and Tajiks than Pathans. These general differences did not interest Barth, who had relinquished cultural history and civilisational analysis for the detailed study of concrete social processes; instead, he was fascinated by the frontier areas between cultural areas, and in particular the ecological adaptations which develop when Kohistanis and Gujars share an overlapping space with each other and with Pathans.

Before leaving Swat, Barth bought food for the journey, since there was no cash economy in the mountains. He also needed to bring a couple of armed guards to protect the food. In addition, Kashmali naturally came along. Initially, he had made arrangements to bring a donkey driver who would carry the food, but after just an hour, the man – who had been paid in advance – protested and claimed that the route was inaccessible for donkeys. 'So I had to draw my gun to get my money back – I didn't know what to do, and there was an outrage, and the man said that he could not and would not return my money, and so – well, I remembered from Western films I had seen – you know, if you don't get your will, you have to act like that. And so I got the money back'.[11]

As a result of this minor drama, Barth had to start anew, this time with bearers. His reasoning around the bearers and the food succinctly exemplifies the Barthian attention to process, which would become a trademark in his subsequent research. The problem was simple. All the food they were going to eat during the journey had to be carried out of Swat, since there was nothing to be purchased en route. Since the bearers themselves ate their share of the food, you needed more bearers the more food you brought. So far, so good. However, by the time they had reached the end of the valley, Barth realised that he had to buy additional supplies, but this meant that he had to hire an additional bearer. In the event, they left the valley with six bearers. Had the bearers not had to eat, three would have been sufficient. On the other hand, if a bearer had only been capable of carrying the same amount of food that he ate himself, it would have been silly to bring bearers at all. As the journey unfolded, it turned out that Barth's calculations were proved accurate: 'To my great pleasure and sense of triumph, when we re-emerged at the other end of Kohistan, I only had one bearer left; I had "eaten up" the five others on the way and sent them home'.[12]

The group had four armed men apart from the bearers – Barth had his pistol, and Kashmali had an old blunderbuss – and they must have looked like a small army, too intimidating to be an interesting target for Kohistani robbers lurking on the mountainsides. Otherwise, they might well have been attacked and killed. A Kohistani whom Barth met readily admitted that an important source of income for them had always consisted in robbing caravans and traders. The region was anarchic ('without a ruler') or acephalous ('without a head'), to use the terms commonly used in social anthropology at the time.

While Pashto is an Indo-Iranian language, the Kohistanis spoke Dardic languages, while a third group, the Gujars, spoke Gujri, an Indo-European language related to Rajasthani. Kashmali did not know any of their languages, but Barth had also brought with him Aurang Zeb-Mian, the son of a saint, who spoke one of the Kohistani languages. Besides, the Kohistanis were usually bilingual in Pashto, so communicating with them was perfectly feasible. While on this expedition, Barth collected 'three to four languages', as he puts it, as a gift to Professor Morgenstierne. He also developed an analytical model which would inspire a renewed interest in ecological anthropology, concerning the relationship between Pathans, Kohistanis and Gujars.

'Ecological Relationships of Ethnic Groups in Swat, North Pakistan' was written in four weeks, and was published in the leading journal *American Anthropologist* in 1956, the year before Barth defended his dissertation at Cambridge. Stylistically, the article is sober, almost dry; it is concise, stringent, and in its time it represented an early attempt to connect the concept of the ecological niche to the analysis of the relationship between discrete ethnic groups. What Barth observed in the higher hills and mountains above Swat Valley was in fact an ecologically based division of labour between groups, whereby each group had carved out a political organisation and economic adaptation adjusted to the ecological conditions. Since group identity was connected to political structure and livelihood, it was impossible to cross ecological boundaries without at the same time changing ethnic identity. Thus, two of the groups – the Kohistanis and the Gujars – could live in almost complete mutual isolation, even though physical distances were short.

A decisive factor for the third group, the Pathans, for maintaining their identity was the ability to grow two crops a year. Only a few, isolated groups of Pashto speakers lived above this ecological limit, since even a simplified version of Pathan political organisation, with landowners, tenant farmers and a fairly complex division of labour, presupposes two annual crops. The Kohistanis grew crops, but animal husbandry was equally important for them, and like many marginal farmers elsewhere (the Norwegian mountain farmers with whom Barth spent a summer during the war come to mind), they had a transhumant (semi-nomadic) adaptation, moving with their animals twice a year between summer and winter pastures.

The Gujar group raised some issues. They were more mobile than the others, and in regular contact with Pathans. Like the Kohistanis, the Gujars combined raising livestock with a bit of agriculture, but some Gujars had become fully fledged nomads, relinquishing agriculture and permanent settlements, like some Central Asian peoples further north. As Barth noticed, the relationship between Gujars and Pathans was complementary and unproblematic. On the other hand, it would appear that Gujars competed for the same niches as did the Kohistanis. The fact that open conflict or assimilation did not take place between the groups seemed to be caused by the Gujars' avoidance of the relatively low-lying areas of eastern Kohistan. They could exploit marginal land just above Pathan settlements, which the latter were unable to use for themselves, and due to their flexibility and mobility they were also able to survive in the cold high mountains in western Kohistan, which were similarly unappealing to the Kohistanis.

The article, based on a few weeks' hiking in the mountains north of Swat, was rightly seen as innovative. The influential American anthropologist Alfred Kroeber had previously written about cultural areas and ecology, especially in North America, and the neo-evolutionist Julian

Steward had studied ecological adaptations among the Shoshone Indians of the Nevada desert. But, as Barth has pointed out, Steward's analysis lacked 'theoretical richness'. For his own part, Barth ends his article with a few general points about ethnic groups, ecological niches and power. Today, these points may seem self-evident or even banal. For example, it seems pretty obvious that 'if different ethnic groups are able to exploit the same niches fully, the militarily more powerful will normally replace the weaker, as Pathans have replaced Kohistanis'.[13] However, the article was important in two respects. First, Barth introduced the niche concept from biology, a concept with which he might have become familiar through his father-in-law, Warder Clyde Allee, as a means to describe competition and complementarity among distinctive peoples occupying the same area. Secondly, he highlighted the importance of including material, naturally given factors in a social science analysis without succumbing to the temptation of reductionism, that is simply explaining complex cultural and social phenomena through biological or ecological factors. Caste, language, technology, religion and history are all brought to bear on the account when necessary. The material is complex, the analysis simple without cutting corners. In its very simplicity and complexity, this early paper remains an impressive piece of work. It reminds me of a formula Barth described to me years ago, and not merely as a joke, concerning how to go about writing a scientific article. He cited his father as the source. Well, he said, an article should be shaped like a fox, with a pointed snout at the start, that is a probing question. Then there is some stuff in the middle, but what matters is that, at the end, it must be equipped with an impressive tail; it should end with a flourish. A good article, in other words, should open up the field rather than closing it. Besides, it should be added that Barth's articles from the 1950s and 1960s are parsimonious almost to the extreme, with no chattiness or superfluous digressions, almost like Hemingway's short stories, compressed and powerful.[14]

Barth's period of fieldwork in Swat Valley was doubtless the most important one he undertook in terms of his subsequent career. It was more thorough than his Kurdish fieldwork, led to far more publications, and it took place in the local language. It revealed, to himself and others, that he was capable of handling data from a complex society without losing sight of individuals, their strategies and ongoing processes at the micro level. The publications from Swat come across as challenging and inspiring even today. Barth's theoretical interests were to a great extent shaped by the political games he witnessed in Swat until well into the 1970s, perhaps longer. In the valley, he entered a world where the ongoing power games between cunning and less cunning strategists were the engine governing many aspects of social life, a world of maximising actors well endowed with the inclinations of the alpha male and a profound fear of losing face and honour. Readers of Barth's later work have encountered similar characters, certainly throughout the 1960s. The question, to which we must return later, is whether this perspective on Swat Valley and the human dramas unfolding there mainly says something general about the human condition, something important about Swat, or something about the author of *Political Leadership*. As I have suggested, other analyses of politics in the valley would also have been perceived, in the anthropological community, as credible. They might not have led to debate and change in the discipline, but they might have pleased Evans-Pritchard and the old guard of British social anthropology far more.

In November 1954, Barth left Swat Valley. An efficient and target-oriented fieldworker, he has always tended to stay in the field no longer than he has deemed necessary. Yet the place, the environment and the themes he had worked with there would follow him for many years, indeed intermittently throughout his career. His last book, *Afghanistan og Taliban*, not yet published in English,[15] was partly inspired by the massive ignorance about Afghan circumstances he witnessed as a professor in Boston at the time that he lived and worked there; but analytically, it is to a great extent based on the insights he gained into political dynamics and forms of loyalty among Pashto speakers (who are the largest language group in Afghanistan) during this fieldwork and on brief visits in the 1960s and 1970s.

After leaving Swat, Barth went home to Oslo. His son Tom was three, and he now also had a baby daughter, Tanja. Barth would spend the winter and part of the spring of 1955 in Oslo before taking the family with him to Cambridge, where Leach, now a lecturer, became his thesis supervisor. In Oslo, he resumed contact with the 'attic group' at the Ethnographic Museum. There was no social anthropology in Norway apart from this small group, which had been slightly augmented since his last visit.

The mainly male group of anthropology students at the museum were acutely aware of the fact that they would be forced to create the new discipline of social anthropology in opposition to the establishment, represented by Gutorm Gjessing. Axel Sommerfelt was especially well read in current British research, and was working on a critical reanalysis of Fortes's studies of kinship and politics among the Tallensi of Ghana. Sommerfelt would also contribute, in his magister dissertation from 1958,[16] a clutch of new technical terms in Norwegian, such as the indispensable word *ættelinje* (lineage). Jan Petter Blom and Henning Siverts, meanwhile, were given decisive input for their dissertations by Barth, while Harald Eidheim, later a key figure in the development of ethnicity theory, received supervision from Barth on his material on the Sami. Whether he wished it or not, Barth immediately became a leading figure in this informal group at the museum.

As the 1950s wore on, new recruits arrived at the museum. Arne Martin Klausen later became an important figure in the popularisation of anthropology in Norway, and would produce the first textbook in social anthropology for secondary schools in the country.[17] Klausen also established contact with Johan Galtung, another precocious academic, a couple of years younger than Barth, and the still embryonic world of Norwegian development assistance. Klausen's main scientific work would be an analysis of an early Norwegian development project in Kerala, India, which had not sufficiently taken local social relations and cultural values into account.[18] Klausen thereby instigated a tradition in Norwegian social anthropology which remains influential even today, of critical perspectives on development aid (and, increasingly, the concept of development itself).

To the energetic and ambitious Barth, the museum seemed somewhat sedate and sluggish. After all, it was a museum, where history moves at a cautious pace. At one time, Blom staged a small, self-deprecating sketch meant to illustrate how the museum was a quiet place whenever Fredrik was not there. 'At a certain moment, when I came back to the museum, he [Blom] placed everybody around the room, and they knew that I was on my way, so they were ready, and they stood perfectly still for a few moments as I was entering the room, and they then, suddenly, all began to move around and talk to me'.[19]

In the spring, Barth went to Cambridge, chiefly in order to work with Leach. The fact is that although the University of Cambridge, then as now, was among the world's finest, its Department of Social Anthropology had for years been relatively marginal relative to the innovative research environments at Oxford and the LSE.[20] The simplest explanation for its marginalisation in the interwar years and during the Second World War was that the department had received the mixed blessings of premature success. The Torres Strait Expedition in 1898/99, an early foray into field-based anthropology in the UK, was organised from Cambridge. Besides, Sir James Frazer (1854–1941), the author of the path-breaking work *The Golden Bough* (published in a series of revised and greatly expanded editions between 1890 and 1915),[21] had a life-long connection to Cambridge, although he never held a chair there. Frazer had a major influence on ideas about cultural variation in the decades before the Second World War, especially in Britain, and not least outside anthropology. Both Ludwig Wittgenstein and T.S. Eliot were inspired by Frazer's analyses of myth and ritual, and Freud used Frazer's *Totemism and Exogamy*[22] in his own late work on taboo, but Frazer's impact on his own discipline would be short-lived. When Radcliffe-Brown and Malinowski published their respective monographs about the Andaman Islanders and the Trobrianders in 1922, it soon became clear that the subject had taken a new direction, and Frazer's main work would be recontextualised as a majestic obelisk for a defunct Victorian anthropology.

The slimmed-down, sharpened subject was first institutionalised at Oxford and the LSE, through people like Evans-Pritchard and Fortes, Firth and Isaac Schapera. In Cambridge, the renewal had to wait until Fortes was offered the chair there in 1950. By the time Barth arrived at Cambridge in 1955, Leach and Jack Goody were also present, two younger anthropologists who would both, in rather different ways, exert a strong influence on the subject in the decades to come. The group of doctoral students, whose ranks Barth joined, included Nur Yalman, who had done research in Sri Lanka and would later become professor at Harvard. Another was Jean LaFontaine, who had carried out fieldwork in Uganda and would later become even better known for her work on sexual abuse suffered by children in religious sects in England. Barth's closest friend at Cambridge was the Canadian Bill Dunning, who wrote his dissertation about the Ojibwa in Canada. Retrospectively, Barth speaks of this research environment, comprising a handful of Ph.D. students, as 'incredibly stimulating'. While he was busy writing up his material on Swat, he was on several occasions invited to London by Firth to present it at seminars, though no invitation came from Oxford. He nevertheless came into contact, through a shared acquaintance, with one of Evans-Pritchard's Ph.D. students, Emrys Peters, who wrote about the Bedouins of Cyrenaica, eastern Libya. As a matter of fact, Evans-Pritchard had himself written a monograph, his least well known, about segmentary opposition in the Sanusi Sufi order, based on limited fieldwork while he was doing war service in Libya. Peters's work also began through war service in North Africa, but it entailed far more comprehensive fieldwork and a good knowledge of Arabic. Barth and Peters met on several occasions, comparing notes about Swat and Cyrenaica.

Many years later, Barth would return to Peters, who died in 1987, enrolling him as a silent witness in a posthumous critique of the hierarchies ruling British anthropology in general and of Evans-Pritchard's authority in particular.[23] Barth himself had at least a couple of personal reasons to be unhappy about Evans-Pritchard's way of exerting his authority in social anthropology. First, the Oxford professor contributed to the rejection of Barth's doctoral thesis about the Kurds. Only a few years later, Barth apparently failed to receive an award because he had shown Evans-Pritchard insufficient respect.

The Curl Essay Prize was awarded annually, and in 1958 Leach – who had won the prize in 1951 and 1957 – encouraged Barth to submit his article 'Segmentary Opposition and the Theory of Games' to the prize committee. In the article, Barth argued that mathematical game theory could shed light on political strategies in a segmentary society (Swat). The paper may well have been the best contribution the prize committee received that year, but the committee decided not to award the prize, and akin to the reasoning of a Pathan landowner, Barth believes that this decision may have signalled that Evans-Pritchard's authority should not be challenged.

In Cambridge, Barth presented two possible synopses for his doctoral dissertation. He had read Gregory Bateson's work on schismogenesis, and was considering an analysis of the relationship between chiefs and saints along the lines proposed by Bateson. Bateson (1904–1980) was somewhat of an anomaly in anthropology, and increasingly became an interdisciplinary system theorist with a knack for creative metaphors and innovative ecological thinking about the fundamentals of living systems, but in the 1950s he was still a member of the anthropological guild. In the monograph *Naven*, based on fieldwork among the Iatmul of New Guinea, Bateson developed a dynamic model for the study of conflict, seen as self-reinforcing spirals or 'armament races'.[24] He distinguished between two forms of schismogenesis, a symmetrical and a complementary form. The relationship between chiefs and saints seemed to fit the concept of complementary schismogenesis well, since the two types of leaders acted differently and had different power bases.

The other alternative consisted in looking at leadership, strategy, notions of honour and alliances, with the main focus on the landowning chiefs. Professor Fortes supported this second plan, and that is how it went. However, Barth was invited to give a seminar paper in Manchester while working on his Ph.D., and there he chose to present an analysis of the competitive relationship between saints and chiefs, or 'foxes and lions'.

The department in Manchester had fairly recently come under the leadership of Max Gluckman (1911–1975), who had formerly directed the Rhodes-Livingstone Institute in Lusaka, Northern Rhodesia (now

Zambia). Gluckman and his students made major contributions to the reformulation of the structural-functionalist programme in ways which resembled Barth's activities at this time. They introduced network theory in social anthropology to facilitate a close study of what individuals actually did, and with whom they did it; and they had produced early studies of situational ethnicity in mining towns on the Copperbelt in Northern Rhodesia. At the same time, Gluckman was loyal towards his teacher Radcliffe-Brown and his friend and sponsor Evans-Pritchard, and the seminar at Manchester was not known for its politeness when outsiders came to present their research. They were politically radical, went as a group to Old Trafford when Manchester United played home matches, and had a reputation as earthy, pragmatic, sharp and polemical intellectuals. Almost like Barth himself, one might say, had it not been for the fact that he had aligned himself with Cambridge and Leach, who also happened to be Gluckman's main antagonist in the small, tight world of British social anthropology. The presentation in Manchester went 'reasonably well', says Barth, who did not encounter any major difficulties in finishing his doctoral work in spring 1957 either, and he also produced an article about caste for a volume under Leach's editorship during the same period.

Although British academia even today remains invested with considerable formality and strives to maintain old traditions and some of the hierarchies that go with them, doctoral defences or vivas are far less formal and solemn than in many other countries, such as the Netherlands and the Nordic countries. In a country like Norway, a viva is a major public event, where both the candidate and the opponents (examiners) are formally attired, while the dean or proxy dean in charge of the disputation wears a gown and reads a formula in Latin, and the actual examination may take on the character of a ritualised performance rather than a genuine dialogue. In England, the entire viva seems permeated with British understatement. There is little by way of formalities surrounding the event, which is not public, and the candidate is not obliged, subsequently, to organise a party resembling a wedding or a formal birthday party. The first time I was asked to examine a Ph.D. student in England, I jokingly asked the institution if I could wear my old Sex Pistols tee-shirt at the event. They answered, reluctantly, that if I really must, they reckoned that I could. Barth had an internal and an external examiner, and the external was the de facto opponent in this case. Barth's external examiner was Isaac Schapera (1905–2003), one of Malinowski's early collaborators and a renowned authority on kinship and politics in Southern Africa. Barth knew Schapera from his earlier sojourn at the LSE, and remembers the viva as 'enjoyable and stimulating'. On this occasion, there was no doubt as to whether the candidate would pass or fail. The thesis was published in 1959 as *Political Leadership among Swat Pathans*, and it is still being read. Some consider it Barth's best monograph.

Towards the end of his stay at Cambridge, Barth made the acquaintance of Christoph von Fürer-Haimendorf, an excellent cultural, rather than social, anthropologist, originally from Austria, who headed the anthropology department at the School of Oriental and African Studies (SOAS) from 1950 to 1975. In a notice published in the journal *Man*, Fürer-Haimendorf had criticised Barth's limited use of literature in an early publication from his student days at Chicago,[25] and thus they came to know each other. Barth took a course in Islamic law with him, and when Fürer-Haimendorf was approached by UNESCO about a proposed study of nomadism, he recommended Barth for the job. 'So there I got my next chance even before I had completed the previous one', Barth comments.[26] He had also recently been awarded a three-year research fellowship from a Norwegian research body, and could scarcely at this moment feel that he did not get the institutional support he deserved, although he did sense that there were certain persons, on both sides of the North Sea, whom he should try to avoid as best he could.

UNESCO's Arid Zone Project concerned the relationship between nomadism and sedentarism in Iran, and its stated objective was to produce applied research aimed at solving practical problems. The Iranian state, briefly, wanted the nomads to settle permanently. The relationship between a modern state and nomadic groups is always problematic, as the strong contemporary resentment against gypsies (Roma and Sinti) in Europe indicates. Barth gratefully accepted the offer, but he first returned to Oslo with his family, to reconnect with the 'attic group' and for an intensive course in Persian with Georg Morgenstierne.

When he arrived in Oslo, Barth found that changes were afoot on the upper floors of the Ethnographic Museum. The 'attic group' had begun to find their way into the academic job market. Sommerfelt had completed his magister degree and travelled to Africa, where he would spend several years, at first working on a Ph.D. with Max Gluckman, later as a lecturer in Salisbury (now Harare) until he was evicted for political reasons by Ian Smith's Rhodesia. A position as a curator at the museum was taken up by Klausen. Barth remarks, laconically, that he had not even heard about this vacancy until it had been filled, which may have had something to do with Gjessing not wanting him around. 'He was profoundly ambivalent because I was better than him. It was no fun to be professor in a subject that you know that you don't really know, but where you have a lot invested both politically and personally, and then to be outshone analytically by a youth. Very difficult'.[27]

By autumn 1957, the 28-year-old Barth was a doctor of social anthropology, he had published articles in some of the best international journals, he had one monograph out (about the Kurds) and another on its way. He had completed two thorough ethnographic studies and was about to embark on his third. It may easily be assumed that he was perceived as an overachiever in his surroundings, and not just by the standards of the 'attic group'. In a very frank and direct letter to his senior Ph.D. student Nur Yalman, Leach commented on his new crop of students. He had mixed feelings about most of them, it seems, but he was confident that 'Barth, with stuff from Surat [Swat], is obviously going to be A++'.[28]

Largely for practical reasons, it was often difficult for Barth to include his family in his professional plans. They joined him in Cambridge and on other trips abroad where hygiene and other practicalities were not a major challenge, but never on fieldwork. To an anthropologist of our time, this kind of arrangement seems somewhat odd. Most contemporary anthropologists who have a family are familiar with the challenges of combining family life and fieldwork. Some take their family along, but not all families are mobile. Most anthropologists' spouses these days have their own careers or projects, and cannot easily be 'brought along' to Mali or Malawi because the husband or the wife plans to live there in simple conditions for a year or so. There are solutions to these dilemmas, but they come at a price, professionally as well as domestically.

Molly and Fredrik Barth had four children between 1951 and 1959 – Tom, Tanja, Jørgen and Elisabet. In this period, Fredrik went away for several months on fieldwork three times. Molly never had her own professional career, and besides, as Fredrik expresses it, 'it was not just a decision, but it was an impossibility that she should have chosen to come actively along to remote places'. Molly rarely complained, and stayed at home with the children throughout the 1950s, and also in the 1960s. In his second marriage, to the anthropologist Unni Wikan, Barth would become, in this respect, an anthropologist of the contemporary era, with a different kind of division of labour in the domestic sphere. To this we shall return later.

Many consider 'Segmentary Opposition and the Theory of Games', the article submitted for the Curl Essay Prize and later published in the *Journal of the Royal Anthropological Institute*, to be Barth's most important short work. It was not directly based on his doctoral research, but further developed the formal analysis of strategies in the dissertation, drawing on mathematical game theory.

Game theory, still a vital tool in the social science toolkit today, was originally formulated by John von Neumann and Oskar Morgenstern in the 1940s.[29] The aim was to create a few simple formulae which could explain, and ultimately predict, behaviour, especially in microeconomics. The theory presupposes that people act rationally, trying to the best of their ability to maximise utility, and that they develop individual strategies combining cooperation and competition in the most beneficial ways possible. Game theory is often described as a form of utilitarianism, which entails a view of social life where individual calculations are considered the most significant driving force. It has been objected that game theorists regard people as egotists and underestimate solidarity and community as goals in their own right. This critique is far from irrelevant, but it is inadequate. Game theory does not purport to be a complete anthropology (knowledge about humanity), but is an attempt to simulate strategic action based on the assumption that people will tend to make the most of their opportunities.

It is easy to see why Barth, with his approach to knowledge strongly influenced by the ideals of natural science, was attracted to game theory. He had never seen the mere description and documentation of cultural variation as an end in itself. However, he viewed wide-ranging theories about cultural evolution as too rough, speculative and normative to be analytically useful. At the same time, he had a desire to understand which factors generated variation, and how an existing social form could be described without invoking an abstract, somewhat mystical 'social logic'. For an explanation to be credible, in Barth's view, it had to build on observable facts, and in social science this entailed that individuals and their actions became the necessary starting point. Game theory, which identified mechanisms for individual strategic action and their implications, seemed worthy of further exploration in this respect.

It nevertheless needs to be pointed out that it is by no means evident that game theory is useful in social anthropology. In conventional microeconomics, the goals of strategic action are taken as givens, and Durkheim in his time criticised the utilitarian social theorist Herbert Spencer for not having understood that the very objectives of economic action were socially defined.[30] There was, accordingly, no such thing as pure economic maximisation, since the norms and values defined in society determined which goals were worth pursuing. Even goal-rational acts have an element of value-rationality (to use Max Weber's distinction).

In economic anthropology, this insight is a commonplace. Which resources are considered scarce, and especially valuable, vary from place to place, and the goals of every strategic act are culturally defined. Religion and magic may have immense importance for people's individual strategies, and which resources are considered scarce also depend on the technology, livelihood and ecological conditions of the society in question.

This does not mean that the notion of maximisation, and game-like strategies, are necessarily useless as comparative concepts. In the article in which he first uses game theory, Barth shows that the objection about culturally defined goals is not relevant for his analysis. In the first part of the article, he carefully lays out the main characteristics of the local conditions – what he would later speak of as incentives and constraints – making it clear, before the analysis as such, what is at stake for the actors, which alternatives they are likely to be aware of, and what will be the probable consequences, intended and unintended, of different strategies. Given the conditions for competition over clients and land in Swat, it is possible to specify fairly accurately when it will be profitable for a particular landowner to enter into an alliance with another, and when it may be beneficial to confront him instead. Three weak landowners may, on a lucky day, and with a mutually binding strategic alliance, thwart the hopes of a mighty man.

In the introduction to the article, Barth signals a position which was radical in the British anthropology of the time. Fortes, Evans-Pritchard and Gluckman, the leading experts on African lineage-based societies at the time, were concerned to explain cohesion in stateless societies. Lineage theory, when it was applied to unilineal descent groups, as the case tended to be in Africa, indicated how kinship created stable corporate groups, strong political communities which acted in a coordinated way on the basis of shared ancestry and a finely meshed network of mutual obligations. The segmentary oppositions appearing both within and between lineages could be drawn upon to solve and mitigate conflicts. The ultimate aim was to show how stateless societies were integrated. Barth refers to this research and makes it clear that he builds on it, but he then adds, 'With a view to the particular orientation of this essay, the implications of unilineal descent may be expressed in terms of their significance for individual choices'.[31]

Patrilineal descent gives a man a well-defined position in society, but says nothing about his course of action in a given situation. He has to consider several aspects of a particular decision and a field of action which offers several options. Besides, it is a fact that the patrilines in Swat do not produce stable, balanced oppositions as they do among Evans-Pritchard's Nuer, but instead an unstable situation where alliances are continuously shifting, and where nobody can trust that today's friend will not morph into tomorrow's enemy.

The examples in the analytical part of the article show that games about prestige and social rank cannot be compared directly with games involving land and clients. Some chiefs who see a chance to increase their prestige may relinquish land they might have claimed, while others will claim the land even if it results in a somewhat weakened reputation. The outcome cannot be predicted in advance. Even if there are strong normative admonitions against brothers competing on opposing sides, this does occasionally happen. Such processes can only be analysed *post hoc*, retrospectively, as strategic games. Just as every move in a game of chess cannot be predicted, a game involving two, three, four or five parties in Swat cannot be simulated in advance, but – like the game of chess – it may be analysed using game theory in retrospect.

In order to understand Barth's view of science and the possibilities of knowledge, it is important to understand this distinction. Although he preferred, at the time, explanation and comparison to description and interpretation, and although he would later be accused of positivism, he never argued that social science could predict human behaviour. For this to be possible, cultural contexts, social constraints and possibilities, and even the human mind in all its complexity, would have to be bracketed.

Barth wrote 'Segmentary Opposition' while still at work on his Ph.D. It is easy to see why Leach liked the article. He had a background in engineering himself before joining Malinowski's group of students, and remained, throughout his life, more interested in mechanisms than in general descriptions. In a comparison between Radcliffe-Brown and Malinowski, Leach once wrote that whereas Radcliffe-Brown produced catalogues where he classified and described all kinds of timepieces, from wristwatches to grandfather clocks, Malinowski tried to find out how clockwork functioned.[32] Barth's approach to lineage theory and segmentary opposition had more in common with Malinowski's than with Radcliffe-Brown's perspective, and must have pleased Leach's engineering brain.

The article became a standard reference in the literature dealing with the relationship of individuals to systems, and contributed to no modest extent to the identification of Barth with a position he later has tried to extricate himself from, namely methodological individualism, the view that all social phenomena can, in the last instance, be explored by looking at individuals and relationships between individuals. Its dialectical opposite is methodological collectivism or holism, where social and cultural phenomena are viewed as supra-individual and irreducibly collective by nature. It should be pointed out that already in 'Segmentary Opposition', Barth takes care to emphasise normative and structural constraints on individual choices. At the same time, it is clear that he went further, perhaps further than any other social anthropologist in the 1950s, in seeing individual agency as the most fundamental feature of social life.

The Cambridge years were productive for Barth. While at work on his dissertation, Barth also wrote another major article, 'The System of Social Stratification in Swat, North Pakistan'.[33] It was included in a volume edited by Leach about caste, and although it is less theoretically bold than 'Segmentary Opposition', it showcases a very thorough and systematic ethnographic fieldworker. In this article, Barth presents, in minute detail and with tabular and graphic overviews, the relationship between caste membership and actual professions, the frequency of caste exogamy (people marrying out of their caste, more widespread in practice than in theory), the flow of goods and services between castes, and the statistical caste distribution in four villages. He would follow up a couple of themes from the article in later publications. The flow chart depicting economic circulation is reminiscent of the more famous diagram at the core of the analysis in the later article 'Economic Spheres in Darfur',[34] while the final discussion (the tail of the fox), about social differentiation, introduces a topic to which Barth would devote attention in different ways until the mid 1970s.

Choosing to speak of social stratification in the very title of an article about caste was in itself not uncontroversial. Many India experts considered caste primarily as a kind of ritual and religious categorisation of people, with its foundation in the Hindu religion. The fact that Muslims maintained caste systems in spite of not being Hindus was explained with reference to the broad influence of Hinduism, extending from Bengal to Afghanistan.

Barth did not disagree with this general view, and in his chapter he distinguishes between pure and impure castes in ways which indicate the affinity between caste in Swat and Hindu castes. For example, tanners are at the bottom of the caste hierarchy in Swat, which makes sense within Hindu cosmology but not in Islam. Tanners handle dead cows, which are ritually problematic to Hindus but not to Muslims. Moreover, the category of 'saints' in Swat, which comprise a caste on their own, is strongly reminiscent of that of *sadhu*s in Hinduism. As elsewhere in Pakistan, the population in Swat had been Hindus before becoming Muslims, and the new religion did not entail a total renovation of local social organisation or the simple excision of traditional notions of purity and impurity.

At the same time, Barth argues that caste should primarily be understood as a kind of social differentiation connected to the division of labour. He analyses it as a social phenomenon, not as a religious one. In Swat, this obviously makes sense, since Islam in theory is an egalitarian religion which holds that all are equal before God.

Towards the end of the article, Barth sketches a typology which resembles Radcliffe-Brown more than it does Malinowski, and yet the editor, Leach, would have accepted it. Barth distinguishes tentatively between three types of social organisation. First, the egalitarian, where only individuals, not groups, can distinguish themselves (ten years later, he would himself encounter such a society in New Guinea). Secondly, he describes systems where clusters of statuses are delineated and associated with sub-groups in societies (castes or similar). The third form involves complex systems, where different statuses can be freely combined, which he associates with a monetary economy. This is our kind of individualist system, at least at the level of the model.

Barth had by now written three excellent scientific articles, about ecology, political games and caste, which elaborated on and expanded the analysis in his doctoral dissertation, soon to be a monograph. He would later publish more from Swat and, not least, other places, but with these early publications he had built a name for himself internationally before his thirtieth birthday. On both sides of the Atlantic, Barth was now considered one of the most exciting younger anthropologists and one who could be counted on for renewal and innovation in the discipline. In the years to come, this reputation would be confirmed and strengthened through a stream of publications, provocations and fieldwork in ever new locations.

The 28-year-old Fredrik Barth who was preparing for fieldwork in southern Iran in the autumn of 1957 was largely the same person as the 22 year old who had followed Braidwood to Iraq in 1951. He had the intellectual habitus of the classic naturalist and held inductive ideals of research, whereby empirical facts were given priority over theoretical constructions. He was also driven by the same curiosity and openness to other people's lives that had brought him to Iraq six years previously. As he says to Hviding about his experiences in Swat: 'I had a very strong experience there and then, as is indeed always the case when I do fieldwork, the problem consists in making sense of that which is there. And then theoretical formulations emerge out of this. But it is in the attempt to get a grip on what is actually *there* that theory comes into being'.[35]

By subscribing to this inductive approach to knowledge, Barth distanced himself from leading social theorists, not just in social anthropology but in the neighbouring disciplines of sociology and social philosophy as well. The great name in Anglo-American sociology in the 1950s was Talcott Parsons (1902–1979), who built ambitious systemic theories about social integration, but rarely mobilised experience-near examples which would have enabled the reader to catch a glimpse of the actors who were, after all, necessary for the system to reproduce itself. Both Parsons and his colleague Paul Lazarsfeld exerted a considerable, direct influence on Norwegian social science in the 1950s in general, and on the recently established Institute of Social Research in particular. These academic visits by prominent Americans contributed to a decisive shift, which might have come about anyway given the outcome of the war, from a dominant orientation towards German scholarship to that coming out of the USA. Before the war, many Norwegian academics wrote their dissertations in German; after the war, English became by far the most widespread international language in the Norwegian academy, a development paralleled in other countries as well.

Lazarsfeld had visited Oslo in 1948, and contributed to the establishment of the Institute of Social Research together with, among others, the philosopher Arne Næss and the social scientists Vilhelm Aubert, Erik Rinde and Stein Rokkan. Lazarsfeld was especially influential in Norwegian research on voting behaviour. Parsons, who was inspired by both Weber and Durkheim, developed a kind of structural-functionalism which might be said to resemble both Malinowski's biopsychological functionalism and Radcliffe-Brown's theories. His schemata identified individual needs that needed to be satisfied (like Malinowski), and functions that must be maintained for a social system to survive and thrive (like Radcliffe-Brown).

Barth had little time for grand theory of the Parsonian type, and quantitative research on voting behaviour lacked an analytical sophistication or originality that might have attracted his interest. There was little contact between Barth and the sociologists and other social scientists now busy setting up shop in Oslo. However, there are some interesting parallels between Barth's epistemology and the philosopher Næss's programme for social scientific research. Both were critical of abstract, continental social theory and were all the more enthusiastic about simple, mathematically based models that might be applied to a wide range of concrete cases. Næss, who would later revise his position and re-emerge as a philosophical sceptic and a founder of the deep ecology movement, was at the time – and rightly so – considered a positivist. He assumed that social matters could be studied, described and analysed using methods from natural science. Barth would later also be considered a positivist, and his recurrent emphasis on the naturalistic 'watching and wondering' ideal may easily give such an impression. Since the mid 1970s, Barth has explicitly distanced himself from such an interpretation of his work, but neither should the early Barth be considered a positivist. As an ethnographer, he knew that local worlds are always unique and peculiar in ways that limit the validity of general explanatory models. Still, Barth and Næss shared an inductive view of science where direct observation was promoted at the expense of speculation and unempirical theorising. They were both empiricists, Næss being a product of the pre-war Vienna School, Barth of the naturalist principles he had learnt through his father and his father-in-law.

It is a fact that Barth, already in his works about the Kurds and Pathans, but also later, seeks a strictly naturalistic description; he wishes to reduce the creative interpretations of the anthropologist to a minimum in order to be able to grasp *that which is there*, assuming that it is available to direct observation. It is also clearly the case that he at this time considered causal explanations as a goal of research. In this, he was out of step with a growing tendency in British anthropology, formulated most clearly by the later Evans-Pritchard, to relinquish natural science models and remain contented with *Verstehen* instead of *Erklären*, understanding instead of explanation.[36] Evans-Pritchard's perfectly sensible justification of this shift was that Radcliffe-Brown's optimistic programme concerning the discovery of 'the natural laws of society' had so far yielded not a single such law, clearly a result of the fact that social life was more unpredictable and ambiguous than processes in nature. Barth's project has rarely, if ever, been seen as a direct continuation of Radcliffe-Brown's. It could be said, however, that he turns it on its head by beginning with the individuals and their interaction rather than the system as a whole, but sharing some of Radcliffe-Brown's basic epistemological assumptions.

So far Barth could perhaps be accused of positivism. He also shared, with Næss and others, a belief that an accurate language was available and necessary for a description of social life. Others were more sceptical, in so far as they held that language contributed to creating reality, and that no language could be completely context independent.

At the same time, there are aspects of Barth's early work which point beyond positivism. Above all, as shown, he accepts that cultural variation governs the strategies of individuals in decisive ways. The values they seek to realise are culturally defined, and the constraints and incentives within which they act are functions of the person's place in a social structure they have not created themselves (but contribute to maintaining and modifying through their actions). Moreover, Barth does not assume that it is possible to predict the actions of individuals, no matter how much is known about their situation. Their choices, in other words, are real. It is tempting to conclude that Barth wanted to be a positivist, but that he was too good an anthropologist to succeed. Social life always carries with it an unpredictable and ambiguous dimension, but you have to come very close to the individual actors to discern it. Powerful novelists like Dickens and Dostoyevsky know this, describing people who make the reader blush and squirm through their irrational, silly and unexpected acts.

The intellectual trends of the 1950s came and went without leaving much of an impression on Barth. Naturally, he was aware of Sartre, Camus and the Parisian existentialists, but found nothing in them that he could use. He did not relate very actively to Karl Popper and his programme for scientific research either, but one does sense that a deeper familiarity with Popper might have strengthened Barth's own programme. Popper's most important contribution was arguably his principle of falsification: it is impossible, he said, to prove the truth of a hypothesis.[37] The best a researcher can do, therefore, is to subject his hypotheses to tough criticism and critical testing in attempting to falsify them. The more unsuccessful attempts at falsification that have befallen a hypothesis, the stronger it stands, but it will never be proved once and for all. This is why militant atheists are wrong when they argue that God's existence has been disproved. Barth may use a similar method of analysis when critically discussing his own findings, but he tends to work with 'that which is there', rarely trying out alternative interpretations.

It also seems to be the case that Barth's tight integration of ethnographic method and anthropological theory, that is his insistence that theoretical insights emerge from observations of everyday life, would have been strengthened had he been more familiar with the new philosophy of language which gained influence in Britain during the postwar years. The young philosophers J.L. Austin and John Searle, in particular, analysed the meaning-content of spoken language in order to show how ordinary language acts shape people's life-worlds. Barth would have been aware of them, but did not spend much time on ordinary language philosophy.

The fact is that Barth never considered himself a learned man. He has a pragmatic, tool-like relationship to other people's research and thinking. In fact, he would occasionally advise students not to read too much about the field before embarking on fieldwork, in order to avoid being too strongly influenced by the pre-understandings and theoretical formulations of others.

Whereas Barth was not particularly interested in the wider intellectual trends of the 1950s, he had a more active, but sometimes strangely detached, relationship to contemporary anthropology. He had a broad overview, but rarely entered into a thorough discussion of the work of others. With Leach, he had learned about Claude Lévi-Strauss's structuralism, which received enormous attention in France at this time, and would be a major influence in the Anglo-Saxon world over the next decade. Leach himself was on the brink of entering into an intellectual dialogue with the Frenchman, which would last until the end of his life. Barth followed with interest the new currents in American anthropology, represented in Julian Steward and Leslie White, who revitalised an evolutionist, materialist anthropology which had been in the doldrums ever since Boas took the reins at the beginning of the century. When it came to American mainstream anthropology, represented by figures like Alfred Kroeber and Clyde Kluckhohn, Barth had moved some distance from it during his Cambridge years. Their emphasis on symbolic culture rather than social relations seemed to him a dead end.

On the other hand, it is true that Barth has continued to relate to American anthropology, and later in his career he would spend more time at American universities than at British ones. At the same time, by the late 1950s, he came across as a representative of the British school. The major influences on his own work consisted in the legacy of Malinowski, especially his methodology and his emphasis on actual individuals; Firth's interest in economic strategies, improvisation and flexibility in social life; and, finally, the collaboration and discussions with Leach.

It is by no means obvious why Barth should have aligned himself so closely with Leach at Cambridge. Among the other anthropologists at the department, Fortes was the most powerful, and Goody the most prolific of the younger generation. However, Fortes remained loyal to Radcliffe-Brown's programme after Evans-Pritchard had jumped ship, and oriented his research towards the understanding of stability rather than change and improvisation. Goody (b. 1919), a West Africanist who would later work with large, comparative themes concerning the state, the family, writing and literacy, and the differences between Africa and Eurasia, wrote, like

Barth, about kinship and politics at this time, but he and Barth never became close.

Leach was respected for his brilliant mind, but he was also feared for his bluntness and arrogance. Leach never hesitated to dismiss work he found seriously wanting. Today, he is above all remembered as an uncompromising and bold thinker and polemicist. Throughout his life, he had an ability to twist problems in unexpected directions, reformulate questions and take established truths in new directions. His first major book, *Political Systems of Highland Burma*, showed, among other things, that it was possible to change one's ethnic identity, and that there was no necessary fit between the actual organisation of a society and the ideas people might have about their society. He would later publish a monograph on Sri Lanka and many influential articles about ritual, communication and myth. Unlike the structural-functionalists, Leach did not see it as obvious or natural that a society should be in stable equilibrium; indeed, he wrote in *Political Systems*, Kachin society in upper Burma was chronically unstable. This view was not uncontroversial, and Leach had a tendency to make provocations in other situations as well. During Barth's period at Cambridge, the relationship between Leach and Fortes turned from indifferent to icy. They would nevertheless remain colleagues at the department until Fortes's retirement in 1973. The relationship between Leach and Goody was not particularly warm, either.

Being a university academic can be trying. Professional disagreements may evolve into personal animosity or vice versa, and yet academics often work in the same place throughout their careers and are forced to sit with their old enemies in the common room, in committees and meetings, year in and year out. The low homicide rate among academics must be a result of the fact that they are inclined to lives of reflection, rather than murderous outbursts.

It was not so much the substantial themes Leach was working on that fired Barth, but his evident intellectual power. Barth recalls Leach as a fantastic conversationalist, always surprising, provoking and inspiring with his twists and turns, erudition and novel approaches. Although Barth would build academic friendships later in life as well, he always returns to Leach (as well as his own father) when talking about his models and sources of inspiration.

The early Barth may profitably be compared with a successful landowner in Swat Valley. There is no doubt that he was goal oriented and efficient. Only five years after the rejection of his doctoral dissertation in Oslo, he was an established, respected scholar on his way to his third major field site, among the Basseri nomads in southern Iran. But he had not reached this far merely as a result of high ambitions and an ability to realise them in practice. He had also been lucky. Had Tom Barth not been offered the chair in Chicago, the son would not have become a student there in 1946, and would also not have accompanied Braidwood to Iraq. He might instead have turned into a good sculptor. Moreover, had the dissertation about the Kurds been accepted in Oslo, it is perfectly possible that he would not have applied for – and won – the scholarship enabling the sojourn in Cambridge. And had he not been in England and made the acquaintance of Fürer-Haimendorf, he would also have missed the opportunity to do fieldwork in Iran. Yet, it would be misleading to explain Barth's exceptional early success as a result of 'pure luck', as he himself has called it. Like a competent Pathan chief, he had an ability to identify opportunities when they came his way and grab them at the right moment. One should also not underestimate the fact that Barth must, even at a young age, have possessed a confidence, a charismatic radiance and a physical presence that convinced those around him that he had something going for him.

Although the aviation pioneer Ludvig G. Braathen was arguably a generous man who also had a keen interest in research, not everyone got a 50 per cent discount on long distance flights twice in a row. This time, however, in 1957, the invoice was picked up by UNESCO. In addition, it might seem as if Barth for once was out of luck.

3

Nomadic Freedom

For it has been my view that if you arrange yourself in such a way that you do not participate as if you were one of them, through what you eat and how you behave and how you sleep – the physical equipment you need in order to exist – then it is obvious that you create barriers between yourself and them.[1]

Everything seemed to be in order before the departure. Barth had been to Paris and obtained his medical certificate at the eleventh hour, after having been interviewed by the renowned anthropologist Alfred Métraux about the assignment. The project, part of UNESCO's Arid Zone initiative, had as its point of departure the problem with nomadic groups, seen from the perspective of the state. They are by definition difficult to govern. In most cases, nomads have no fixed address, no regular wage work and their children do not receive a formal education. They do not submit to the power monopoly of the state unless forced, pay little tax and do not respect official political boundaries. Across the world, nomadic groups have increasingly become a problem for the state, as its dominance has become ever more complete; conversely, the state has increasingly become a problem for nomads. The aim of the Arid Zone Project was to study how nomads could be made to be sedentary so that they could be ruled more efficiently and make more useful contributions to the national economy. In a broader sense, the UNESCO project concerned how we humans could better exploit the arid zones of the world, which cover nearly half the land area of the planet, but are thinly populated, often by nomads.

Then, unexpectedly, the paper mill ground to a halt in Tehran; Barth failed to get his research permit, and was forced to spend weeks and eventually months in the capital waiting for his research permit. He did little of consequence during this period. He spent much of the time in his hotel, read novels and resisted the temptation to do some fieldwork in the markets of Tehran. He was also careful not to attract the attention of the authorities. After nearly three months of patient waiting, he was

3.　With Ali Dad among the Basseri (photo reproduced by
permission of Fredrik Barth and Unni Wikan).

finally permitted to travel to the Basseri area, but before he could start
his fieldwork, the Ministry of the Interior demanded that Barth obtained
permission from the chief. Technically, the chief had lost his power, and
the army had taken over the formal administration of the area, but in
practice the Basseri chief was still the executive power. Finally, Barth got
the green light from the chief, travelled back to Tehran for the necessary
rubber stamps, and could finally begin his fieldwork among the Basseri.

The Basseri were one of many nomadic or semi-nomadic peoples
in Iran. One reason that they were chosen for this study was the fact
that they spoke Farsi, but they were also typical in terms of their way
of life. They consisted of roughly 16,000 persons, and as regards their
social organisation, they could be located somewhere between the most
hierarchical and centralised groups in the fertile and well-watered areas
in the west of the country and the loosely organised, anarchic peoples

living in the eastern semi-desert. As a general principle, a people is more differentiated the greater economic surplus it is capable of producing, and this pertains not only to the division of labour, but also to economic inequality and power discrepancies. Seen from the perspective of cultural history, it has been the surplus from primary economic activities, be they hunting, agriculture, horticulture, pastoralism or something else, that makes the division of labour possible. This is why the social system is at its most egalitarian and least differentiated in societies that are only barely capable of producing enough for their own survival. With the industrial revolution and subsequent economic globalisation, the potential for labour differentiation and hierarchy has increased even further. Rich industrial leaders in our world may earn as much as 200 to 400 times as much as an ordinary employee; in deeply unequal societies such as the USA and Brazil, it is even more.

The primary social grouping among the Basseri is the nuclear family, which possesses its own tent, the symbol of an autonomous unit, and its own herd. The shared identity of the society is based on kinship and way of life, and as mentioned, it was at the time of Barth's fieldwork still de facto headed by a chief. Their traditional territory stretches about 450 kilometres in a south-easterly direction from the lower parts of the Kuh-i-Bul massif, and ends west of the town of Lar. The nearest major city is Shiraz. Since they move seasonally with their animals, only a tiny fraction of the total area is utilised at any time. The rhythm of their lives, in other words, is governed by climate and ecology. They spend the winters in the dry and relatively barren areas in the south-east, the summers in the juicier pastures in the north-west. Moreover, they are culturally related to other nomadic groups in the province of Fars, and have periodically teamed up with them in loose federations.

Change had affected the Basseri before. Reza Shah, the grandfather of the shah who was deposed by the Islamic revolution in 1979, forced all nomads in the country to become sedentary in the 1930s, an arrangement that ended when he was forced to abdicate during the British–Soviet invasion of 1941. Most of the nomads then returned to their earlier way of life, but during the years of sedentarism they had not only lost most of their livestock, but also some of the features of their political system.

Good research assistants are not to be underestimated, although their role tends to be under-communicated in anthropological publications. In Swat, Barth had been lucky to have Kashmali to teach him the essential dos and don'ts, make introductions and explain the conflict pattern among wealthy landowners. Although Barth spoke passable Persian, he wanted an assistant who would be capable of interpreting, if it turned out to be necessary. 'So I brought a fellow called Ali Dad, who was a boy from a different tribe, and who had a good intellect and personal ambition, and who had learnt English without formal training, but as an errand-boy in an engineering company; and he came along with me'.[2]

Ali Dad had lived in Shiraz, and he was of great assistance, not so much by making introductions, for he had no personal network among the Basseri, but as a cultural guide. For example, the problem of hospitality emerged at an early stage. This is a familiar dilemma among anthropologists. They enjoy other people's hospitality, and are thus obliged to give something in return. But it is not always good form to pay money to one's confidantes, as the medium of money tends to redefine a friendly relationship as a contractual one, which creates embarrassment on both sides of the transaction. Among the Basseri, the problem of hospitality and the return gift appeared in an immediate and urgent way. One day, Barth finally arrived in the Basseri camp as a guest. They had heard that he was coming, and suddenly he was there in front of them. As he tells Hviding:

> The chief drove me out there, had my luggage thrown out of the Land-Rover, and called out to some people that 'here is that fellow, he's going to live with you'. And he then drove off. And there I was, right, and I was a guest, and what ought I to do, since it is unthinkable to pay a Persian nomad for his hospitality. So what should I do, considering that I was going to stay with them for months? And then Ali Dad said that 'the next time we pass by a market, I'll go and buy a bag of sugar and place it in the tent, and in this way, there will not be a problem for either of you'.[3]

Gifts and return gifts must be properly calibrated. This has been common knowledge among anthropologists for a long time, at least since Marcel Mauss wrote his famous essay about gift exchange in 1923.[4] They should be neither too big nor too small; they should be personal and sensitive and symbolise the relationship between giver and receiver. When you arrive in a new place and are unfamiliar with local customs, it is nearly impossible to guess what the norms of exchange are. Among the Basseri, a bag of sugar was obviously appropriate.

The visiting anthropologist was received with great hospitality and treated with respect. He could scarcely ride, but he had to. 'And, unfortunately, I should say, I got the chief's stallion, so I rode an elephant of a horse which was so randy that it was impossible to control'.[5] It must have been quite a sight. Every morning, the anthropologist had to ride in front, so that his horse did not catch a glimpse of any of the mares.

Like other nomadic pastoralists, the Basseri live in a kind of symbiosis with sedentary farmers and traders. Since nomads appear to live technologically simple lives with few possessions and implements, it is common to assume that pastoralism is older than agriculture. This is wrong; the first to domesticate animals were farmers, and it would often be the wealthiest farmers who turned to pastoralism. Raising livestock is less labour intensive than traditional farming, and the returns may often be larger. The nomads receive produce, tools and textiles from farmers and traders in return for their animal products. Their most important animals are sheep and goats, but the Basseri also keep donkeys (for transportation), horses (for men), Bactrian camels (for wool and heavy transport) and dogs for security.

In the 1950s, not many good anthropological studies of nomadic pastoralists existed. One who had carried out such a study just before Barth was Derrick Stenning. He had studied the Fulani of West Africa, and his monograph was published in 1959.[6] He had been instructed by his supervisors at Oxford to follow the Fulani from east to west and back, which required him to spend a full year in the field. Barth only spent a few months among the Basseri, following them from their winter pasture to the summer pasture, but he did not return with them. Although the preface to *Nomads of South Persia* states that the field period lasted from December 1957 to July 1958, the three first months were, for bureaucratic reasons, spent in Tehran. He arrived at the Basseri camp only in March.[7]

Barth himself comments on his unusually quick and efficient fieldwork periods, that 'I suppose I've been somewhat easy in that I haven't stayed very long in the field, but my excuse is that I always stayed there until I got it'.[8] He always worked with clearly delineated, sharply formulated research questions, and he had an exceptional ability, in his friend and colleague Gunnar Haaland's words, 'to use his eyes to see how people behave in different situations'.[9] Verbal communication tends to be less important than direct observation in Barth's ethnographic methodology.

Stenning's most widely read article concerns household viability among the Fulani.[10] The aim was to show the upper and lower limits enabling a household to reproduce itself, and he identifies the maximum and minimum number of animals for a given number of active workers. A family with three sons able to work can, naturally, keep more livestock than a family with only one son able to herd. And since the division of labour follows gender, the number of daughters will also be decisive in determining how many animals can be milked and how many products, for sale or for use, the household is capable of producing from hides and wool.

The economy of the Basseri was entirely dependent on goats and sheep. They also engaged in other activities, such as collecting truffles one week during the spring, but both their livelihood and their trade were based on goats and sheep. The characteristic, black tents were made of goat's wool, which was easy to move, water resistant in winter and cool in summer. The women carded and wove carpets, which could in principle be sold, but were often kept.

When travelling through a village or town, the main goods the Basseri sold or exchanged for things they needed would be dairy products, wool, meat and skins. By default, they could not hold on to more possessions than those they were able to carry with them on their annual treks from lowland to highland and back. Some of the richest did own some land, but they would let others cultivate it for a rent varying between a third and a sixth of the crop, depending on the quality of the soil and the availability of water. Like other nomadic peoples, the Basseri were not strongly attracted to farming as a livelihood.

The contrasts with Swat were many and obvious. Although they had chiefs and camp headmen, the political organisation of the Basseri was fundamentally egalitarian and decentralised, and the tent – the nuclear family – was the operative political entity. If a family wished to move to another camp, they were able to do so, provided the head of the other camp accepted it. Decisions were taken after long and exhausting discussions, often without a clear conclusion. A man owned his own capital, namely his livestock, and he did not need to work for others.

The relationship between genders was also different among the Basseri compared to the Pathans and Kohistanis. Among the Pathans, gender segregation created watertight seals between men and women outside of the internal family sphere. Pathan women wore the burka, so whenever they left the home they saw the world through a blue or white grid. Regarding the Basseri, Barth describes the relationship between men and women as being 'natural and relaxed'. When he and his assistant Ali Dad, both of them men unrelated to their hosts, moved in with Ghulam Islami and his family, there was no sign of a moral concern. Even when Ghulam's young and beautiful daughter moved into the tent with her newborn child, no discernable gossip emerged from the other tents.

As should be recalled, the assignment from UNESCO amounted to an evaluation of the conditions for sedentarisation of the Basseri and other nomadic groups. The better Barth got to know his hosts, the greater the dilemma. He found it easy to understand and appreciate the high value placed on freedom of movement among the Basseri, who had taken up seasonal migration immediately after the end of enforced sedentarisation, even if they had scarcely any animals left. Barth also noticed that the Basseri were better off materially than most sedentary peasants and labourers. They enjoyed good health, a wholesome diet and a healthy life with plenty of fresh air and exercise. Their quality of life was high, and they relished their independence, knowing that it did not exist among the sedentary villagers. When Barth has been interviewed about his many fieldwork experiences, he has sometimes mentioned his long trek with the Basseri as the most fulfilling one at a personal level. He has also spoken of the Basseri as the happiest people he has studied. They lived uncomplicated, independent lives close to nature, placed a great value on hospitality and had strong family ties.

In the winter months, the Basseri are scattered over a fairly large territory. As Barth alighted from Chief Hassan Ali Zarghami's Land-Rover in March 1958, he could not discern anything resembling a nomadic camp. His host was present to receive him, but apart from his tent, none of the 16,000 Basseri was to be seen anywhere. Far away on the plains one could nevertheless glimpse numerous black dots, which would turn out to be the tents of the other Basseri. The winter pasture is sparse, and as a result, the flocks need as much space as possible.

Following the Basseri showed Barth that they lived in close interaction – it is tempting to speak of harmony – with the surrounding nature. When pasture was meagre, they scattered; when it was lush, they gathered in larger groups. Politically, they converged according to need, and the most important task of the political leaders consisted in functioning as a kind of traffic police, ensuring the just allocation of pasture and, not least, water. Rites of passage, such as weddings, invariably took place in the fat season.

Since the assignment from UNESCO consisted in studying the possibilities for and consequences of sedentarisation, the fieldwork focused on economy and ecology. Barth estimated that a household needed at least 100 animals, goats and/or sheep, to get by, while 200 was optimal. Should the herd become too small, it would not produce enough meat, wool and dairy products, but if it grew too large, the animals might become undernourished because they lived too close together, and they would also become more vulnerable to disease. Rich nomads could own as many as 800 animals, but they would need hired help to herd them. These hired hands did not, however, feel the same responsibility for another's animals as they would for their own, and this might lead to reduced productivity and embezzlement. Many stories were told about paid herders who sold animals and subsequently claimed that they were 'gone'. In other words, there were sound economic reasons to sell animals when the herd grew too large.

The money could be converted into jewellery, but buying land was more common. The more land a Basseri owned, the greater the temptation to settle as a landlord in order to gain better control of the land they leased out. No Basseri admitted that this was something they desired, but it did occur. Conversely, Basseri with flocks that were too small to provide a comfortable living, often a result of droughts or epidemics, might be forced to settle permanently, but in their case it would be as poor labourers.

To nomads, land has value, but no price. Animals are simultaneously investment capital and dividend. As is the case among other pastoralists, the Basseri are reluctant to slaughter animals, since it means a reduction of their capital. At the same time, meanness is looked down upon. One of the richest of the tribe, 'who dresses poorly, rides a mule, never gives food to visitors, and works as shepherd of much of his flocks, is known by the delightful nickname of D.D.T. Khan, with the implication that he is so miserly he eats his own lice'.[11]

Barth discovered that many Basseri who could have converted their animals to land and become sedentary chose to divide their flocks among their children. Rich men tended to have more than one wife and, accordingly, many children to divide the animals between. Among those who sold their animals and settled as farmers, many lacked male heirs. In other words, there was a clear cultural preference for continuing with the nomadic way of life. Barth's research, moreover, indicated that the Basseri exploitation of their land was optimal and efficient in that the intensity of the grazing was adapted to the carrying capacity of nature. Here, it should be interjected that there is no automatic ecological equilibrium involved in nomadism, and many areas, not least in arid zones, have become ecological disaster areas owing to overgrazing. Among the Basseri, by contrast, both the population and the herds were kept at an ecologically sustainable size.

The way Barth viewed it, there were no good reasons for the Basseri to settle and become farmers, as the Iranian government wished. When he returned to Europe that summer, he discussed the issue with Métraux, who supported Barth's ideas but advised him to downplay the role of UNESCO in the monograph. In late summer 1958, he wrote a report for UNESCO, in which he explained the relevant parameters concerning economy, ecology and the utilisation of arid regions. Afterwards, he wrote the monograph, in which the role of UNESCO is, as Métraux had suggested, downplayed, apart from a short description of their project in the introduction. In the monograph, he took the report as his point of departure, but expanded it so that 'practically every sentence became a paragraph', as he puts it. The manuscript was submitted in the autumn of 1959, but it was published by the Ethnographic Museum is Oslo and by Little, Brown in Boston only in 1961.

When it finally reached its readership, the monograph about the Basseri was received with great enthusiasm. Although it was the result of an applied research project, it gave a rich and diverse description of Basseri life. The ethnography was written in simple language, it was experience-near and punctuated with anecdotes and depictions of telling events. Carleton Coon wrote, in the *American Anthropologist*, that Barth's book provided the reader for the first time with the opportunity to understand how Persian nomadism functioned,[12] and many have since found inspiration in the book, which is concise but touches upon most aspects of Basseri life. Barth writes about gender and religion, envy and conflict. He has a short chapter about a gypsy group which periodically accompanies the Basseri on their travels, he describes their political structure and ritual life, and establishes a clear contrast between the logics of sedentarism and nomadism respectively.

Nomads of South Persia, Barth's third monograph in six years, shares many characteristics with the preceding two. It is brief (150 pages) and written in a sober language without much in the way of stylistic flourishes. Although the main theme, in accordance with the assignment from UNESCO, is the nomadic economy, the book is holistic in the sense that the author also treats relevant contexts. And, it should be added, context is to the anthropologist what location is to a real estate agent. The relationship between nomads and settled people, and between nomads and the state, is an obvious contextual dimension which has to be understood before anything else. Moreover, it is impossible to understand the economy of the Basseri without knowing their political organisation, which offers many options and a great deal of flexibility to the household. Politics in its turn cannot be understood fully without understanding the kinship system, which is patrilineal, but without the formation of strong alliances or corporate groups based on clan or lineage membership. Kinship, moreover, cannot be understood without knowledge of the division of labour between the genders and the rules and practices governing marriages and the transmission of property through inheritance. Religion, which is discussed only in an appendix, is not a very prominent feature of Basseri life, in itself a highly interesting omission to an anthropologist, who tends to expect traditional peoples to have a keen interest in religion and the supernatural. The Basseri are 'generally uninterested in religion as preached by Persian mullahs, and indifferent to metaphysical problems'.[13] They do follow the Persian annual cycle and celebrate *Nawroz*, the Persian New Year; they circumcise their sons; and a *sayyid* is paid to administer the marriage rites; but religious rituals are on the whole not foregrounded in Basseri life. Towards the end of the appendix about religion and ritual, however, Barth turns the question on its head and asks if the regular migratory process itself and its surrounding activities might not be said to have ritual value. It may be argued that this migration in itself gives a meaning to existence as a whole, and that it may thus function as a full cosmology, in spite of its obvious practical and pragmatic dimensions. In this way, Barth tries to integrate the curious absence of ritual activity both with the totality of the Basseri way of life and with a tentative critique of conventional anthropological approaches to religion. His own background in middle-class Oslo society, where active engagement with nature is valued highly while only a minority are practising Christians, may have given Barth a comparative advantage in understanding the symbolically meaningful aspects of the regular migrations.

Nomads of South Persia shares with Barth's earlier monographs an unusual parsimony in the use of sources. The list of references fills just one page and consists of a grand total of 23 references, of which Barth himself has written three. Most anthropological monographs in the 1950s had several pages of references. Fourteen of the sources cited in the book concern nomadism in Iran or Iran in general. Stenning's article about household viability is cited for a comparative perspective on pastoralist economy, and Radcliffe-Brown's classic about the mother's brother in Southern Africa is cited for its perspective on kinship. Further, the human geographer J.S. Furnivall is cited for his perspective on plural societies. His famous description of the complex societies of South-East Asia, where different ethnic groups had little in common but met in the marketplace, was compatible with Barth's observations in Iran. Leach's highland Burma monograph is also included, in the appendix on ritual and religion, and is quoted for the author's argument that ritual may be understood as the communicative aspect of action, in other words, that which does not have an instrumental function or goal. Finally, Barth found inspiration in the sociologist G.E. Homans, known for his contractual view of interaction, where social life comes across as a series of exchanges. None of these authors is the object of a larger discussion, but nor are they the subject of polemic or criticism.

The actual period Barth spent with the Basseri only lasted three to four months. At first, he had waited for nearly three months for his research permit, and from the beginning of June he was in Tehran and went on shorter visits to other peoples in the region. Considering the quality and depth of the ethnography in *Nomads*, this is nothing short of sensational. Nobody has, to my knowledge, accused Barth of having been guilty of oversimplification or gross misunderstandings in this monograph, and the descriptions of everything from marriage rites to handicrafts and migration rhythms are accurate and convincing. The inevitable conclusion is that Barth was an exceptionally competent and focused fieldworker, who gathered a body of empirical material in just three months which might easily have taken another ethnographer a year. However, with the exception of Swat, where he could easily get along in Pashto in any conversation, his limited command of language has been Barth's Achilles heel as a fieldworker. Even with the competent help of Georg Morgenstierne and Linguaphone, he never achieved fluency in Persian (Farsi), which he readily admits both in the monograph and in later writings. As a result, he was far from able to understand all the nuances in other people's conversations, although he may well have been able to understand their answers to his questions and carry out an ordinary conversation himself. He would have depended greatly on his bilingual assistant.

At the same time, Barth tended to make the most of his observations and experiences in the field, and his Basseri fieldwork was no exception. Apart from the monograph, he wrote several articles, which only partly overlap with the book. The most important is 'Capital, Investment and the Social Structure of a Pastoral Nomad Group in South Persia', which shows why it is not only existentially rewarding, but also economically meaningful, for nomads not to turn themselves into sedentary peasants.[14]

A reading of Barth's first three periods of fieldwork and the rich crop they yielded not only tells the story of a gifted ethnographer and a shrewd analytical thinker, but indirectly how useful it may be to hire a local assistant in the field, and how lucky – or skilful – Barth was in finding excellent collaborators again and again. In Kurdistan, he received invaluable assistance from Baba Ali Shaikh Mahmoud, who shared his considerable network of contacts with Barth, but who had also studied political science and had a genuine interest in Barth's study. In Swat he worked with Kashmali, and among the Basseri he had Ali Dad with him continuously. Kashmali especially may be described as a key informant, but there are sound reasons to assume that Ali Dad also helped Barth greatly in entering and understanding the local community quickly and efficiently. To young ethnographers, who have been told more or less explicitly that they have to do everything themselves (and spend at least a year in the field), it must be liberating to hear Barth's story about his high-octane, high-speed fieldwork periods with the close collaboration of key informants. Barth has been more explicit about his use of interpreters and key informants than most other anthropologists, showing that the quality of the ethnography may indeed be enhanced through the complicity of a local trickster or cultural translator.

In autumn 1959, when the Basseri monograph was completed, Barth and Klausen began to teach anthropology at the undergraduate level in Oslo. The students were few, but enthusiastic. Among the first were Knut Odner and Jan Brøgger. The interdisciplinary Odner, who throughout his life was just as much an archaeologist and cultural historian as he was a social anthropologist, would later teach for many years at the University of Oslo, while Brøgger had a dual education in psychology and social anthropology, and eventually became the founder and undisputed paterfamilias at the Department of Social Anthropology in Trondheim.

Around this time, a readership was announced at the University of Oslo. It was unspecified, but attached to the Faculty of Humanities. Now, social anthropology is usually classified as a social science, but its identity has never been obvious, and there are some anthropology departments which are part of humanities faculties. Moreover, the Faculty of Social Sciences was not founded in Oslo until 1963. In the 1950s, the kinship between anthropology and subjects such as archaeology and ethnology was generally seen as closer than that with sociology and politics. Gjessing was an archaeologist himself, and Blom received his magister degree in ethnology. The readership was not announced openly, as would have been the case today, but instead, there was a round of nominations among senior academics. Morgenstierne nominated Barth, who would have accepted the post happily. However, the historians made up 'a strong group', as he puts it (in accordance with the alliance dynamics he had studied in Swat). They wanted the theoretically oriented historian Ottar Dahl for the post. He was clearly a strong applicant, and his candidacy won in the end. Barth suspected that Gjessing might have played a part here. Just as he felt that the powerful and highly respected Evans-Pritchard had opposed him from Oxford, the academically less significant but influential Gjessing was an opponent in the competitive struggle over scarce resources in Oslo.

Around the same time, a group of influential men were meeting to discuss the future of the new University of Bergen (founded in 1946) and its potential comparative advantages in a broader Norwegian and Scandinavian context. The philosopher Knut Erik Tranøy, based in Bergen, had come into contact with cultural anthropology during his studies in the USA. He received Barth's curriculum vitae and publications from Oslo, and took them to the university's director, Arne Halvorsen. It may also have helped that Barth's old comrade from the 'attic group', Henning Siverts, now held a fellowship at Bergen Museum and spoke at length and with great enthusiasm about this hugely gifted young man to Tranøy and other influential people. Indeed, Siverts would later be nicknamed 'John the Baptist': he who spoke of the imminent coming of the Saviour. Halvorsen happened to know Barth's father Tom from committee work in Oslo, and came to believe in his son. As a result, Barth received a personal offer of a temporary post as a reader in Bergen, but with the possibility of tenure, and promotion, if things worked out well.

However, just as this was unfolding, Barth received a letter from Jean Pehrson, Robert N. Pehrson's widow. Pehrson and Barth had become acquainted in 1953, and they shared an interest in the region where the Middle East merges into the Indian subcontinent. Pehrson had also cultivated an interest in the Sami of northern Scandinavia, and had published about them, but he had been planning fieldwork in south-western Pakistan when he and Barth met. He was doing fieldwork there, in Baluchistan, from the autumn of 1954 until he died, following a brief illness, in 1955. Jean, who had accompanied her husband to the field, edited and wrote out 200 pages of fieldnotes, and approached Barth to ask if it might be possible to do something with the material. Barth studied Pehrson's fieldnotes and realised that it would be difficult to get a proper grip on them without first-hand knowledge of the field. Therefore, he applied to the Wenner-Gren Foundation for Anthropological Research (an organisation from which he would later benefit considerably) for a grant to travel to Pakistan. The application was approved, and in spring 1960 he went to Baluchistan in order to find a way of giving final shape to Pehrson's fieldnotes. Luckily for Barth, the Baluchi with whom Pehrson had worked were bilingual in Pashto and Baluchi, so he could communicate with them easily. The tragic circumstances of Pehrson's fieldwork also contributed to his being received by the Baluchi in a warm, hospitable and respectful way. *The Social Organization of the Marri Baluch*, written out and edited by Barth but published in Pehrson's name, was eventually published in 1966.[15] The enthusiastic reviewer in *American Anthropologist* concluded his review by saying that he believed that Pehrson, 'in his quiet way', was proud of the collaboration.[16]

Barth also managed to utilise Pehrson's field data and his own visit to Baluchistan for an article of his own, 'Competition and Symbiosis in North-East Baluchistan'.[17] It applies some of the same methodological devices that were also used in the article on ethnicity and ecology in Swat, as well as the Basseri monograph. The article shows how political power, ecological conditions and economic calculations govern niche creation and socio-economic relations between the three main groups in the region – settled Pathan farmers, Powindah nomads and Marri Baluch, who combine farming and raising livestock.

Several things had now happened nearly simultaneously. First, the readership in Oslo was given to someone else. Second, Barth was offered a temporary readership in Bergen. Third, he travelled to Baluchistan for the sake of Pehrson's legacy. Finally, Barth received an invitation from Columbia University to spend 1960 there as a visiting professor. Barth accepted the invitation, but because of the project in Baluchistan, he had to wait until the autumn to travel to New York. Around this time, Klausen travelled to India on fieldwork, and Blom took over the undergraduate teaching at the museum.

At Columbia, Barth encountered a diverse, energetic and self-conscious academic milieu with many eccentrics, but little pomposity. The impetus behind the invitation came from the 1956 ecology article, but students and colleagues would soon discover the more recent Basseri monograph. Among the faculty were Harold Conklin, a founder of ethnoscience, a branch of anthropology that studies knowledge systems and 'native science', and Andrew P. (Pete) Vayda, who had a background in biology and wished to use ecological accounts more systematically in anthropology. Barth shared an office with Marvin Harris, who would soon make his name as a writer of popular anthropology and as an uncompromising, controversial materialist. Barth wrote and taught, and admits retrospectively that the environment at Columbia was quite demanding, since the students worked hard, were talkative and intelligent (he once spoke of them as 'typical New York Jews'), and he learnt from them as well as teaching them. One of these students was Roy ('Skip') Rappaport, who would later develop innovative analyses of pigs, humans and ecological sustainability in New Guinea.[18]

On the eve of his departure from Columbia in spring 1961, the head of department, Charles Wagley, organised a farewell party. He ended his speech by offering Barth a position at the department. Columbia University, so high up on the Upper West Side that it almost rubs shoulders with Harlem, is one of the finest in the USA. It belongs to the exclusive club of Ivy League universities, and has an anthropology department where Franz Boas presided for four decades. A tenure-track position there would rank much higher internationally than a temporary readership at the newly founded, provincial university in Bergen. Being American by birth, Barth's wife Molly may well have found the proposition enticing. Yet, it does not seem as if Barth even considered the offer. He says that accepting a position in New York would have entailed becoming an American and being enrolled in a highly competitive, achievement-oriented system, where the chance of pursuing one's own interests doggedly would probably be much less likely than in the backwater of Bergen. For this reason, he opted to view Bergen as a golden opportunity rather than as a last resort, and accepted their offer.

What drew Barth to Bergen was, above all, the belief that he would be able to 'rely on his own capabilities', as he puts it. Barth was very much his own man, which he had now demonstrated through three books and several articles. Moreover, he knew that the temporary post as a reader might eventually develop into a professorship, and that in Bergen, of all places, it would be possible to build a new research environment without having to deal with the kind of heavy historical baggage that encumbers creative souls and inhibits innovation elsewhere. It was tempting, as he phrases it in a retrospective: 'I was … attracted by the challenge to create the first anthropological department in Norway, indeed in all of Scandinavia. This was a chance that I could not pass up'.[19]

His father Tom warned him. He himself had seen colleagues go to seed academically by moving to the small, provincial university of Bergen. Perhaps this warning indirectly served as a motivation? Barth was now a celebrated anthropologist, at 32 a father of four, but he was still determined to show his father what he was made of, and he cared little about formal rank. Tom Barth was a person of significance, one of the good and the great, in the Scandinavian natural science world – according to his colleague Henrich Neumann, he was far better known for his scientific contributions than for the American cars he struggled to get up the hills toward Holmenkollen in the winter months.[20]

Yet, Barth maintained a connection with Oslo in spite of moving to Bergen. Throughout his life, Barth has been deeply attached to the forests of eastern Norway in general, Nordmarka, outside Oslo, in particular. He would never feel entirely at home in rainy Bergen, with its long-standing German connection through the Hanseatic League. At the end of the

1950s, he bought a house in the upmarket area of Holmenkollåsen, on the western outskirts of Oslo, near his parents' house and on the very border of Nordmarka, a large protected area of forests and lakes, with a panoramic view of the lake Bogstadvannet. He would not move into the house for another twelve years, but the purchase was a tangible sign – observation data, not interview data – indicating that he did not intend to spend the rest of his life in Bergen.

4

Entrepreneurship

You shouldn't look at what makes the entrepreneur, you should see what the entrepreneur makes.[1]

When Barth arrived in Bergen, its fifteen-year-old university was located on a low hill near the city centre. Norwegian society, with its rural history and modern national identity associated with nature and rural life, has serious difficulties in handling urbanity – with Bergen a main exception. The main campus in Trondheim is located in an open field about 10 kilometres from the city, the University of Tromsø is closer to the airport than to the city, and in Oslo most of the departments are at Blindern, surrounded by apple trees and middle-class suburban bliss. New university colleges, from Vestfold to Lillehammer, are built just far enough from the nearest town that the students do not have to feel part of an urban community when they go to lectures. In Bergen, however, the social anthropologists were setting up shop in an older building in Fosswinkels Gate, within immediate reach of pubs, squares and shops.

In 1961, there was no department of social anthropology as such, and the discipline was attached to the Department of Philosophy. However, it went almost without saying that Barth's primary task, from the university management's perspective, consisted in creating a professional social anthropological environment at an international level. Henning Siverts was already in place, but left for fieldwork in Mexico in the same year that Barth arrived. Otto Blehr and Robert Paine were the first to arrive. Blehr had studied anthropology in British Columbia and taken his magister degree in ethnology in Oslo. Paine, an Englishman, held a doctorate from Oxford, but since he wrote about the Sami in Northern Norway, he not only knew Barth, he knew Norway. Both men wrote about Scandinavian issues, and their early presence in Bergen would serve as a reminder that anthropology 'at home' (or 'near home') has not always been considered a last resort or second-rate in Norwegian anthropology. Having been a reasonably prosperous country even before the discovery of North Sea

4. In Bergen, 1967 (photo reproduced by permission of Bergen University Library).

oil in the 1970s, Norway had the possibility of funding exotic fieldwork early on, and those who chose not to travel far did so out of desire, not necessity.

By the following year, Blom brought his research fellowship with him from Oslo, and the Inuit specialist Helge Kleivan also joined the growing group of anthropologists in Bergen. However, the rest of the 'attic group' remained in Oslo, and several of them would soon take centre stage in the development of social anthropology in the capital. Axel Sommerfelt remained in Africa and would stay until he was evicted by Ian Smith's police, but Arne Martin Klausen had steady employment at the museum and continued, along with Ingrid Rudie and Harald Eidheim, to build social anthropology there. The Department of Ethnography (soon to be the Department of Social Anthropology), was founded in 1964.

In Bergen, the circle around Barth continued to grow. In 1963, a lectureship was announced. Many thought that it was meant for Kleivan, being the most senior and most accomplished in terms of formal qualifications of the group below Barth, but he did not wish to stay in Bergen. Perhaps he needed to liberate himself from Barth's charismatic leadership, or perhaps it was his Danish wife who wanted to go home; be that as it may, Kleivan went to Copenhagen, where, in 1968, he founded the International Work Group for Indigenous Affairs (IWGIA), an influential NGO. Thus Blom felt he had to apply, did so, and got the lectureship.[2] Over the decades to come, long after Barth had left Bergen, Blom would play an important role as a teacher, supervisor and institution builder in Bergen.

Barth realised early on that social anthropology had to be made relevant for Norway and Norwegian conditions if it were to have a future in the country. There was some anthropological research on Norway, such as Paine's work and Eidheim's studies of Norwegian–Sami relations, as well as John Barnes's study of Bremnes, a fishing hamlet in the west. But there was little else, apart from a large body of ethnological literature, much of it descriptive, some of it openly nation-building in character. Barth says:

In a way, we had to identify ourselves with a series of tasks in Norwegian society. And it was theoretically defensible to say that Norway is a place in the world and thereby just as ethnographic as any other place. So there was no theoretical contradiction here; it was, put in so many words, explicitly, our view of anthropology. And I remember how we laughed at Lévi-Strauss, who gave a famous lecture where he said that anthropology finally reaches enlightenment when its object disappears – the last tribes vanish or dissolve, and at that point, anthropology no longer has an object of study. We thought this was an incredibly silly thing to say. Which, as a matter of fact, it was.[3]

Two projects on Norwegian society saw the light of day during the first couple of years in Bergen. The first concerned fisheries. Barth had recruited the sociologist Øyvind Hansen to contribute to it, but in the first instance he got Ingrid Rudie to carry out a six week pre-study of social interaction in fishing boats on the north-western coast, before joining her later.

The idea for the fisheries project came to Barth after having read Erving Goffman's *The Presentation of Self in Everyday Life*,[4] a book that has inspired generations of sociologists and anthropologists since its first publication in 1959. Barth, who had known Goffman superficially at Chicago, was especially impressed by the sociologist's ability to develop interesting and revealing perspectives on apparently trivial situations. Goffman shows how we humans have a tendency to exaggerate (over-communicate) whatever it is that we want others to notice, while we play down (under-communicate) that which we would rather others did not pay too much attention to. His focus is on situationally defined courses of action with a strategic element. What you want your girlfriend or boyfriend to notice about you is unlikely to be identical with whatever it is that you over-communicate towards your employer.

The main idea, honed and refined by Rudie during her weeks on the Møre coast, consisted in studying the relationship between status and role in the interaction on-board a fishing vessel. In anthropology, status refers to the formal position of a person in a social system, while role refers to that person's active, often strategic and improvising, application of status to achieve particular goals. In the fishing boat, there were three types of relevant statuses: the skipper, the fishermen and the net-boss, who had a kind of trickster role. It was his job to sense or feel where the shoals of herring stood. Sonar was not available on fishing vessels at this time.

Barth went fishing and returned, and seminars were given in Bergen about role behaviour and strategic choice. No major publications emerged out of the fisheries project, but a few years later it would provide the empirical basis for the first chapter in Barth's main theoretical work, *Models of Social Organization*.

The other project focusing on Norwegian society, by contrast, almost immediately bore fruit. In January 1962, Barth organised a symposium about rural entrepreneurship, and in the following year, *The Role of the Entrepreneur in Northern Norway* was published. The perspective was clearly formulated, and Barth's international positioning in the world of anthropology could not have been more clearly stated than in the introduction to the book, where he says that what is interesting is not whatever it is that creates the entrepreneur, but what the entrepreneur creates. While others would begin by looking at the system, or the norms, or the social structure (or, a few years later, property relations), Barth begins with the tangible, acting and desiring agent who finds himself in the middle of some social situation.

The entrepreneur is a slightly different kind of character in social science than in the construction business, although the two have something in common, occasionally quite a bit. Barth found a definition in the work of the historian Cyril Belshaw that he could use, where the entrepreneur is described as a risk-taking leader of an enterprise, who instigates innovation and is driven by the hope of big profits. These aspects of the entrepreneur, Barth writes, show that the entrepreneur initiates and coordinates a string of activities, and that a corporate group coalesces around them (the term network might also have been used). Entrepreneurship is an aspect of a role, sociologically speaking; it is not, as in everyday language, a profession or a person.[5]

The book about entrepreneurship in Northern Norway is short even by Barthian standards (82 pages), and contains five articles, including Barth's introduction. He there shows both why he might be accused of positivism, and why, in the final instance, he is not a positivist. A maximising logic of action is presupposed both in the description and in the analysis, and the reader may get the impression that people in general are fundamentally strategic and selfish. Such a critique has been directed at the entire discipline of economics, and the answer is simple: there is no assumption to the effect that people are per se selfish strategists, but an important element in economic research is maximising behaviour. Economists rarely study the informal interaction taking place between parents and children, but they frequently look at capital investment and financial speculation. What is peculiar about the book on entrepreneurship (and many of Barth's other early writings) is the fact that a social anthropologist should take this approach to the study of economy. After all, when anthropologists have studied 'primitive economy', they have typically either searched for its socially integrative role (as in Mauss's *The Gift*) or the culturally specific forms of exchange and norms regulating transactions (as in Malinowski's Trobriand research). They have frequently followed the economic historian Karl Polanyi and his important book *The Great Transformation*, where individual profit-maximising under large-scale capitalism is contrasted with earlier economic systems, where values other than individual utility were given pride of place.[6] As elsewhere, Barth assumes in this book that humans everywhere operate within a recognisable, universal logic of action: people will everywhere tend to make the most of their opportunities, and this may well be studied as strategic, maximising behaviour.

At the same time, this logic is obviously expressed differently in different cultural worlds. This means that even anthropologists who assume that the logic of action is the same are obliged to learn about local conditions, with their accompanying systems of values and norms. Barth's early focus on maximising actions may well be discussed, and has been discussed thoroughly in anthropological circles, but there is no basis for accusing him of seeing just utilitarian maximisation. In an interview conducted many years later, Barth explains in few words why anthropology cannot be positivist; it cannot, in a word, search for objective, universal regularities with the aim of predicting behaviour: 'We were what is now described as constructivists. We say that people interpret their situation by means of their culture, and that does not lead to a positivist science'.[7]

A partly implicit theme in *The Role of the Entrepreneur*, which Barth would develop further a few years later, concerns the entrepreneur as mediator. The entrepreneur is the person who sees opportunities that nobody else is able to identify. They are willing to take risks and are a skilled networker. They create connections where they would otherwise not have existed, and are capable of making others see new possibilities. The entrepreneur, as Barth and his contributors present it, usually functions in the economy, but in one of the chapters, namely Eidheim's article about entrepreneurship in Sami politics, the concept is opened up to include strategic mediation in other fields as well. In the introductory chapter, Barth expresses some scepticism towards the use of the concept of the entrepreneur in the study of political careers, but he nevertheless describes Eidheim's chapter as a 'clarifying *tour de force*'.[8]

The empirical field in which entrepreneurship takes place in this book is that of Northern Norway, and 'certain general ecological, economic and cultural themes recur in most of the case material which limit its range of forms, and should be understood as a common ethnographic background for the material'.[9] Located inside the Arctic Circle, the region is ecologically marginal, but economically it swings irregularly between scarcity and 'Klondike-like' outbursts of sudden wealth. The fisheries are the key in both kinds of situations. Ethnicity is also a topic, especially in the northernmost county of Finnmark, where Eidheim had already carried out comprehensive fieldwork. His chapter describes a Sami political entrepreneur who exploits the precarious, special situation of the Sami, as an indigenous people, in order to obtain political allies, clients and voters.

The remaining chapters in the book, written by Ottar Brox, Paine and Rudie, suggest that the tiny group of anthropologists in Bergen was beginning to extend its reach. In his comparison between 'Eastfjord' and 'Westfjord', Brox shows his local knowledge – he was born and raised in the area – and shows how 'Eastfjord' is an atomistic and individualised society permitting a great deal of autonomy to the individual fisherman, while 'Westfjord' is controlled by a powerful businessman, the hamlet owner (*væreier*). Brox, later a member of parliament for the Socialist Left Party (1973 to 1977) and an active social researcher, frequently visited

Bergen. Throughout his life, he says, he has benefited from Barth's inductive, processual way of thinking. Brox had met Barth in 1959, thanks to an introduction by Robert Paine. At the time, Brox was based at the Norwegian College of Agriculture (now the Norwegian University of Life Sciences), and had written an article about his home island, Senja, north-east of Tromsø, that he asked Barth to read for him. Somewhere in the text, Brox had written that 'society resists changes'. Barth immediately reacted to this sentence, pointing out that 'society' is incapable of acting on its own. This apparently innocent comment had major consequences. Today, Brox says that this early meeting with Barth changed his intellectual orientation permanently, and became the start of a life-long engagement with Barth's thinking.

In spite of his interdisciplinary background with little anthropology proper, Brox was employed for a few years as a lecturer at the department in Bergen, and he made a difference. He published less than Barth, and mostly in Norwegian, but after he published a political book about southern Norwegian 'neo-colonialism' in Northern Norway, *Hva skjer i Nord-Norge* ('What's going on in Northern Norway?') in 1966, he had become an influential political voice in that part of the New Left which had a rural and national orientation.[10] Brox also responded in a critical and undogmatic way to other people's research, and represented a conduit of sorts between the academic world and the world beyond.

In his chapter, Paine describes entrepreneurship in the coastal Sami community of 'Nordbotn', with particular emphasis on new technology. He distinguishes between two entrepreneurial types: the free-holder (who is a farmer and/or fisherman), and the free-enterpriser, a speculator who has no immediate interest in having good and stable relations with the locals, and who can therefore to a greater extent switch between strategies, depending on where the greatest profit is to be had. Rudie's chapter adds a further dimension to the image of ownership, competition and scarce resources in the coastal areas of Northern Norway, and shows, in ways reminiscent of Barth's analyses of Swat, how partnerships connected to boats, trade agreements and fishing cooperatives give birth to different kinds of strategies, and – not least – how difficult it can be to withdraw profits from a growing business.

Only a few months after the symposium about the entrepreneur, a new opportunity arose to develop the anthropological study of Norwegian communities further. In 1962, Brox had just taken up a post at Tromsø Museum in the far north, and 'he wanted to stir up a bit of action, and so he invited a group of us to the great journey from Narvik, through the Lofoten archipelago, up to Tromsø'.[11] The trip took place that summer, and Barth recalls it as 'ten wonderful summer days, with continuous sunshine'. This far north, sunny days also entail sunny nights in midsummer. Brox introduced the Bergen anthropologists to various north Norwegian communities, and to many interesting people. However, it does not seem as if these introductions were ever followed up by subsequent research by members of the Bergen department.

The small, but powerful book about entrepreneurship was produced in the classical Barthian way, that is efficiently, focused and competently. First of all, Barth circulated a short, mimeographed sketch where he gave a short account of the issues at hand. At the next stage, the contributors submitted their draft chapters, which were discussed thoroughly at a two-day symposium in Bergen. When the revised chapters had been submitted, Barth wrote the introduction.

This edited volume was published by Universitetsforlaget, to this day the largest Norwegian academic publisher. Were Barth to have begun his career now, he would probably have made certain to establish a stable relationship with one of the larger Anglophone academic presses as early as possible. In the present day, publishers are ranked according to prestige. Besides, not all have equally competent editors or equally good distribution and marketing; and Universitetsforlaget, which chiefly published books by Norwegian academics in Norwegian, was in no position to be represented properly at large international conferences. At this time, the field was less crowded in anthropology, the turnover rate was slower, fewer titles were published, and it was less difficult to be noticed. The anthology about the entrepreneur may be Barth's least known book, but in Anglophone anthropology people knew about it, and many read it. Although it concerned Norway and was part of Barth's plan to make anthropology relevant to that country, it was also intended as a theoretical contribution to the growing field of economic anthropology.

By the time the book about the entrepreneur went to press, Barth had spent about three years in Bergen, and was by now well established there. He took an active part in the planning of a separate faculty of the social sciences, and also invited well-known anthropologists to give lectures and seminars at his university. The department as such would be founded only in 1965, the same year that Barth obtained his professorship. Among the visitors in the early years were Edmund Leach, naturally, and also Raymond Firth, equally naturally, but also colleagues like Peter

Worsley, Gerald Berreman and Adrian Mayer. Barth himself also began to receive invitations to give prestigious keynote lectures both in the USA and in Britain. Bergen was about to become internationally visible as an interesting anthropological environment, and it is to a great extent a result of Barth's efforts in Bergen that Norwegian anthropology today is considered an integral part of the international, that is Anglophone, professional community.

5

The Global Theorist

The idea for the project on entrepreneurship came to Barth after a Wenner-Gren symposium on economic anthropology, to which Raymond Firth had invited him. The Wenner-Gren Foundation for Anthropological Research was founded by the Swedish businessman Axel Wenner-Gren (who is, incidentally, often described as an entrepreneur) in 1941, then under the name of the Viking Foundation. Between 1958 and 1980, more than 80 conferences and workshops within all branches of anthropology, including biological anthropology, were organised at Burg Wartenstein castle in Austria. Barth was invited to several of these symposia, and he mentions that it had been suggested, tongue in cheek, that one should restrict invitations to Barth to a maximum of one event a year.

Raymond Firth (1901–2002) was a key figure in twentieth-century British anthropology. Born in New Zealand, he wrote his first academic work about the economics of the freezer, as it was now increasingly used aboard cargo ships, enabling New Zealand to export meat and fish overseas. Given the remoteness of New Zealand, it is hardly surprising that this newly invented technology was potentially of great importance with regard to the island's meat exports. Firth then became one of Malinowski's first students at the LSE. His first major ethnographic work, *We, The Tikopia*, published in 1936, was based on fieldwork on a Polynesian outlier, the southernmost of the Solomon Islands. Firth would soon become one of the strongest critics, if always polite and mild-mannered, of the abstract models of the structural-functionalists, arguing that people's actual behaviour does not necessarily follow norms, but emerges in the interstices between norms and cultural limitations, opportunities and personal idiosyncrasies. If this sounds familiar, that is no coincidence. Barth read Firth's *Elements of Social Organization* soon after its publication in 1951, and found himself in broad agreement with Firth's main arguments. The two also had a shared interest in economic anthropology. However, Barth missed a clear analytical focus in his older

5. Fur women on their way to the market (photo reproduced by permission of Fredrik Barth and Unni Wikan).

colleague's work, and would spend the next 15 years developing such a focus himself.

Firth, who died a month before he would have been 101 in 2002, was a student of Malinowski, a friend of Leach and had strong professional views, but he was socially easy-going and built networks both within the sometimes divided small tribe of British social anthropologists and across the Atlantic with American cultural anthropologists.

Since his first degree had been in economics, Firth was determined to develop economic anthropology further, with Malinowski's early contributions as a point of departure, but making it compatible with the discipline of economics. So far, anthropology with an economic focus had mainly concentrated on societal aspects of the economy; it was delineated through its contributions to the totality of society. Economy was seen simply as production, distribution and consumption. Although Mauss had written about individual strategies in *The Gift*, its greatest contribution lay in a deepened understanding of inter-group alliances, the maintenance of communities and of relationships. Firth, conversant with neo-marginalist (neo-classical) economics, wished for a similar approach in anthropology, where the motivation of the agents and their calculations of gain and loss were crucial. Eventually, two 'schools' of economic anthropology were formed, dubbed substantivists and formalists.[1] The substantivists regarded the economy as something substantial and physical, namely production, distribution and consumption. The formalists, on their part, regarded economy as a maximising type of action, and regarded economic processes as something to be studied as transactions between agents, not as systemic processes.

In this dispute, Barth was perceived as a formalist, and Firth wished to enrol him on his side. However, Barth was interested both in individual strategies and what was peculiar and unique about societies, and retrospectively he feels that the opposition was not very productive. Seen in a larger perspective, this debate in economic anthropology nevertheless refers to a more fundamental distinction in anthropology specifically, and in the social sciences generally, between an actor-oriented and a system-oriented approach. According to Malinowski and his successors, society was chiefly created by humans. In the view of Radcliffe-Brown, Lévi-Strauss and many others, humans were chiefly the products of society. It is easy to see that both perspectives can be illuminating – in the same way, perhaps, that light can be seen both as waves and as particles – but when dealing with complex ethnographic material, the researcher has to choose an approach. You simply cannot say everything, you have to decide on your story.

It was arguably because he saw an ally in Barth that Firth invited the Norwegian to give a lecture series at the LSE during the winter of 1963. At any rate, Barth delivered three lectures where he refined and clarified his processual, generative perspective on social life. The existentialist Sartre had, just after the war, formulated the slogan that 'existence precedes essence',[2] and Barth might well have made the motto his own. In his case, it was essential to drive home the point that process was prior to form. What needed an explanation was the existence of stable social forms – systems, societies, structures – and how they came about. In the final instance, Barth saw them as by-products of intentional actions and strategic projects. The three lectures, subsequently published, were the clearest formulation hitherto of the perspective known as generative processual analysis or transactional analysis, and are considered his most important, and most hotly debated, theoretical statement.

The first lecture, subsequently the most controversial one, introduced *the transaction* as an analytical term. Taking as his point of departure the situation aboard a fishing vessel off the west Norwegian coast, Barth argued that the particular status distribution aboard the boat was the outcome of strategic transactions between the parties – the skipper, the net-boss and the fishermen, who all had an interest in appearing as highly competent key actors in the joint activity of fishing. Barth referred to Goffman's concept of impression management to indicate how the actors over-communicated certain forms of role behaviour to show beyond doubt that they knew what they were up to. In other words, he presented an economic perspective on social life, where the maximising behaviour of individuals was a driving force ultimately generating social form.

The second lecture raised the question of cultural integration, asking how shared norms and values within a population arise. The focus here is on negotiations of value where the total opportunity situation of each participant, and their evaluations of their options, entails a conventionalisation of value, whether what is at stake are goods, services or other scarce resources. The main example is from Swat, but Eidheim's study of the political entrepreneur in Finnmark is also cited in order to demonstrate the struggle over value evaluations when different values are incommensurate. For example, a certain politician may regard Sami culture as an inalienable value in itself, while the politicians from the established parties (Labour and Conservative) focus on roads and schools. Barth concludes that it remains unclear which standard will be normatively dominant in the future, and with hindsight we may add that to this very day there is an ongoing struggle between Sami identity politics and tendencies to downplay the boundaries between ethnic groups in Finnmark.

The third and final lecture took on the problem of comparison. Barth pointed out, as he had done before, that comparison is the anthropological version of the experiment in natural science. In two social worlds where there are many similarities, but certain variables differ markedly, it is possible to study the social process in order to explore causal connections in an accurate way. Two of the examples come from Barth's fieldwork in Kurdistan and Swat, both being patrilineal, Muslim, agricultural societies. The question raised concerns the circumstances under which strong, descent-based corporate groups are formed in such societies. The analysis seems to show that such corporate groups tend not to be established when the land is owned collectively and is allocated temporarily to farmers, who have usufruct rights without private property rights. This was the situation in the Kurdish mountain area. On the other hand, strong corporations, and eventually feudal societies, emerge in societies where land is privately owned and inherited through the agnatic line.

The third example, the Basseri – an otherwise comparable group (patrilineal, Muslim, from the same ethnographic region) – indicates how distinctive social organisation becomes when capital consists of animals rather than land. Since there is an upper limit to the number of animals people can usefully own, no permanent, ranked status groups appear here, at the same time as the circumstances force the Basseri to coordinate their activities to a greater extent than the Kurds.

The main point of all three lectures was that the focus of inquiry should be shifted from research on existing social systems as such to the social processes leading to a particular form. Thereby, by isolating the decisive variables and factors, anthropology would be capable of demonstrating how a particular form of social organisation emerged.

Barth did not speak explicitly about prediction in these three lectures, but he came close to doing so. What held him back was, I believe, his acknowledgement of the unpredictable element in courses of action. In Bergen, Barth had used his colleagues as a sounding board to discuss the ideas in the lectures before giving them, and also afterwards, during their preparation for publication. Blom was now employed as a lecturer, and had the main responsibility of teaching the still very few students who appeared in the anthropologists' seminar room. This turned out to be a happy decision. Blom was a lucid and always well prepared lecturer, and he soon developed into a respected professional authority in the Bergen community.

Barth's own professorship was not yet in place, and he thus remained in a temporary position. On this occasion, however, he was not worried about the lack of tenure, although he remembered having been bypassed in Oslo when he had applied for a fellowship there just a few years earlier. He was now in a position to pick and choose between job offers. In 1963, there was scarcely an anthropology department in the world that would not gladly have recruited Barth, still a young man of 34, but with considerable academic merit, both in terms of his comprehensive ethnographic material and regarding his independent approach to theory and method. A couple of years after his arrival in Bergen, nobody could doubt his capabilities as an institution builder either, as he revealed himself to be a cunning strategist who understood both the intrigues and intricacies of university politics, and knew what it took to create an intellectually stimulating academic environment.

The small Bergen community continued to grow as the 1960s went on. Advanced students were recruited from other disciplines. Gunnar Haaland had been planning a magister degree in political science when he studied anthropology for a year as a supporting discipline in Oslo and was smitten by Eidheim's fascination for the kind of detailed empirical stuff that only anthropologists are capable of dishing out. Following advice from Eidheim, he applied for a transfer to Bergen and a switch to social anthropology. Haaland in turn recruited his friend and fellow student from Stavanger, Reidar Grønhaug, who had previously studied German and philology. Soon, Georg Henriksen would also make his appearance, bringing with him a strong political engagement on behalf of indigenous peoples in the Arctic region. Several distinctive personalities would eventually show up in Bergen, people like Ottar Brox and Jan Brøgger, both of whom built careers as public intellectuals – Brox on the socialist left, Brøgger on the libertarian right – in addition to their academic lives. Seen from the perspective of the 2010s, the 1960s was a time when eccentrics were still admitted into academia, provided they had sufficient professional knowledge, some originality and were able to explain it in a reasonably lucid way. Brox, with his political engagement as a 'leftist populist', and Brøgger, whose anthropology had a strong psychological element and sometimes seemed strangely out of date because of its unflinching admiration for the sociological classics, would not have easily fitted in with today's far more streamlined academic world. And although Bergen was unique in some ways, it would have been typical of provincial universities anywhere in the Western or North Atlantic world. The academic quality of the university was uneven, but at its best, it might, on a good day, look Oxford or Harvard in the eye without blinking. In the social sciences, it was not only Barth who made his mark internationally, but also the political scientist Stein Rokkan, who built a research environment with an international impact largely based on his theory about centre and periphery in European politics.

In spite of the steady trickle of new recruits, Blom was Barth's main conversational partner in the early years. Working on the formal modelling of language, dance and folk music, Blom once said to me that the ultimate aim of his research consisted in working his way through the substance in order to be able to identify the main formal relationships and mechanisms driving the processes. Although Blom had derived inspiration from structural linguistics and semiotics, there is an obvious kinship between his thinking and the models Barth developed in his LSE lectures and the publication that led from them.

A decade earlier, John Barnes had remarked, 'Norwegian social anthropologists can be counted on a mutilated left hand'.[3] This was now changing fast. As a result of Barth having a handful of reliable colleagues in Bergen, he was now free to travel. In 1963, he was approached by UNESCO about a possible visiting professorship in Sudan. The agreement, which was eventually signed with the University of Khartoum, specified that Barth was to teach for half a year, followed by four months of fieldwork. (In reality, he only got to spend two months in the field.) Anthropology was already reasonably good in Khartoum, and it had originally been developed by Evans-Pritchard, who had done long-term fieldwork in various parts of Sudan.

The institutional cooperation between Khartoum and Bergen has continued to this day, and several researchers, both from the University of Bergen and from the development research institution, the Christian Michelsens Institutt (CMI), would eventually carry out research in Sudan. Sudanese students came to Bergen, and the first doctoral degree awarded in social anthropology at the department was defended by the Sudanese scholar Abdel Ghaffar Ahmed in 1973. Ahmed is currently associated with the CMI, but has spent most of his academic life as a professor of social anthropology at the University of Khartoum.

While he was in Khartoum teaching anthropology, chiefly political and economic anthropology, Barth wrote up his LSE lectures with a view to publication. There were a few other European anthropologists in the city, and Barth remembers his collaboration with Ian Cunnison in particular. Talal Asad, who would later make his mark as a radical critic of Barth's analysis of Swat, was also there at this time. The Czech anthropologist Ladislav Holy, later known for his writings on kinship, comparison and methodology, once told me that Barth's lectures in Khartoum had made it possible for him to leave structural-functionalism behind once and for all.

Finally, Barth was ready for fieldwork. He had explicitly demanded of UNESCO that the visiting professorship should include fieldwork, since anthropologists depend on it, and the requirement was met. Barth had found an area in the Darfur region which seemed promising. It appeared that there might still exist remnants of a traditional political system there, in the old Fur sultanate, which had officially been defeated by the British as late as 1918. Barth spent four to five days in the Land-Rover on his way west, through the Sudanese part of the Sahel, before arriving at the isolated Jebel Marra massif and the surrounding villages. Upon arrival, it soon became clear, to his disappointment, that not the faintest trace remained of the ancient Fur sultanate. He was left with no other option than to change his topic, something anthropologists probably do more often than most outsiders are aware of. He changed his focus to economic processes, which were also worth taking a closer look at. He had immediately noticed that people, who were cereal farmers, had granaries attached to their huts, and was astonished to discover that husband and wife filled separate granaries. He then became curious about what happened to the grain afterwards, which in turn put him on track for a study of economic change.

During his short fieldwork in Darfur, Barth became acquainted with a group of aid workers working for the United Nations Food and Agriculture Organisation (FAO). He contacted them, by his own account 'to get hold of coffee or chocolate or something else I felt like', and discovered that they had designed an ambitious project for local development. However, they had no anthropological competence in the programme, 'and had no clue as to what was going on. I had spent a few weeks there, and was able to tell them fundamental things about the agrarian society in which they were making their intervention'.[4]

The people in charge of the project realised that Barth's insights might become valuable, and wished to collaborate with him. In this way, Barth became a consultant for the FAO in Darfur, and received funding for an anthropological project on economic change in the region. This funding would lead to Haaland's first job in the anthropology of development. For his own part, Barth was never especially attracted to Africa as an ethnographic region. He would in the following year visit several East African countries as a member of a Norwegian development aid delegation in Kampala, and he would visit Haaland in the field. He also went with NORAD (the Norwegian state development organisation) to Africa in the 1980s, but never returned to the continent for fieldwork.

The period in Darfur, however, was productive, with the main outcome the widely read article, 'Economic Spheres in Darfur'.[5] In this article, he managed to mobilise most of his academic interests, from the exploration of strategic action as the driving force of society, entrepreneurship as mediation or bridging, and the generative processual analysis he had lectured on at the LSE. The article also clearly demonstrated Barth's formalist perspective on the economy.

There existed a small, but interesting literature on 'economic spheres'. In the 1950s, Paul Bohannan had written about this phenomenon among the Tiv of Nigeria, where different goods circulated in relatively isolated spheres.[6] Things in the same sphere could be exchanged for one another, but not for things in a different sphere. Among the Tiv, brass rods and a costly white fabric circulated in one sphere – and could thus be exchanged for one another – but could not be bought with grain or chickens, which were part of a different sphere, one of lower cultural value. When the money of the colonial power – pounds, shillings and pence – was introduced, the spheres of exchange economy soon started to collapse. Suddenly, pretty much everything could be paid for or bought with money, although labour and land were kept outside the market sphere for a long time.

In Jebel Marra, the economy was diverse and thriving. Unlike the surrounding arid areas, the villages near the volcanic mountain were blessed with enough water for irrigated farming, and it rained from June to September. The inhabitants, who spoke the Nilotic-Saharan Fur language, lived in villages of around 500 residents. They grew millet, fruit, vegetables and some wheat. In addition, they had a few animals, chiefly pigeons and goats, as well as donkeys for transportation and some cattle. Not all the residents were farmers, and agricultural produce was traded in traditional markets a couple of times a week. In the market, people could also buy imported commodities, such as fabrics, tools and sugar, from itinerant traders.

A somewhat controversial commodity was millet beer. Some women sold beer in the market, which was considered morally problematic, not because the beer contained alcohol (the Fur are Muslim) but because brewing is considered an intimate activity whereby women brew beer for their husbands in the domestic sphere.

Many activities outside of the market sphere must also be considered economic. When a man needs to have a new hut built, which happens regularly, it is done as a form of community work. The owner himself erects the skeleton, which is wooden, and the wife makes the clay walls with other women. However, the roof is built and covered with straw by the man and his friends. As a reward for their labour, the participants are invited to drink millet beer with the owner through the night. The beer is brewed by the house owner's wife.

There are thus (at least) two clearly discernable economic spheres in the Jebel Marra region, and there are moral sanctions inhibiting conversion between one sphere and the other. However, unlike the spheres of the Tiv, the spheres in Darfur are not clearly ranked. Bridewealth tends to be paid in cash (unlike the situation among the Tiv, where women could traditionally only be exchanged for women), and valuable prestige objects such as swords circulate in the monetary sphere. Still, it is clear, although Barth does not say so, that the sphere containing beer and communal labour refers to activities where what is being maximised is not economic profitability, but more opaque values such as moral capital and social belonging.

In the absence of technical innovations and access to remote markets where prices may be higher, there are not many opportunities for economic growth within this system. The most obvious option for many Fur consists in accumulating livestock for sale. Animals are a costly investment, but the returns are (as witnessed among the Basseri) generally superior to those from farming. Another option may be to grow more fruit and less cereals.

A third alternative may be to shift the boundary between the two economic spheres by expanding the sphere where labour is being exchanged for beer. A couple of years before Barth's fieldwork, an Arab trader (likely a member of the Baggara people) had asked for permission to spend the rainy season in a village, and he was allocated some land to grow tomatoes. He brought with him large amounts of millet, which he had purchased elsewhere at a low price, and his wife began to brew beer. He then began to organise communal work parties, not to build houses but to grow tomatoes, for which the payment was in beer. Barth made a simple calculation showing that this activity was very profitable for the Arab. The market value of the tomatoes far exceeded the cost of the millet beer. The Arab came across as a successful entrepreneur, an innovative person capable of carving out a profitable niche in the interstices between the spheres.

From a different perspective, the Arab may, naturally, be considered an immoral person who cynically exploited the sense of moral obligation in the local community and their norms of friendship to make money. This might have been a conventional anthropological view of the changes, but instead of lamenting the fact that yet another traditional society was on its way to market-driven modernity, Barth saw an exciting, new possibility for creating a generative model of change.

Returning to Bergen, Barth found that his situation was more complex, but above all better, than ever before. There seemed to be no limit to what he could accomplish. Soon after his return, he negotiated an agreement with the CMI about introducing anthropology into the burgeoning field of development research, and simultaneously began to collaborate with NORAD about funding anthropological research as an integral part of development projects. Georg Henriksen, whose main ethnographic interests were in the Arctic, did fieldwork in Turkana, northern Kenya, in this context, and wrote *Economic Growth and Ecological Balance*,[7] an excellent critique of a development project destined to fail. But as Barth remarks, it had no discernable practical consequences. Later, Barth would also, under the agreement with NORAD, recruit Eirik Janssen to study development projects in East Africa.

Barth also resumed his involvement in university politics upon returning from Sudan. In 1965, he finally got his professorship, and the Department of Social Anthropology was founded. The Faculty of Social Sciences would have to wait for another five years. The small band of students grew, but anthropology remained a fairly well-kept secret. It was taught in a decentralised way. As Haaland expresses it, everybody went to every lecture. In the first few years, most of the teaching was done by Barth and Blom. Barth could draw on his extensive fieldwork experience and his analytical brilliance, while Blom's lecturing was appreciated for his ability to identify the essence of complex ethnographic material. At the seminars, advanced students were often asked to summarise an article or book they had read recently. In this way, the production of knowledge became a collective endeavour to which everybody was expected to contribute. Haaland and Grønhaug were asked to contribute to the teaching at an early stage, indeed before having submitted their magister dissertations, and would in turn recruit those who were a couple of years behind.

Yet the hierarchy was very real. The sociologist Gudmund Hernes commented years later that it had taken the Baktaman of New Guinea two months to figure out that this tall, pale creature was actually a human being and not a god, but that his students at home might not have discovered it yet.[8]

Several of the advanced students began to leave for fieldwork in the mid-1960s, and, in Bergen, Barth received two prestigious invitations almost at the same time. In Great Britain, the Royal Society had just started up a lecture series entitled the Nuffield lectures. The first lecture was due to be given in March 1965 by the economist R.M. Solow (later a Nobel laureate), and Firth had succeeded in convincing the august committee that the anthropologists should be given the second one. The audience for these lectures were academics from different subjects, and since social anthropology was not an established discipline within the Royal Society, the contribution from the anthropologists had to convince sceptics in other disciplines that the subject actually had something important to contribute, and did not merely consist in unreadable, second-rate travel writing, as uncharitable critics had claimed. The decision was made to invite Barth, who describes this invitation as a high point in his life; that he, as a foreigner, should be given the role of standard-bearer in British social anthropology. (Incidentally, a similar invitation would come his way, from Halle in Germany, nearly 40 years later.)

The lecture, delivered in October 1965, was given the title 'Anthropological Models and Social Reality'.[9] It is formulated in such a way as to be clearly directed towards an interdisciplinary academic audience. In the introduction, Barth explains that social anthropology, unlike for example moral philosophy, does not 'comment and evaluate', but 'discovers and registers'.[10] Others would have put it in different terms; here, Barth's ideals from natural science are again in evidence, but he succeeds in identifying a defining trait of social anthropology: it is not in itself normative, and this is precisely why so many are provoked by the cool and detached style in which anthropologists often comment on controversial phenomena. Already in one of the first paragraphs, Barth reveals what distinguishes anthropology from natural science, namely the fact that the objects of study are intentional, acting humans, and that it is necessary to interpret their life-worlds in order to understand what they are doing. Interpretation and empathy, what Weber described as *Verstehender Soziologie*, 'a sociology of understanding', is thus necessary in the very process of data collecting, and also in the subsequent analysis.

Nonetheless, Barth presupposes that actors tend to be utility oriented and rational in an economic sense, and that social structure (or, if one prefers, regularities in social form) cannot be taken for granted, but is the accumulated outcome of individual strategies. In the main part of the lecture, he sketches a genealogy for his own position, interestingly enough beginning with Evans-Pritchard and not Malinowski. In his famous study of the Nuer, Evans-Pritchard shows how the social system is integrated as a result of segmentary oppositions operating at several levels of scale, from the lineage segment to the clan, depending on the situation at hand. Later, Gluckman would reinterpret the Nuer material, arguing that cross-cutting ties could also mitigate conflict.[11] Since a man had his social identity embedded both in his village and in his lineage group, he had an immediate interest in preventing conflict between lineages, as he would otherwise risk a conflict with his own neighbours. Cross-cutting ties thus strengthened social cohesion. However, Barth continues, it should be emphasised that the facts on the ground need to be studied with a focus on individual strategies, seen in the context of the varying opportunity situations in which people find themselves. The logic of action is universal, but the circumstances vary.

When teaching methodology, anthropologists often stress that it is not sufficient to listen to what people say; it is just as important to observe what they do. In the Nuffield lecture, Barth distinguishes between three kinds of data, or models: (a) legal rules, including formalised norms, rights etc.; (b) cognitive categories, that is a central part of what we tend to think of as culture; and (c) the system of interaction, that is to say the social process viewed in the light of personal strategies and constraints on them.

The Nuffield lecture was a condensed and clearly argued version of Barth's view of science. He expressed deep scepticism towards assumptions about invisible deep structures, whether they were social or mental, of the kind found in Radcliffe-Brown and Lévi-Strauss respectively. To Barth, truth lay in that which was visible and observable, as long as it was properly understood. But Barth, too, presupposed some premises or axioms that could not themselves be observed or tested, namely the notion of the rational actor, that is the conviction that people generally act in accordance with their 'enlightened self-interest', as Adam Smith put it. This conviction, expressed clearly at the meeting of the Royal Society, was the most controversial aspect of Barth's position in the 1960s and into the 1970s.

The delivery of the Nuffield lecture was powerful. One of the students present, now a seasoned professor of social anthropology, recalls that Barth was standing tall at the rostrum, his expansive mane of dark hair flowing from his head in a light which made it resemble a halo.

Models of Social Organization would be the most important, most widely read and probably the most misunderstood source for Barth's visions for anthropology. *Models*, based on the 1963 LSE lectures, was published early in 1966. Evaluated from its exterior appearance, it is not a particularly striking publication. The pamphlet, wrapped in a green cardboard cover with a hint of grey, comprises just 32 large, dense pages. When I studied at Oslo in the early 1980s, the entire pamphlet was read by first-year sociology students, while the social anthropology students only had to read the first chapter, the one on transactions. It was one of the first texts I read as a sociology student, and to those of us who had begun to grow accustomed to the student-friendly, almost chatty style in much of the curriculum, the encounter with Barth's dry, concise writing came as a shock. That text offered nothing but a promise of hard work. From the beginning, the reader has to find a way to digest condensed formulations such as, 'a model whereby complex and comprehensive patterns of behaviour (roles) may be generated from simpler specifications of rights (statuses), according to a set of rules (the requirements of impression management)'.[12] Even the simple relationships aboard the fishing vessel are described in a pared down, technical style which makes it difficult to visualise the fishermen, the skipper and the net-boss. The book about the Basseri, published half a decade earlier, was far more engaging. But *Models* was his most ambitious theoretical text, and it may seem as if Barth made an effort to write it out without a superfluous word. In this he doubtless succeeded, but as a result students had to attack it with hammer and chisel.

In *Models*, the reader encounters an attempt to make a science of social research without reducing social life to tables and numbers. Everyone who seriously read the pamphlet understood that they were in the presence of a thinker who was, at one and the same time, strictly inductive – he made no claims which were not embedded in empirical findings – and generalising: he was searching for general mechanisms and a handful of simple, but efficient models enabling the comparison of social forms. A common reaction to *Models* consisted in complaining that the concept of transaction was unduly foregrounded, turning human beings into something like business school economists. For this reason, it took a long time before many of the readers (myself included) understood the implications of generative processual analysis, where what is foregrounded is the very movement in social life, not its coagulated form, and that social form is only fleetingly maintained by continuous, but evolving, goal-directed interaction.

Many social scientists before Barth had emphasised strategic choice and maximisation. The term utilitarianism is often used, usually in a deprecating way, about their work. Barth's original contribution chiefly consisted in the generative aspect, that is the premise that individual strategies (a) are being executed under circumstances which are so diverse that one almost has to be an anthropologist to understand it, that they (b) create different social forms under different conditions, and that (c) a central task in research must consist in accounting for this variation.

Barth's models would be extensively criticised, but the main thrust of the criticism would take a few years to be published. The pamphlet first had to be read and digested, and as history seemed to take a sharp turn to the left in 1968, the criticism would be tinged with a political urgency that had not been anticipated in 1963, when the lectures were given, or in 1966, when they were published. For the time being, *Models* existed only as Barth's most principled, thorough and programmatic contribution to anthropological theory.

The other main invitation, apart from the Nuffield lecture, was a request to give a plenary lecture, with Max Gluckman as the other speaker, about social change at the American Anthropological Association (AAA) meeting in the autumn of 1966. Both scholars had worked with processes of change. Gluckman, a direct intellectual descendant of Radcliffe-Brown, had liberated himself from some of the constraints of structural-functionalism by focusing on the dynamics of concrete social situations, but he continued to assume a societal drive towards integration. Barth, who was inclined to see society as a fairly unstable entity, always in the making, went further. He sometimes speaks of society simply as the 'aggregate effects' of strategic action. It is said that Gluckman was profoundly nervous before the event, sensing that his delivery could never match the charismatic authority of his younger colleague.

This would be the largest audience Barth had ever lectured to, with an audience of a couple of thousand. The title was 'On the Study of Social Change',[13] and like the Nuffield lecture of the previous year, it was programmatic in its intent. The approach and topic were nevertheless different. Whereas the Nuffield lecture has much in common with the first chapter of *Models*, the AAA lecture takes up the same topic as the second chapter, namely questions to do with continuity, integration and change. Barth here says, mostly using examples from Darfur, that the stability of social systems is at least as puzzling as their change or instability. He speaks of change as a result of entrepreneurship and the discovery of new opportunities among individuals, often as a result of contextual change, but he also speaks of continuity as a result of stable opportunity situations. Others might have emphasised the power of habit, the need for security or the inherent inertia and resilience of established social systems. But these others were not the views of Fredrik Barth, an unusual individual who knew what he was talking about, not least owing to his own engagement with the world.

The mid 1960s were the busiest period in Barth's professional life. He wrote and lectured at home and abroad. The lectures in London and at the AAA were the most important ones, but he also travelled elsewhere, as well as keeping the conversation going in Bergen. In 1964, he wrote a chapter about the economy of the Basseri for a volume edited by Firth and the economist Basil Yamey,[14] and in the same year produced an article about ethnic processes on the boundary between Pathan and Baluchi territory, published in a festschrift for Georg Morgenstierne.[15] He also wrote another couple of articles about the Basseri and a lengthy article about the Middle East for a Danish reader in regional ethnography. Notwithstanding the year in Sudan, he undertook no long stint of fieldwork during this period. At the same time, these hectic years seemed to have brought nothing but success. It doubtless strengthened his confidence, but he also discovered something other busy people may be able to subscribe to, namely that the person who does many things always finds the energy required to do a bit more, provided that they succeed at what they are doing. This phenomenon would later be described through the psychology of flow. Barth himself describes the mid 1960s like this:

It was a very rich and inspiring and challenging period, and a lot of what happened could perhaps be said to make me a bit vain and inflated, since things moved really fast, and sort of led to success each time, I seemed to get there every time – in the field and in the Royal Society and in the AAA and at the department and in the committee that made [the] social science [faculty], and everything. There seemed to be no limits as to what one could accomplish.[16]

For Barth, his appetite grew while he was eating. The stories about his discipline and productivity reached mythical proportions, but the truth is that he considers himself a fairly leisurely, almost lazy person in his basic character. He had to give himself deadlines and goals, and force himself to reach them. This seems to have worked reasonably well. On the other hand, if Barth's prolific writing and lecturing in the 1960s indicated a great and sustained burst of energy, his colleagues in Bergen were noticeably less productive. One exception was Cato Wadel, who published widely, but not very ambitiously and eventually exclusively in Norwegian. The sociologist Øyvind Hansen, who had been employed at the fisheries project, never submitted a finished publication. Blom did not publish much, but produced a few articles, among them a classic article in sociolinguistics with John Gumperz. Later, Haaland, Siverts, Grønhaug and Henriksen would all publish monographs and articles, but never as ambitiously as Barth. In the common room and corridors of Bergen, it was sometimes said, especially in retrospect, that people wrote for their desk drawers because they feared what Fredrik would say about their efforts. To what extent this is an excuse or an explanation is hard to judge; the answer is likely to be a bit of both.

If he failed to turn his colleagues into prolific writers, at least Barth ensured that they did their fieldwork. During the 1960s, Haaland went to Sudan, Siverts to Mexico and Peru, Blom to the mountain valleys of Norway and the Bahamas, Grønhaug to Turkey and Afghanistan, Wadel to Newfoundland, Henriksen to the Naskapi (Innu) in Canada, and Yngvar Ramstad to Melanesia. Gunnar Sørbø did fieldwork in Sudan, Sigurd Berentzen did the same a few years later in a kindergarten in Bergen, and Ørnulf Gulbrandsen went to Botswana. They were all well schooled methodologically and theoretically up to date, if somewhat selectively so. In the space of five to six years, Barth had succeeded in establishing a vibrant anthropological community, in a peripheral, small university, that many were envious of.

Barth was still in his thirties, but he had been active in anthropology for 15 years, and he had established himself as a major figure. So when, early in 1967, he applied to the Wenner-Gren Foundation for funding to organise a symposium about ethnic relations, with participation by a dozen Scandinavian colleagues, the application went through instantly. Indeed, he had been encouraged to put in an application. The result eventually became a publication which to this day is among the most cited anthropological texts in the world, namely the edited volume called *Ethnic Groups and Boundaries*.

6
Ethnic Groups and Boundaries

It was mainly from his colleagues and students that Barth sought – and received – inspiration on an everyday basis. The sociologist Stein Rokkan worked, like Barth, with comparative models, but he worked historically at the macro level, and their relationship was respectful, but restricted. Other 'professor entrepreneurs' in the burgeoning social science departments of the new university were useful allies in the effort to establish a faculty of social science at Bergen, but there was no intellectual affinity. The philosopher Knut Tranøy was a loyal ally and a personal friend, but there were no intellectual synergies to speak of with him. The anthropologists would have felt closer to another philosopher, the phenomenologist Hans Skjervheim, but contact was limited here as well. Admittedly, social scientists from different disciplines did attend each other's seminars during the first years, but as their circles grew and student groups were consolidated, 'history and philosophy and anthropology would no longer sit around the coffee table, right, since there wasn't a large enough coffee table anywhere, and my group also became somewhat legendary, on its daily walk from the department to [the cafe] Paletten and back'.[1]

The connections with social scientists in Oslo were also restricted. Barth felt no strong affinity to the growing anthropological community there, although Harald Eidheim was often invited to Bergen, on the other side of the mountains, as an examiner. Among the sociologists, a major figure was Vilhelm Aubert, who had briefly taken part in the project on entrepreneurship, and who shared Barth's enthusiasm for Goffman and seemed to share some of his perspectives on microsociology. But, as Barth sums it up, 'Aubert and I were somewhat shy towards each other, in a benevolent way. We were obviously empire builders of different kinds, with different academic views, different theoretical positions, politically with very different profiles. I was perceived as a conservative, for some reason'.[2]

Although he was fascinated by mathematical game theory, ecology and sociological thinkers from Weber to Goffman, Barth never became an interdisciplinary entrepreneur. He enjoyed participating in settings where

6.   First edition of Ethnic Groups and Boundaries,
      published in 1969 (photo reproduced by permission of
      Universitetsforlaget).

several disciplines were represented, but always took on the part of the
anthropologist promoting the ethnographic way of producing knowledge.

The 1960s was a decade of fast growth in academia almost everywhere
in the Western world, Norway being no exception, and there was no need
to perceive the situation between the disciplines as a zero-sum game
where one person's breath was another's death. There was fast expansion
across the board. By the second half of the decade, social anthropology
in Bergen had reached a critical mass of faculty and students, and could
be relatively autonomous both professionally and socially. Fieldwork was
carried out on all continents. The first to study anthropology in Bergen

from beginning to end was Sigurd Berentzen, who received his magister degree in 1969.

The anthropological milieu in Bergen had a reputation for analytical and methodological severity bordering on puritanism, in its outspoken distaste for wide-ranging theorising and untestable assumptions. Under Barth's leadership, they collectively developed a critical attitude to structural models from Oxford, French structuralism and generalising American cultural anthropology with poor sociological grounding. Knowing the different traditions of the discipline well and being well read in a classical sense did not earn any brownie points in this environment. What Barth appreciated was the ability to cut through the empirical data and develop accurate analyses of specific social processes. There was something about this milieu that, seen from a distance, might be described as intellectually frugal, even ascetic. Students and colleagues took great pains to write concisely, express themselves accurately, avoid digressions and contribute to theory in a way that never lost sight of their original data. Gunnar Haaland's magister dissertation of 1966 was delivered to the secretary as a 60-page hand-written manuscript. In its typed version, it became a 49-page pamphlet, without so much as a superfluous comma. It seems beyond doubt that the social anthropological version of Occam's razor at this time resided in Bergen.

Apart from Barth's models and his 'transactionalism', two main trends in social anthropology were especially influential at this time, the eve of student radicalisation and feminist scholarship. Lévi-Straussian structuralism became increasingly well known in the Anglophone world, and several of his books were translated. His *chef d'oeuvre* on kinship was nevertheless not translated until 1969. Structuralism was a doctrine about the structures of the mind, not of society. Lévi-Strauss himself had his limitations as a fieldworker – he had tried and failed – but he was a strong reader and a bold thinker whose intellectual origins could be traced to Kant and Rousseau. Inspired by French sociology and structural linguistics, he had developed a complete theory about the functioning of the mind, which he believed could be documented through empirical studies of phenomena such as kinship, myth and totemism.

Barth respected structuralism as the major intellectual effort it doubtless was, but did not feel that he had much to learn from Lévi-Strauss. To him, structuralism was too intellectualising and detached from ongoing social processes and tangible life-worlds. Yet there are some intriguing, striking parallels between generative processual analysis and structuralism. Both aim to reveal rules of transformation in a particular process. In Lévi-Strauss, this is expressed, for example, when animals, characters or events in particular myths are replaced by structural equivalents, which he tries to document by comparing different versions of the same myth. In Barth, the rules of transformation can be identified in the basic circumstances that delimit social processes and give them a particular direction, so that changes in property rules or those regulating inheritance lead to changes in other parts of the system. In Barth's case, the universal is embedded in the particular, that is the very social process, while Lévi-Strauss was far more interested in the underlying conditions for thinking, which he assumed to be universal.

The interest in formal systems of relationship in Bergen, which was especially marked in Blom, but which Barth also shared, is also reminiscent of structuralism. In both cases, the objective is to establish a set of logical models which may contribute to explaining the substantial facts. The difference is, clearly, that in Barth's case, the models are immanent in social processes, while Lévi-Straussian models are transcendental. If Lévi-Strauss represents a kind of anthropological Platonism, Barth is definitely an Aristotelian, feet firmly planted on the ground.

The other tendency that began to make its mark was interpretive anthropology. Barth had been present when Clifford Geertz gave the lecture, later developed into a famous article, 'Religion as a Cultural System',[3] in 1965, and found the perspective interesting. Instead of explaining religion by referring to its social functions, or with a focus on power and dominance, Geertz took the meaningful content of religion at face value, proposing a method of interpretation reminiscent of literary studies. Geertz recommended a hermeneutical method in the study of cultural systems. This project, inspired by phenomenological philosophy and Boasian anthropology, might seem far removed from Barth's more sociological research interests, but he saw the originality in Geertz's perspective and appreciated his willingness to take native representations seriously. In the same way that Barth generally held that actions were what they purported to be, neither less nor more, Geertz held that religion or other 'cultural systems' could be fully understood on their own terms.

There were points of convergence between Barth's anthropology and other tendencies in the 1960s as well. One of Gluckman's students, F.G. Bailey, had started to do research on political strategies in Orissa, India, and published on deceit, caste 'climbing' and leadership. In his celebrated and perceptive history of British social anthropology, Adam Kuper points out that Bailey developed 'a thread of Manchester theory until it converged with Barth'.[4] Gregory Bateson, who had inspired Barth since his student days with his concept of schismogenesis, now developed dynamic system theory where both feedback (reinforcement) and negative feedback (absence) were integral processes in the functioning of a system. Like Barth, Bateson was oriented mainly towards process rather than form in his thinking. Yet, no close relation developed between Barth and either Bailey or Bateson.

Other tendencies in the anthropology of the time would appear less relevant to Barth and his crew. The great debate in Oxford in the middle of the decade was the so-called rationality debate, which concerned whether or not a certain form of rationality was universal, that is to say whether different peoples reasoned in different ways.[5] Barth regarded this debate as too philosophical and in the last instance a dead end, since rationality, in his view, was always locally embedded. Nonetheless, it may well be argued that he might have had something to contribute, and to learn, from the debate. The transaction model presupposes a shared, universal rationality, namely a goal-oriented rationality which may, according to the model, be discerned everywhere, even if the context and circumstances should vary hugely. He did not, in other words, favour a radical cultural relativism, but presumed the existence of a universal human nature.

Soon after, another tendency began to gain momentum, namely Marxist anthropology. As a theoretical basis for anthropological research in the West, Marxism had been dead, or dormant, for nearly a hundred years – almost to a day since Marx, and then Engels, died. The Marxist theory of historical change is evolutionist and materialist. It describes the cultural evolution of humanity in terms of a series of stages, and the stages succeed one another through changes in technology and property relations. Most anthropologists felt that Marx and Engels had asked the wrong questions, since their interest in cultural variation was negligible. (This is only partly correct. Engels developed some interesting ideas, partly borrowed from Morgan, about family organisation and economic systems.) Since the 1950s, however, a group of anthropologists, especially in the USA, had worked with perspectives which were clearly Marxist, even if they did not say so. Communists would not get tenure in the USA of the 1950s. Younger anthropologists like Eric Wolf and Sidney Mintz refined research programmes they had inherited from Julian Steward and Leslie White, and became increasingly interested in the historical processes that had created the contemporary world. They were interested in slavery, plantation societies, oppression and revolt, with a geographical focus in the Caribbean and Central America.

In France, a different form of Marxism began to develop. It took its cue equally from Marx and from structuralism, and French Marxists such as the Africanist Claude Meillassoux and the Melanesianist Maurice Godelier had a limited interest in world history. To them, the essential project consisted in analysing and comparing modes of production from a Marxist perspective, with a particular focus on the relationship between infrastructure and superstructure.

The Marxist projects, especially the French ones, bored Barth. They contained little of that curiosity-driven process of discovery which he considered to be science at its best. The Marxists often seemed to him to have the answers in advance, so that the actual research became little more than an exercise in connecting the dots. At least once, following a seminar at the Marxist-dominated department in Lund, Sweden, Barth exclaimed, exasperated, that the students didn't have to go to the field at all; they already seemed to know all the answers.

By contrast, Barth was enthusiastic about the recently returned Haaland's material from Darfur. In the Jebel Marra area, two groups co-existed, the Fur and the Baggara. The boundaries between the groups were clear-cut since the Baggara were Arabic-speaking nomads, but under specific circumstances it was possible to cross the boundary, so that a Fur could become a Baggara. It was conversations with Haaland about his fieldwork in Darfur that gave Barth the idea for a symposium intended to lead to a joint publication.

The participants in the symposium about ethnicity, held in Bergen in 1967, were mostly Norwegian, but there were also a few from the other Scandinavian countries. Barth sent out a loose theoretical sketch in advance, as he had done a couple of times before. He says himself that the secret behind a lively and productive workshop consists in distributing a sketchy, incomplete but tantalising invitation that may contribute to liberating the intellectual creativity of the participants.

Eleven anthropologists took part in the symposium; one from Aarhus, two from Gothenburg, one from Stockholm, three from Oslo and four from Bergen. All submitted draft papers to be circulated in advance, but just seven submitted revised versions for the planned publication.

Most of the major ethnographic regions were represented at the symposium, and the book is characterised by this breadth. Karl Izikowitz wrote about ethnic relations in Laos, Siverts about boundary processes in Chiapas, Mexico, Karl-Eric Knutsson about porous boundaries in southern Ethiopia, Jan Petter Blom about mountain farmers and valley farmers in southern Norway, Haaland about Fur and Baggara, Eidheim about Norwegians and Sami; and finally, Barth himself contributed a chapter about the physical and ethnic boundaries of Pathan identity, as well as the subsequently famous introduction.

Anthropologists and other social scientists had long written about ethnicity. The Chicago School of urban sociology had studied ethnic relations in its hometown since the First World War. Leach had written about the boundaries between Kachin and Shan and how they might be transcended. Gluckman and his collaborators had, moreover, written about ethnic stereotypes and degrees of social distance in ethnically mixed townscapes in the 1940s. Besides, the human geographer J.G. Furnivall and the anthropologist M.G. Smith had written about 'plural societies' for 20 years. In the 1960s, finally, a stream of books were published, usually by American social scientists, arguing that the early modern idea of 'the American melting pot' at best needed to be modified. Even the grandchildren of immigrants (often *especially* the grandchildren) experienced a strong identification with their ethnic group, even if they no longer could speak the language of their grandparents.[6] Barth and his contributors were aware of this literature. They quoted Leach and Gluckman, but as usual Barth did not spend much space discussing other people's research, preferring to concentrate his energy on chiselling out his own perspective.

The most original, counter-intuitive insight in the introductory chapter is the view that ethnic differences do not correspond to cultural differences. Although Leach, but also Gluckman, had intimated as much, it was Barth who formulated this view most lucidly and polemically. The key concept was *boundaries*, not understood in terms of cultural boundaries, but as social ones. The boundaries become discernable since interaction is reduced and often meticulously circumscribed across them. On both sides, groups maintain stereotypes about each other. This is not about objective cultural differences, but perceptions of cultural differences which are socially significant. Blom, Eidheim and Haaland reveal, in their chapters, why this is an essential insight.[7]

Eidheim's chapter, the most frequently cited one apart from Barth's introduction, shows how coastal Sami identity is under-communicated in public contexts because it is stigmatising. The politically dominant Norwegians regard the Sami as dirty, drunken and ignorant. As a result, observable cultural differences between Norwegians and Sami are almost non-existent, especially in public settings. At the same time, ethnic boundaries are being maintained. Informal networks, marriages and political alliances follow ethnic identity and rarely transcend it.

Blom's chapter demonstrates, interestingly, the mirror image and the logical implication of Eidheim's argument. He compares mountain farmers and valley farmers in a Norwegian locality, showing that they are quite different from each other in cultural terms, partly because of different ecological adaptations. Yet they consider themselves, and are seen by the surroundings, as members of the same ethnic group, and there are, for example, no sanctions against marriage between highlanders and lowlanders.

Haaland's chapter, based on the research that gave Barth the idea for the symposium to begin with, takes on the relationship between sedentary Fur and nomadic Baggara. To anyone who remembers the genocide in Darfur in the early 2000s, this is disturbing reading. The Arabic-speaking Baggara were used, by the regime in Khartoum, as mercenaries with extended rights to kill, intimidate and conquer areas with intransigent populations, not only in Darfur but also in South Sudan before that country became independent. In the 1960s, the relationship was nevertheless peaceful and based on economic complementarity, as the situation tends to be in societies where pastoralists and farmers live next to each other. It was primarily livelihood that defined some as Fur and others as Baggara. Therefore, a Fur family would slowly change their ethnic identity to Baggara if they acquired enough livestock to become full-time nomads.

Most of this may sound almost trivial today, decades after the publication of *Ethnic Groups and Boundaries*, but it had wide-reaching implications when it first came out. In his introduction, Barth stressed that goods, ideas and persons could move across boundaries, which nevertheless remained intact in spite of the traffic across them. He also points out, doubtless inspired by role theory, that ethnicity is simultaneously imperative and situational. It cannot be abandoned at will, but it is relevant in some situations and not in others. Ethnicity is, in other words, as Eidheim used to say, an aspect of a relationship and not something you carry inside yourself. And when Bateson says that he does not have five fingers, but four relationships between fingers, he expresses the same way of thinking.[8] It is not that which is *inside*, but that which is *between*, which creates social life, identity and exciting topics to explore for anthropologists. Leach essentially said the same thing in an article about a quantitative survey in Sri Lanka: the smallest entity we study in social anthropology is not the single individual, but the relationship between two individuals.[9]

It is contact, not isolation, that leads to ethnicity, and it is whatever is socially effective, not actual cultural difference, that contributes to the importance of ethnicity. In a retrospective, Barth writes:

We documented situations where people changed their ethnic identities under pressure, or as a result of ecologic change, or where they clung to them in minority situations by careful impression management, or used impression management to deny patent cultural differences that might have been given ethnic significance.[10]

In reality, the book showed that ethnicity could not be chosen consciously and reflexively, but that it might be manipulated strategically.

This strictly sociological perspective on ethnicity, where cultural content becomes a resource which is not always made relevant in interaction, which may be under-communicated or over-communicated as circumstances permit or dictate, has proved enormously stimulating for later research on both ethnic relations and relationships between groups that carry a collective identity. Identity now came to be seen as more plastic and malleable than before, as something flexible and shifting in an almost chameleon-like way. It is not exclusively because of *Ethnic Groups and Boundaries* that research on ethnic processes became a major activity for anthropologists in the 1970s and later, but the book did play an important part. At the same time, it should be noted that the Barthian perspective on ethnicity also raised a few unanswered questions. The very concept of boundary, so pivotal that it is featured in the title of the book, has been the subject of many discussions following the publication of the book. Some have suggested replacing it with the less clear-cut concept of *frontier*, where it is often unclear what is inside and outside the limit, and where there may be no absolute criteria of membership.[11] Following up on this objection, it has also been pointed out that none of the contributors to *Ethnic Groups and Boundaries* discusses those who do not fit in, that is people of mixed descent or cultural identity, who may be neither/nor or both/and. In later years, many of those who stand on Barth's shoulders have given ethnic anomalies their due attention.

A more fundamental objection came from Marxists and others who claimed that Barth and his collaborators were downplaying the structural – economic, political, historical – causes of particular ethnic identities, hierarchies and configurations. This is both correct and misleading. As in his other analyses, Barth refers to contextual conditions that provide constraints and opportunities, but as usual, the focus is squarely on persons and their ability to make the most of their situation. The other contributors to the symposium, and subsequent book, reasoned along similar lines. Nobody thought it useful to write as though people acted in a historical vacuum.

Most later anthropological research on ethnicity takes Barth's introductory chapter as its point of departure, and it is also quoted frequently by historians, sociologists, social philosophers and others writing about the field. The book has been widely translated: the Spanish edition, published in Mexico, has had a sustained and deep impact on Latin American research. The book is nothing short of a constitutive text within an area of inquiry.

Barth's familiar actor orientation is also clear in the book about ethnicity. A short example may illustrate how this is an active choice on his part, and not merely something that grows organically out of the empirical material, as he sometimes seems to suggest. Consider a person of mixed ethnic origin in a society where the ethnic contrast between two or several groups, in theory mutually exclusive, is fundamental. This person may be both/and or neither/nor. In my research on ethnically complex societies, such as Mauritius, I have known many who fall into this category. I once knew a Mauritian who was half Creole, half Tamil. His first name was Catholic, his surname Tamil. He was involved in small-scale business and politics, and once explained to me how he over-communicated his Catholic identity in certain situations and his Tamil identity in others. He could, in other words, be described as a typical entrepreneur, if we accept that the term may be allowed to travel beyond economics. He saw possibilities where others would have seen constraints.

At the time of the publication of *Ethnic Groups and Boundaries*, Barth represented a well-defined position in social anthropology, and was widely understood to be a Weberian individualist concerned with agency, by contrast to those who, following Durkheim, were interested in the cohesion of societies. In the same year that Barth published *Models of Social Organization*, another book was released which would exert a huge influence on anthropology and beyond, and which illustrates the contrast. The book was *Purity and Danger*, the author Mary Douglas.[12] Douglas had studied with Evans-Pritchard, and would defend the main features of structural-functionalism until her death in 2007. In her view, societies created people, not the opposite. In *Purity and Danger*, she speaks on several occasions about anomalies, that is phenomena that do not fit into established systems of classification. In their way, they are simultaneously neither/nor and both/and: flying mammals; even-toed ungulates who do not chew the cud; and, perhaps, people who are a bit Tamil and a bit Creole, and who do not fit in anywhere in the classificatory system. In Douglas's nomenclature, they become anomalies; with Barth, the same people become potential entrepreneurs. Both perspectives may shed useful light on the situation of someone like my Mauritian friend. What you discover when leaving your house or desk to discover 'what is there' depends to a great extent on what kind of conceptual apparatus you are looking through.

This is not a trivial insight, and a reading of Barth's academic development seen in relation to his own biography and personality makes it nearly impossible not to see a connection. 'It takes one to know one', as the saying goes, and this is no less true of anthropologists than it is of other people.

Barth's intellectual position had grown out of his major fieldwork experiences among the Kurds, the Pathans and the Basseri (Darfur and Møre were too short to count here), through a kind of dialogue between him and the field. In Kurdistan, he met a tribal people living on the outskirts of state power, where the honour of men depended on their ability to defend themselves and their women and children. Kurdish peasants and chiefs must in their way take responsibility, not lose face, control their inferiors and make the right decisions. In Swat, he met leaders who were compelled to make fast decisions when confronted with tricky and complicated situations, but who could never allow themselves a break or a holiday, lest someone might take advantage of their momentary lapse. Among the Basseri, Barth met a people who worshipped freedom and mobility above all. Unencumbered by fixed property, they lived a life of movement.

It is easy to see that Fredrik Barth could identify in different but overlapping ways with the Kurds, the Pathans and the Basseri, and that he learned something from them. His articles may sometimes be dry as parchment, but the monographs are bursting with life, written in an almost intimate way with visible compassion for the actors and a meticulous attention to detail. Barth was himself a man of honour, a Kurdish alpha male, a strategic planner of Pathan ancestry, an ascetic nomad who never took more baggage with him than he knew he would find use for. It was no coincidence that it was Barth who organised the symposium about the entrepreneur.

The book about ethnicity easily found its place on the shelf next to Barth's previous books; lucid, accurate, analytically sharp, concise and focused on social process and acting individuals. Yet change was already in the air. Subjectively speaking, ethnic identity does not merely concern social boundary processes and the strategic use of culture as a resource. It is also, often primarily, about meaning: eating the same food, laughing at the same jokes, sharing some solemn and joyful moments, smells, childhood memories and musical pleasures; in brief, the meaningful commonalities people develop by virtue of living close together in the same place. In the introduction to *Ethnic Groups and Boundaries*, Barth dismisses, or brackets, this substance as 'cultural stuff' which might, strictly speaking, have been anything at all as long as it does the job, but in practice, he mentions several examples, both from Swat and from other places, of aspects of ethnic identity which are not primarily instrumental and utilitarian, but emotional and meaningful.[13]

It was not long after the symposium about ethnicity that Barth decided to change his focus. In the following year, he found himself in New Guinea, not in order to study strategic actors and rational men, but to try to penetrate and understand an alien knowledge system.

Part 2

An Anthropology of Knowledge

7
Baktaman Vibrations

By now, I felt that I had done rationality and strategy and actor and choice and those things long enough. And I also thought that I had done ecology and economy and politics long enough. And the interest in anthropology had also moved, and increasingly so, towards symbols and rituals and religion and value, and I wanted to try to transform the economical concept of value to a deep cultural analysis, and I wanted to shift my entire professional weight over to what I guess I then would have described as the other half of the story. Not what people do and how they articulate with the world, but how people think and how they thereby model the world.[1]

In 1968, more than ten years had passed since Barth had carried out long-term fieldwork. He had been aboard a fishing boat and studied economic spheres in Darfur, but had not carried out a larger ethnographic work of the kind that produces monographs, anecdotes for methodology seminars and cases for theoretical articles since the Basseri.

He needed to expose himself to something new. Barth has rarely mentioned wanderlust as a motivating factor in his professional life, but that must be because he takes it for granted. For it is difficult to imagine that he would have exposed himself to the many deprivations, discomforts and frustrations entailed by exotic fieldwork if he had not also been driven by an insatiable curiosity about the world and an urge to travel that was ultimately caused by the awareness that the world brimmed with potential new experiences and insights. Barth is an untypical social scientist in this respect, but this quality about his life has also turned him into something of an anthropologist's anthropologist. Among colleagues, it has sometimes been said that there are three kinds of anthropologists: those who have done fieldwork in one location; those who have done fieldwork in two or three places; and then there is Fredrik Barth.

Barth has always developed his thinking and moved ahead intellectually by travelling and immersing himself in new and strange settings. It is only

7. With Kimebnok, the initiation master, among the Baktaman
    in New Guinea, 1968 (photo reproduced by permission of
    Universitetsforlaget).

on a few occasions in his long career that reading or inspiration from
colleagues have set him on a new track. It happened when he met Leach,
when he came across a book about the theory of games in the Cambridge
university library, and when he discovered Goffman's role analysis. These
events apart, he has been unusually independent for an internationally
respected academic. In his articles and books, his lists of references
remain short, he scarcely includes a single discussion of another scholar's
publications, and he delves deeply into his own empirical material and
resurfaces with analyses which are simultaneously tightly interwoven with

the data and point towards something that might be universally human or at least interesting to try out in a different society. Barth's authority in Bergen was unquestioned, but he was no intellectual snob, and remained loyal to his naturalist ideal, originally gleaned from Niko Tinbergen: 'watching and wondering'. He now scrutinised the world map in search of a radically different, challenging place. He was already familiar with the region stretching from Iraq to Pakistan, while Africa tempted him less. Melanesia presented itself to him as tantalising and different in a profound way.

Many of the Melanesian islands, as well as the coastal regions of New Guinea, had long been studied by anthropologists. Just before the beginning of the twentieth century, the members of the interdisciplinary Torres Strait Expedition had studied the Melanesians of the Torres Strait Islands, and respected figures such as W.H.R. Rivers and Alfred Haddon had published on kinship, totemism and other aspects of Melanesian culture. Malinowski later worked in the Trobriands, while the French missionary Maurice Leenhardt had spent many years with the Kanaks of New Caledonia, subsequently publishing several fine works of ethnography. Margaret Mead, Gregory Bateson and many others had carried out research along the Melanesian coast in the interwar years. As regards the interior and highlands of New Guinea, the situation was very different. These areas were difficult to access, with steep mountains, dense forests and narrow valleys. For a long time, it was generally believed that the interior of New Guinea was uninhabited. It was only in the 1930s that it became clear to the outside world, including coastal Melanesians, that the interior was settled by hundreds of small groups, largely horticulturalists who grew tubers and bananas and kept pigs, and who spoke languages that were unrelated to the major language groups. By the 1960s, the New Guinea Highlands had become a field area for the bold and the brave in anthropology, and the literature from the region began to grow. Roy Rappaport went there and wrote an ecological analysis of the Tsembaga, their migrations and the cyclical slaughter of their pig herds. The couple Andrew and Marilyn Strathern (later divorced) wrote about power, kinship and gender in the Mount Hagen area. Roy Wagner was interested in symbols and cosmologies. Maurice Godelier wrote about modes of production in a structural Marxist vein. More was soon to come, and it was commonly agreed that the region was simultaneously fascinating, diverse, demanding and challenging for Western anthropologists.

In the New Guinea Highlands, you did fieldwork without a safety net. It might take you days, sometimes weeks, to travel to the nearest shop for a Coke and a packet of filter cigarettes. The person who decided to do fieldwork in the interior of New Guinea would also have to learn the language from scratch. The languages were not Austronesian, and most people did not speak Tok Pisin, the English-based creole which is a lingua franca in Papua New Guinea. There were neither Linguaphone courses nor dictionaries. The prospective researcher also had to be prepared to spend a year or two in the field (certain departments held that two years was a requirement in such a demanding setting), without electricity, running water, telephones and shops. Barth had a strong desire to go to this region; he felt an urge to do something difficult, to be able to move forward.

The Wenner-Gren Foundation was supportive again. They funded a tour of the region in search of a suitable location. Barth went to parts of New Guinea, New Caledonia, the New Hebrides (now Vanuatu) and Fiji, before taking a trip to Hawaii to visit Bateson, who was then busy studying dolphin communication. At the end of the trip, Barth decided to do fieldwork in an area on the border between lowland and highland, in the northern part of the Fly River catchment area near the border with Irian Jaya, the Indonesian part of New Guinea. The eastern part of this variegated and secretive island was under Australian administration during Barth's fieldwork, and became independent only in 1975.

During the tour in 1967, Barth visited Australia, where he spoke with the linguist Stephen Wurm, who knew New Guinea well from his own research. Barth had decided to go to the Ok Tedi area, and asked Wurm if this would be a difficult task. Wurm looked at him with sad eyes and said, 'Well, I know *one* part of New Guinea that might be worse'.[2]

In this rough, wet and overgrown region there are few roads, and most villages are inaccessible by car. Luckily, there was an airstrip at Olsobip, the local centre, and this is where Barth first arrived. He made the acquaintance of a young man named Nulapeng, who had been raised among the Baktaman for five to six years as a child, and who was, accordingly, fluent both in Baktaman-Faiwol and Tok Pisin. Barth hired Nulapeng, and they left together for the relatively short but exhausting walk to the Baktaman settlements.

Barth had brought as little as possible with him. If he had arrived among these people with an abundance of material wealth, they might have started a cargo cult, a neo-religious kind of movement with the expressed aim of obtaining large amounts of 'cargo' (goods from the modern world) by ritual and magical means. In that case, the entire research project would have failed. Barth had sought out the Baktaman precisely to study their ritual life and cosmology, and he wanted as little noise and interference as possible. So he took with him just 30 kilogrammes of salt, glass beads for women's handicrafts, a few spare bush knives and axes, a blanket and a bucket. Salt was a very common traditional medium of exchange in the New Guinea Highlands, and was often compared to money.

As mentioned, the Baktaman lived between highland and lowland. Generally, pigs and sago demarcate the boundary (or frontier). Highland peoples keep large numbers of pigs, while lowland people grow sago palms. Apart from this difference, peoples in both the highlands and the lowlands have engaged in much the same kind of horticulture, with an emphasis on tubers like taro, supplemented by some hunting and gathering of wild fruit. Breadfruit and pandanus fruit are especially sought after.

The territory of the Baktaman covered an area ranging from about 500 and 1000 metres above sea level, where their villages were, and reached up into the mountains, which might reach 2000 metres. They did grow some sago, but this was not a major activity. Rather, the sago, which took 15 years to grow sufficiently large to be reaped, was a reserve, to be used only if the taro crop failed. They also kept pigs, but to a limited extent and in near symbiosis with the population of wild pigs in the surrounding area. All male pigs kept by the Baktaman were castrated when young, which meant that they depended on catching wild boars to fertilise the sows.

None of the 183 Baktaman spoke any other language than Baktaman-Faiwol. They were, in Barth's estimation, capable of communicating 'more or less fluently with perhaps 1,000 speakers of the same or closely similar dialects'.[3] They had been contacted and 'pacified' by an Australian patrol only four years before Barth's arrival. 'Pacification' entailed, at this time, the Australians threatening to shoot and kill them if they continued to practise war and headhunting.

The tropical mountain forest represented something very different from everything Barth had previously experienced in the field. New Guinea is located east of the Wallace line, the boundary between South-East Asian and Oceanic flora and fauna, and the forests are inhabited by rare marsupials, large lizards and, not least, the feared, aggressive cassowary, an ostrich-like bird about the size of a human. Olsobip is considered to be one of the wettest places on Earth, with about 10 metres (10,000 millimetres) of rain every year. Early in his fieldwork, Barth contracted a fungal infection of the skin: it would be a couple of years after his return before he got rid of it. The smell of mould and decay drifted in the air almost everywhere, and there were few days with no rain, but the clearings the Baktaman had made for themselves were exceptionally fertile and productive for horticulture.

Before leaving for New Guinea, Barth had decided to change track in social anthropology. He would later describe this new project as an anthropology of knowledge. Briefly put, it entailed mapping out and describing native knowledge systems and their world-views from within, in order to make better sense of people's courses of action. Naturally, anthropologists had been interested in world-views and knowledge systems from the beginning. Two of the most widely read anthropologists in the late 1960s, moreover, wrote about such things. Lévi-Strauss's structuralism used the knowledge, myths and classifications of small groups and stateless peoples as a means to develop a general theory about the functioning of the mind, while Clifford Geertz in Chicago (and later at Princeton) was busy developing his anthropological hermeneutics, inspired by continental models such as the social phenomenologist Alfred Schutz and the philosopher Paul Ricoeur.

Barth's approach was different, partly because he had no faith in structuralism and cultural hermeneutics since they failed to take social action sufficiently into account, but also partly because he always searched for vacant niches and alternative perspectives. Geertz, Lévi-Strauss and many other contemporaries took it for granted that society is projected onto the world, which is to say that our image of the world is governed by concepts and categories produced in our cultural universe. Barth toyed with the possibility of turning this view upside down and instead postulating, as a working hypothesis, that it might just as well be the world outside us which, in its concrete materiality, shaped society and social categories.

In Barth's view, Lévi-Straussian structuralism was too tight, Geertzian hermeneutics too loose. Lévi-Strauss tended to crown his analyses with a stylised structural model, timeless and ahistorical, subsuming the richness of the experienced and sensed world beneath it. In Geertz, the procedure of discovery instead consisted in accumulating facts about 'local cultural institutions in the hope that an inherent systematic would gradually emerge'.[4] It must in all justice be added that Geertz was no less systematic than Barth, but searched for patterns of a different kind. Faithful to his scientific ideals, Barth was determined to do the job in his own way, by bringing his own understanding as closely as possible to the actors, their interpretations and their actions, in order to discern what rituals actually meant to them. With the native point of view as his point of departure, he would then try to find out exactly which aspects of the rituals enabled them to express their inherent meaning-content.

Barth's interest in meaning and cosmology was not entirely new, although it seems far removed from politics and economics. Haaland told me that when Barth visited him in the field in 1965, he became interested in a woman who fell into a trance during a ritual. Haaland did not pay much attention to the event, since he was in Darfur to study kinship and the economy, but Barth regarded it as significant and important to understand fully. He now had the chance, albeit on a different continent.

Among other anthropologists who had worked with rituals and ritual symbols, Victor Turner was probably the one whose work resonated the most with Barth's own perspective. Turner (1920–1983) was originally a student and colleague of Gluckman, but emigrated to the USA in 1961. Initially, he had analysed rituals from a chiefly structural-functionalist perspective, showing how they contributed to social integration by creating communitas – an emotional community – and permeated the surroundings with meaning. He later became more interested in meaning and symbols as such, less so through their social expressions and ramifications. Turner, who had done his research among the Ndembu of present-day Zambia, appeared relevant for Barth's current endeavour, and he engaged with his work both before and after fieldwork.

On several occasions, Barth told his postgraduates and junior colleagues in Bergen that it might be a virtue to read as little as possible before fieldwork, apart from trying to learn the language, naturally. You would then avoid being contaminated and tainted by the commonly agreed-upon approach to the field, and could approach it with an open mind and an impartial gaze.

There is something to recommend in this attitude, but at the same time, it must be pointed out that it is not entirely coincidental that much of the research on Melanesia has been about gender, that descent and corporate groups were huge topics in Africanist anthropology, and that scholars of Latin America for generations have written about race, violence and cultural mixing. Clearly, to anthropologists too (and not just to the natives out there), the concrete materiality of their surroundings, for example on fieldwork, may influence their perceptions. Barth did read up about the region, but fairly unsystematically, and he was by no means a fully-fledged Melanesianist when he arrived in the main Baktaman village. He had few specific notions about what to expect.

Among the first things he encountered was boredom. He has never spoken of any of his previous periods of fieldwork as tedious, but speaking about his ten months among the Baktaman, he admits that time sometimes moved very slowly. Barth had travelled to New Guinea to experience the Stone Age, and soon came to realise that in this kind of society, there is little by way of novelty from one day to the next.

> It is curious how the most extraordinary human life becomes banal after two weeks, and you aren't even able to experience how incredibly exotic and different it is … [S]o I sat there among Baktamans, and they have a ritual life which is teeming with activity, and yet, after a short while I could feel that it was excruciatingly boring.[5]

In the late 1960s, it was not yet known how old the human settlements in New Guinea were. Experts assumed that people had lived in the Highlands for perhaps a few thousand years. Yet later archaeological discoveries and DNA testing have shown that the region has been inhabited for more than 40,000 years! They have engaged in irrigated horticulture for at least 10,000 years, probably longer. In other words, we talk about societies where change takes place at a pace so slow that it is difficult to imagine. This, incidentally, would change. Had Barth waited 15 years with his Melanesian experience, he would have met a very rapidly changing society.

The Ok region has already changed dramatically since the time of Barth's fieldwork. The huge Ok Tedi gold and copper mine, which opened in 1984 after years of exploratory drilling, is located just a few days' march from the Baktaman village Barth stayed in. The many small groups living in the narrow valleys near the watershed between the two largest rivers of Papua, the northbound Sepik and the southbound Fly, have thus been exposed to wage work, mass-produced consumer goods and cyanide poisoning. They have been forced to become citizens. Some have left their villages. The Baktaman participate in local football tournaments, and some have become miners.

In 1968, the Baktaman had no knowledge of either money or writing. They owned a few metal implements that they had acquired through barter, but their knowledge of the outside world was extremely limited. And there were just 183 Baktaman people. The division of labour was gender specific and limited. Both sexes worked in the gardens, but rarely at the same time, and only men took part in hunting. Men and women lived in separate huts and had limited contact, barely enough, it seems, to produce children. Of the 183 souls, 82 were children in 1968. Only six of them had at least one living grandparent, and nearly half had lost one or both of their parents. Life expectancy, in other words, was not very high.

Barth did a quick calculation and estimated that about a third of all known deaths were caused by violence. Many others died of diseases that might easily have been healed with access to modern drugs. This society teetered at the limit of sustainability, with no basis for population growth. Perhaps it had been like this for many thousands of years.

The Baktaman did not produce a food surplus, which would have enabled the development of a more complex division of labour. Everybody had to participate in food production. Even by New Guinea Highland standards, where small-scale societies with a basic social organisation are typical, Baktaman society was small and basic.

An ethnographic fieldworker needs, above all, to be patient. They cannot force insights, and if they ask questions which do not form part of the local repertoire, they risk interfering with their object of study, with distorted and misleading conclusions as a result. They then may begin to talk about *their* own interests rather than those of their interlocutors. Barth led a simple life and participated from day to day in the activities of the Baktaman. Apart from practical preoccupations, on which they spent most of their time – food production, child rearing, hunting, handicrafts – the culture gravitated around male initiation rituals. Unlike initiation in many other societies around the world, where both boys and girls go through one major initiation ritual transforming them from children to adults, the Baktaman had seven grades of initiation, but exclusively for men. The relationship between men and women was one of mutual distrust. The men insisted that women should not acquire access to the deepest religious truths, since nobody knew what they would do with them. There was no parallel female cult. As in so many other places, the secret society guarding sacred truths was a male institution among the Baktaman.

Since he was a grown man, admittedly with limited cultural skills – he spoke the language badly and was, by his own account, a terrible archer – Barth was not obliged to pass through the lowest grades. He was present at a fourth-grade initiation, and the chief initiator, Kimebnok, allowed him to move straight to the sixth grade afterwards. Thanks to Nulapeng, he still got detailed descriptions of the three lowest grades. The fifth grade was explained orally by Kimebnok, who then admitted Barth as a novice at the sixth. Great was the anthropologist's sense of relief when, after a suitable period, he had shown himself worthy of being initiated at the seventh and highest grade.

The aim of initiation is to turn ignorant and confused ragamuffins into wise, dynamic men. Already at the first grade, the boys are torn away from their mothers and brought to the men's house, where they are told secrets and some of the mysteries of nature and culture are revealed to them. When the first grade has been completed, which is marked with a feast consisting of a roast pig, the boys move to live in the male part of the village. They may speak with their mother and other women, but not live with her.

The later levels of initiation, which take place when the community leaders deem it necessary, introduces the boys, eventually the young men, to new domains of knowledge, skills and mysteries. They learn about invisible powers and colour symbolism, they learn to deal with fear and pain, and are subjected to ordeals meant to make them fearless. The rituals of initiation establish contact between the novices and abstract entities such as invisible spirits, emotions and inner power, the cosmos and the inevitability of death. These forms of knowledge are always imparted with the aid of concrete objects at the disposal of the ritual leaders, such as the boiled intestines and penis of a dog, water and fire, nettles and the skulls of ancestors. Moreover, they learn of food taboos, such as the ban on eating a mouse-like marsupial (the *eiraram*), as well as ritual incantations to be used before hunting. The fourth grade involves a dancing ritual lasting for four days. It does not make matters easier that the boys are subject to a taboo on water throughout the dance. At this stage, the boys will have traces of facial hair, and much of the symbolism in the fourth stage is associated with sexuality.

The Baktaman carry visible symbols, such as scars and decorations, indicating their level of initiation. The higher they have reached, the more they have understood of the connection between the sacred and the profane, to use Durkheim's old terms. Ever new layers of prohibitions and other rules are added, connected to food, acts, gender differences and the importance of secrecy. The sixth grade of initiation is a secret hunting expedition from which the men return with sacrificial animals. But, and this surprised Barth, 'no Baktaman initiation rite is accompanied by the telling of myths'.[6] Although the initiation rituals are a matter of great concern to the Baktaman, and they invest considerable time and energy in organising them, the rituals themselves are fairly simple, compared to those of other Melanesian peoples. This disappointed Barth somewhat to begin with, but he also saw the advantage of their simplicity, which made the rituals themselves and the ritual symbolism relatively transparent and generally straightforward to understand.

Rituals are always multivocal; as Leach had shown, they simultaneously *say* something and *do* something.[7] If what they say becomes too obvious, the effect is weakened. Like art, rituals must contain a surplus of meaning.

They must contain more meaning than each participant is capable of extracting. For this reason, rituals are often explained by ritual specialists through metaphors, riddles and ambiguities, or simply by a long and meaningful silence. Among the Baktaman, purity and impurity are crucial, along with taboos and other prohibitions which offer an ideological confirmation of social differentiation according to age and gender. For example, certain parts of a pig can only be eaten by grown men.

Especially at the highest grades of initiation, the symbolic relationship between nature and culture is crucial. During the sixth grade, Kimebnok and the other participants showed how the skull of the ancestor (marked with white hair) is symbolically equivalent to the straw roof on the temple hut, while the temple corresponds to fur, and the body of the cuscus (a small marsupial) corresponds to vegetation. The symbolism and the ritual acts connect the people to their surroundings in a sacred way and may add a shimmering layer of something deep and transcendent to the often drab and monotonous experience of everyday life. The metaphors used in Baktaman ritual may resemble modernist poetry, but remain resolutely anchored in the concrete, the Baktaman being illiterate. They help people not only to achieve a larger, mystical knowledge of the cosmos and their place in it, but they also contribute to their transformation as social persons. A person initiated into the seventh grade has, simply, understood more, and carries heavier and deeper secrets, than those who have not reached as far. Among other things, the sixth-grade initiates know that some of the sacred knowledge revealed at the lower grades will later be exposed as lies and deception. The older men are therefore key persons in Baktaman society. They can communicate with everyone, and they possess all the keys.

Knowledge and Ritual among the Baktaman of New Guinea was written over a long period, which was also a turbulent time in Barth's life. It was published only in 1975, more than six years after the completion of fieldwork. Apart from having been written far more slowly than his previous monographs, the book also carries with it an uncertainty, an ambivalence and a tentative form of reasoning which represents something of a new departure in his professional authorship. In virtually all of his earlier work, Barth had relied on, and produced, a clear, logical progression from beginning to end, a clearly delineated research question and an efficient use of data which shed light on the questions posed and allowed for unequivocal conclusions. The Baktaman book does not really have a conclusion. It just ends.

Yet, the book would gain a special place in the literature on Melanesia, and it was well received, although many had initially been sceptical of this expert on Asian Muslim societies and his apparent wish to reinvent himself as a Melanesianist. Besides, many regarded his ten months in the field as absurdly short. The success of his monograph reveals once again Barth's exceptional qualities as an ethnographic fieldworker. For example, he says that he understood early on that food taboos were essential in Baktaman society. When he was installed in a hut in the village, they started to bring him various kinds of food. He needed to eat, but waited for the others to leave before tasting the food, since he had an inkling that they wanted to try out what he ate to find out what kind of person he was. Only several months later did he get an overview of the taboos which are such an essential part of their social organisation, but already at the outset he suspected that food had a deeper meaning than mere nourishment. It may well be that Nulapeng had whispered some advice, but there is no doubt that Barth is endowed with an unusual ability to read other people and social situations, and that he has again and again discovered, often just in the space of a few weeks, what is at stake for people, just by paying attention to what they do – but also by taking in the unsaid and implicit, the nonverbal aspect of communication, that which Unni Wikan would much later describe as resonance.[8]

A key to an understanding of his gift for fieldwork is Barth's naturalism, his desire to observe and describe the world as concretely as possible. This penchant for the observable and tangible enabled him to give a credible account of the symbolic world of the Baktaman, their ritual practice and classification of their surroundings, in a relatively unfiltered way. The reader is given the impression that it actually *is* the world of the Baktaman that is gradually unfolding in the book, their actions, the parts of their surroundings that become especially significant, and the way in which their world becomes meaningful. The key, in Barth, consists in taking his point of departure in the readily observable and show, as he does here, how the abstractions are immanent. In this, he is distant from Geertz's interpretive anthropology, but comes strangely close to Lévi-Strauss, who introduces *The Savage Mind* with a chapter entitled 'The Science of the Concrete'.[9] Lévi-Strauss argues that non-literate peoples assemble their abstract concepts with the aid of tangible things and sensory experiences, since they lack our cognitive crutches (letters and numbers), building a kind of science with what they have at hand.

Barth discusses Lévi-Strauss's approach briefly, but dismisses it quickly, perhaps a tad too quickly. His main objection is that the universe of the

Baktaman is not integrated in a logical way, that their system of taboos, metaphors and ritual symbols does not compose a coherent totality, but is rather incompletely and imperfectly integrated. Besides it is debatable, Barth continues, to attribute a meaning to a symbolic world that cannot be found among the informants themselves. He regards the symbolic world of the Baktaman as the expression of an improvised cultural creativity, where they use whatever they have at hand – cassowaries, skulls, taro (a common tuber, their staple food) and so on. However, so does Lévi-Strauss, but he adds another analytical level which refers to the ways in which the structure of the human mind influences classification, both of the ecological surroundings and of the social world. Up to a certain point, thus, Barth follows almost the same recipe as Lévi-Strauss, but he rejects the Frenchman's notion of structure, believing the human mind to be more plastic and less rule bound than a structuralist would assume.

In this lies Barth's great strength as an ethnographer, but perhaps one of his weaknesses as a theorist. With his open mind and watching-and-wondering ideals, he entered the Baktaman village with no preconceived notions about underlying structures. He took the people's own interpretations at face value, nevertheless starting from a more or less explicit idea about the mental unity of mankind, which is a condition for other people's worlds to be accessible in anthropological research. This feature distinguishes Barth's epistemology in a fairly fundamental way from theoretical edifices such as psychoanalysis, Marxism or structuralism. He also works quite differently from anthropologists whose focus is on semantics and verbal communication. There are few direct quotations from informants in Barth's writings. Among the Baktaman, he says, he could almost turn his linguistic incompetence into a virtue, by being especially attentive when they *did* something, and by taking in the ambience and the non-verbal.

A couple of anecdotes from the Baktaman fieldwork may clarify further how Barth works, both as an ethnographer and as an analyst. One day, he was sitting in the men's hut, asking a Baktaman about a dramatic event in the recent past, that he had heard about from others. The man hesitated and was unable to answer, but in the end, he brought Barth with him into the forest, showing him the place, and telling the story. The passage of time is, thus, connected to the physical location of particularly dramatic events, almost like in old European maps, where events from widely different periods, such as the crucifixion of Christ and the much later sacking of Jerusalem, are depicted side by side at the site of their unfolding.

On another occasion, Barth spoke with a legendary warrior, known for having killed countless people. It then turned out that he had killed a grand total of five persons, and could explain who they were, the circumstances under which he had killed them, and who their relatives were. This told Barth not only that the Baktaman were inhabiting a very small world, but also something about the nature of violence. In a popularised account published in Norwegian, he speaks of the contrast between the tangible violence of the Baktaman and the abstract violence exercised by the war machinery of our time. He then raises the question, obvious perhaps to anthropologists but not to everyone, whether we have the right to claim that we represent a moral advance over allegedly primitive barbarians and their brutal tribal wars.[10]

In both of these short examples, it becomes apparent that Barth refuses to speculate without a basis in fact, and he has throughout his career been consistently critical of what he sees as tendencies to impose a wide-ranging and generalising theory upon a stubborn and resistant piece of empirical evidence. When he was working with the Baktaman material, Barth increasingly began to see human beings primarily as improvising, multifaceted creatures, who may act in goal-oriented ways, but who are not always aware of their own best interests.

One evening towards the end of his fieldwork, Barth was sitting around the campfire with his Baktaman informants and the loyal Nulapeng, when he caught a glimpse of a jet airliner high in the sky. He knew that it had to be the flight from Manila to Sydney. He then knew that in a few days, he would himself be seated aboard a similar plane, on his way from the misty forest, the secret knowledge, the monotonous diet and the small world that made up the known cosmos to the Baktaman – while they would remain on their forest paths, in their clearings, in their simple huts and gardens for the rest of their lives.

Changing into his ordinary clothes on his way to the flight home, Barth noticed that he had grown ten centimetres around the waist and was barely able to wear one of his own pairs of trousers. But at the same time, he had lost as many kilos during the ten months he had spent among the Baktaman. In a word, he was seriously malnourished from having lived on pure starch for almost a year. Fungi still grew on his skin. The transition to a Western academic life would represent a greater contrast than any of his earlier periods of fieldwork. The Kurds, the Pathans, the Basseri and the Fur were in contact with, and partially integrated into, large-scale systems about which they had varying degrees of knowledge. Many in Swat Valley spoke fluent English, and Baba Ali Shaikh Mahmoud in Kurdistan had earned an M.A. in London. Among the Basseri, 'they began to recite classical Persian poets as we went – and then they had heard rumours about Sputniks and wanted to know if it was true that there were artificial moons and hotels up there, and that sort of thing. Their understanding of history also referred to a large conceptual world. With respect to the Baktaman, it was very striking how small theirs was'.[11]

It is evident that Barth struggled with the Baktaman in ways he had not experienced during his earlier stints of fieldwork. They were more radically different than any other people he had worked with. By the time he had learnt the rules of food taboos and ritual symbolism, they were perhaps not so difficult to understand at a superficial and everyday level, but the overlap between his world and theirs could at times feel wafer thin. During his fieldwork, on occasion Barth could almost have subscribed to Lévi-Strauss's description of his frustrating meeting with the Tupi-Kawahib of the Brazilian Amazon in the 1930s. Lévi-Strauss writes, 'There they were, all ready to teach me their customs and beliefs, and I knew nothing of their language. They were as close to me as an image seen in a looking-glass: I could touch, but not understand them'.[12] This barrier operated both ways. What the Baktaman got out of their time with Barth is hard to say, but they cannot have grasped more than a small fragment of his world.

Barth had travelled to New Guinea in order to do something difficult and important. It was not just about contributing to the study of native knowledge systems and ritual life, but also a kind of 'urgent anthropology'. Human cultural diversity is shrinking, something that has occupied anthropologists since Boas and Malinowski. The repertoire of recipes for living is becoming narrower. We become more similar. For this reason it was important, as Barth writes in the preface to *Knowledge and Ritual among the Baktaman*, to document this unique way of life before it was too late.

And yet, Barth had problems finding his feet among the Baktaman. What troubled him most was the feeling that they based their seven-layered mystery cult around an insight – the ultimate truth – which at the end of the day turned out to be fraudulent. At the lower grades, novices were fed secret truths, only to be told, when they reached the higher grades, that they were untrue. And the big truth, which was to be imparted at the seventh grade, did not exist.

Barth returned home just before Christmas in 1968. *Ethnic Groups and Boundaries* was still in press. He was tired. The following three to four years would not be very prolific by his own standards, although he published several excellent articles about kinship and politics in the Middle East based on earlier fieldwork. 'Analytical Dimensions in the Comparison of Social Organizations' was a constructive extension of ideas that had been aired briefly at least since *Nomads of South Persia*, about comparative social forms.[13] In the article, he distinguishes between degrees of complexity in status repertoires, from the most basic, based on kinship and family, to large-scale modern societies with their dizzying number of statuses and extreme degree of differentiation. This article, which may well be one of his best, offers a methodological basis for studying social complexity without relinquishing the ethnographic virtue of focusing on local life and interpersonal relations. Instead of counting people, measuring production capacities and disentangling levels of decision-making, Barth wished to demonstrate that complexity was expressed through the lives of individuals, their status repertoires, their degree of specialisation and networks of relationships with others. This article also pointed ahead towards a later Wenner-Gren symposium about scale, which led to a book publication in the end, but which deserved more attention than it received.

Around 1970, Barth also published a few popularising texts in Norwegian, and edited a volume meant to serve as an introduction to anthropology. Characteristically, the book is called 'Man as a member of society' – *Mennesket som samfunnsborger*, in the original Norwegian – not, for example, 'Other cultures' or 'Societies of the world'.[14] Like his later books written for a general readership, it begins with the individual. In it, he includes his first article based on the Baktaman fieldwork, an account of their ritual system. He also wrote a succinct article in Norwegian entitled 'A Society Must Be Understood on Its Own Terms', intended to help development workers to understand and respect cultural differences in order to do a better job.[15] He was far from inactive following his return from Papua, but the monograph and further academic work from his Baktaman fieldwork would still be long in the making.

While Barth had lived among the Baktaman, in blissful ignorance of events in the outside world, perceptible changes took place at home. The most obvious change was in the students, who had somehow become less respectful and deferential during the past year. The spring of 1968, while Barth had concentrated on the possibilities of being accepted into the seventh grade of initiation, marked a shift which may retrospectively be said to have led to changes in university life and, indeed, in mainstream Western culture. Inspired by the revolutionary situation in France, where students joined forces with workers in demanding a different political system, students across the Western world replaced their dinner jackets and pearl necklaces with army-surplus greatcoats and crystal bangles, declared themselves anti-authoritarian or revolutionary, and began to speak loudly about bourgeois science versus Marxist science. Not all the radicals supported Marxism; some represented a very different world-view in that they saw themselves as part of the anarchist flower-power movement emanating from California. But the new crop of students shared a frustration with the stiff and formal establishment, regardless of their ideological differences; and this wave of revolt and leftism also hit the humanities and social sciences in Bergen.

Anthropology in Bergen was comparatively apolitical. It was true that Barth was engaged in development aid, but it was just as much about showing the relevance of anthropological knowledge, and not least a way of creating jobs for anthropologists, as it was the result of a dream to make the world a better place. He has always regarded the view that the state and capitalism would save traditional peoples as an expression of ethnocentric ignorance and arrogance. Ever the naturalist, Barth saw it as an empirical question whether people's lot would improve through an encounter with the mixed blessings of modernity. But it should be noted that, as an adviser to the FAO in Sudan, Barth had influenced decisions that had consequences for half a million people: the collaboration he started with the University of Khartoum has continued to flourish, and has generated development research of high quality, fuelled by genuine humanistic engagement.

Bergen was, after all, not entirely apolitical. Kleivan had left a legacy of engagement in the Fourth World, that of indigenous peoples, continued especially by Henriksen. Brox was politically engaged on the left. There was applied research, carried out by Haaland, Sørbø and later Gulbrandsen, mostly in Africa. Still, it is fair to say that the department, its teaching and research were fairly disengaged from the burning issues of the day. The Bergen anthropologists did not see it as their task to sign petitions against the Vietnam war, or to criticise the capitalist exploitation of poor countries in the South. They saw themselves first and foremost as scientists.

While the students demonstrated and organised themselves in various radical groupings, Barth was busy thinking comparatively about tropical ecology. Not long after his return from the Baktaman, Siverts returned from fieldwork among the Aguaruna in the Peruvian Amazon. They compared their experiences in tropical forests, and Barth was struck by the contrast between a tropical ecosystem, with its enormous diversity of species, but small numbers of each species, and ecosystems like the Arctic ones, where there are few species but many of each. He tentatively designed a project on comparative tropical ecology, meant to end in a symposium. The idea was innovative and exciting, but nothing came out of it immediately. Actually, such a symposium did take place at the Ethnographic Museum in Oslo in the mid 1970s, but no publication came from it.

They may not have seen it as relevant to their own concerns, but the Bergen anthropologists were eventually forced to relate to student radicalism. Barth remarks:

> We spent a great deal of intellectual energy and time encountering and confronting the Marxist critique and the criticism of positivism in a professional way, and I can understand that we became a strategic problem for the Marxist-Leninists. Since this was a fortress that didn't fall, right, they never conquered it, and different people were instructed to bring us down, but it didn't work. So while other departments either gave in to the students or were destroyed, we stood upright.[16]

It is something of an exaggeration to claim that other departments and institutes were destroyed, but it is true that the student movement of the late 1960s and early 1970s led to major disruptions by demanding a more politically aware, more leftist and, eventually, more feminist and postcolonial approach to knowledge. However, it was not, as Barth says, as easy for the Marxist-Leninists to 'put down' the anthropologists as it might have been to criticise other disciplines. Sociology, politics and history could all be easily dismissed as bourgeois sciences, loyal to the system and obedient contributors to nation-building, each in their own way. With the anthropologists, who studied the world with a main emphasis on non-European societies, and a methodology which placed the lives of ordinary people at the forefront of their research, the situation was different. Even if their research did not always take place on the locals' terms, researchers necessarily found themselves in a close and ongoing dialogue with local people of humble standing. The discipline also seemed to represent an implicit anti-imperialist perspective, since its methodology depended on the view that all human lives have equal value.

Yet, the criticism did come, and much of it was directed at Barth himself. Was it not the case, as radical critics would soon write about in detail,[17] that Barth studied the elites in Swat without caring about the poor and oppressed? And was not his transactionalism really an expression of a Western, liberal individualism where competition was the order of the day? Some also regarded Barth's naturalistic methodology as a form of naive positivism, as if it were possible to study the world in an ideologically neutral way. The politically radical anti-positivists argued, often convincingly, that *all* research had an implicit ideological dimension. When a researcher delimits the field and defines their research question, they have made a choice which will have direct consequences for the process of discovery and the findings.

This criticism did not hit Barth very hard. His research was of a high standard regardless of criteria (dogmatic Marxist-Leninism excepted), and if others wished to study the world from a different angle, that was fine by him; he even encouraged it, as long as what they did was empirically credible.

It was more difficult to counter feminist criticism than it had been to respond to the Marxists. The anthropological community in Bergen had been very masculine throughout the 1960s. Some women passed through it, but none stayed, and no woman made a major contribution to Bergen anthropology in this period. When the new, radical student type made its appearance, it soon became apparent that it contained in its midst a number of young, outspoken women. Some of the most gifted students from this period were Marianne Gullestad, later the finest anthropological writer about Norwegian mainstream culture and a powerful critic of its implicit racism; Elisabeth Eide, later a professor of media studies and a novelist; and Unni Wikan, who would go on to do fieldwork in Cairo.

Something new was in the making, albeit not quite in the way the more utopian Marxists envisioned it. The Bergen community was tight, compact and resolutely masculine. Every day, the department went collectively to their lunch café. As the sociologist (and former cabinet minister) Gudmund Hernes describes it, the anthropologists walked like a flock of migrating geese, in what Norwegians know as the 'snow-plough formation', with Barth at the head and students at the back. Occasionally, they had foreign visitors with them, or advanced students from a neighbouring country such as the Swedes Åke Daun, Orvar Löfgren and Tom Svensson, and the number varied between a dozen and a score. They spoke anthropology incessantly. As Hernes recalls it – he was a young sociologist in Bergen at the time – those lunches were 'seminars on foot and at table'.[18]

There were no clear boundaries between work and leisure, and the colleagues socialised informally when they were not working. Barth's right-hand man remained Blom, whom he had known since the early days in the attic of the Ethnographic Museum. He also appreciated the gifted researchers and active ethnographers Haaland and Grønhaug, and Blehr was a good friend, but it was chiefly from Robert Paine that he got some real intellectual resistance. Paine, who had obtained a D.Phil. from Oxford before arriving in Bergen, had a penchant for historical substance and descriptive ethnography that Barth did not share. He was just as sceptical of Barth's models as he had been of Evans-Pritchard's. A few years later, Paine would write a thorough critique of Barth's *Models of Social Organization* in his pamphlet *Second Thoughts about Barth's Models*, appropriately published in the same series (and with the same off-putting cover design) as *Models*.[19]

Being not a, but *the* professor, Barth was automatically head of department, and he could build it pretty much as he liked at the young university of Bergen, where the skeletons in the closet were few and traditionalist dons were absent. He went for methodological and analytical unity, but geographical and thematic diversity. New positions were announced towards the end of the 1960s, and the department, which had relied heavily on Barth and Blom in the early years, could soon hire Haaland, Grønhaug and Brox in tenured jobs, in addition to a number of research fellows and temporary lecturers, such as Brøgger, Henriksen and Ramstad. The department would continue to grow and prosper in the 1970s, but by then, Barth would have left.

As mentioned, it was through conversations with Haaland about his Darfur material that Barth had got the idea for the symposium on ethnicity, and his next idea for a similar event came from Grønhaug's work. Grønhaug, who had already carried out fieldwork in both Afghanistan and Turkey, had developed an original approach to the study of scale as a variable in social life. Rather than seeing scale as a property of a social system, he saw it as an aspect of a person's status repertoire, which could say something significant about the reach of a person's network. When a merchant from Herat in Afghanistan went on the *haj* to Mecca, he participated in a system of enormous scale, but when he took tea with his neighbour, the reach was much shorter. This theme, about which Grønhaug and Barth had many conversations, seemed a natural extension of Barth's earlier work on roles, social organisation and varying degrees of social complexity. Besides, his recent experience of an extreme small-scale society in New Guinea was still with him, largely unprocessed.

During the 1960s, Barth had become a regular at the Wenner-Gren Foundation's Burg Wartenstein castle in Austria, where he participated at many symposia and became acquainted with influential colleagues, from

Marshall Sahlins to Eric Wolf. It was therefore on the cards that Barth himself should organise an event there. An application was written, and the symposium on scale and social organisation was entered into the programme for 1972.

The planning of the symposium converged with an unexpected event, which must be seen as decisive in Barth's life, both privately and professionally, namely his meeting with Unni Wikan. Wikan (b. 1944), from Harstad in Northern Norway, had studied sociology and social anthropology, and had already travelled to Cairo in 1968, intending to do fieldwork there later. Barth was then in New Guinea. Their very first contact dates to a letter sent on 10 January 1969, where Barth made a suggestion to Wikan. The department wished to deepen its competence in the Middle East and Barth suggested that Wikan do a short, quick piece of fieldwork in an Egyptian village, which might form the basis of a 'short, but adequate' M.Phil. dissertation when she returned. Wikan, who had not even completed her undergraduate degree, applied for a research permit, which she obtained, along with a grant. However, the situation in Egypt precluded fieldwork anywhere but Cairo or Alexandria. She therefore began fieldwork in a poor quarter in Cairo that summer. She was back in Bergen in spring 1970, but did not make Barth's acquaintance then either. In September 1970, she went back to Cairo, where she completed her fieldwork in January 1971. It was only then that she and Barth were properly acquainted.

Unni Wikan was an excellent student with an independent mind, and by now she had also done long-term fieldwork in a challenging environment. In all likelihood, she would have been one of the few people around who had the nerve to express disagreement with the professor in a way he deemed relevant. Barth fell head over heels in love with her. 'And then, a continued marriage with Molly became somehow impossible', he comments many years later.[20]

However, as any anthropologist might predict, the break-up of the Barthian home did not just involve the family members. The department was in complete turmoil when news came that Barth and Wikan had become a couple. Since private and professional networks were closely woven together, and departmental colleagues had multiple (many-stranded) relationships with each other, a major tangle emerged. After all, they socialised in private and knew each other's spouses and children. A gifted student, Wikan must have been perceived as something of a challenge to the boys' club in Bergen. In the event, most of the department sided with Molly. The atmosphere in the common room was uneasy, at times hostile, and Barth sums up the situation by stating that all of a sudden he was standing on clay feet again, almost in the same way as he had when his dissertation about the Kurds had been rejected. 'But', he adds, 'my happiness and feeling of renewal and rebirth are quite important for my biography'.[21] The meeting with Unni Wikan brought Barth into close contact with an emotional repertoire that he had formerly related to in a more diffuse and vague way. This would have consequences for him, not only privately, but also in his subsequent development as an anthropologist and academic.

In 1972, the couple travelled to Yale University for six months; he as a visiting professor, she to work on the material from Cairo. They subsequently lived together for a year in Bergen. This was a difficult time for Barth and the institution he had spent a decade building. Everybody knew that a major change was coming, and that they would lose their leader. To some, there may have been a feeling of relief that the tall tree would soon be gone, since it might be easier for the smaller plants to thrive in the absence of its shadow.

The opportunity came at the right moment, as has been the case so often in Barth's life. When, in 1973, Gjessing retired from his professorship at the Ethnographic Museum, Barth applied for the job. He had been waiting for it, partly unconsciously, for more than a decade, maybe two. He got the job. Barth and Wikan married in January 1974, and moved into the house Barth had bought at the end of the 1950s, but never lived in. He would now live in that house until the summer of 2011.

8

A New Kind of Complexity

During his twelve years in Bergen, Barth organised four major symposia: on the entrepreneur in Northern Norway, role theory, ethnicity and scale. By far the best known is the symposium on ethnicity, thanks to the subsequent book publication. However, the idea behind the scale conference was equally original, and deserved a better fate. The book *Scale and Social Organization*,[1] published only in 1978, is not very well known, even in Scandinavia. The anthropological concept of scale remains underused in a systematic way, even in studies where it would clearly have been useful.[2]

The concepts of large and small scale, as in the terms 'small-scale society' and 'large-scale society', are familiar inside and outside the academic world. However, in the way they are used in everyday speech, the terms chiefly refer to size. An island community in Shetland might thus be considered a small-scale society if it comprises just a few hundred persons, although it is connected with surrounding national, transnational and even global systems in a multitude of ways. Following an anthropological delineation of scale, the inhabitants of the island would participate in several part-systems, or social fields, although the island itself, considered as a social system, is definitely small scale.

It was Grønhaug who initially began to work seriously on the concept of scale in Bergen. He used a systemic concept of scale in his research on Anatolia and later Herat, using it to show how and along which lines villagers and townspeople were integrated into different part-systems.[3] Now, scale as an analytical concept (and not just a word from everyday language) had been used before, especially at the Rhodes-Livingstone Institute, by researchers who would later move to Manchester under Gluckman's leadership. We are again reminded of the kinship between Barth and his generative processual analysis on the one hand, and the Manchester School on the other. Perhaps they were too close for any kind of intellectual intimacy to arise.

8.   Bridegroom preparing for wedding in Sohar (photo reproduced by permission of Fredrik Barth and Unni Wikan).

Scale in a social system, part-system or field refers to the number of statuses that are required for the system to be maintained. In other words, it refers to complexity. Seen from an actor's perspective, scale indicates how far you can reach in your operative networks and connections. We all participate in systems at varying levels of scale, unless we are pre-mining Baktaman. Their world begins and ends near the village. A farmer in Herat, by contrast, participated in and contributed to several fields, some of which stretched all the way to Morocco and Java. He spent most of the time with people he knew well, but he traded with strangers in the market, and took part in a local political system comprising at least 100,000 persons who were dependent on the same irrigation canal. If he went on the *haj*, he participated, at least once in his life, in a field with millions of participants from all over the Muslim world. Scale, thus, is not the same thing as macro and micro, and it refers to complexity rather than size. There are peoples in the world who roughly speaking share the same culture, livelihood and way of life, and whose numbers may be counted in the millions, but who are scarcely connected with each other beyond their local community. Their society is, in other words, organised at a lower level of scale than a town of 20,000 with an intricate and advanced division of labour, where thousands of statuses, from plumber to schoolteacher, are required for the reproduction of the system.

Grønhaug also spoke of social fields. Since Pierre Bourdieu's concept of fields is far better known, it should be noted that Grønhaug's version of the term is sociologically more readily applicable. Bourdieu speaks of discursive or symbolic fields, that is relatively bounded communities of communication.[4] Grønhaug, by contrast, speaks about *social* fields, that is systems of interaction which likewise are bounded, not because communication decreases, but because interaction does. This concerns who does what with whom and for what purpose.

While Barth was planning the symposium about scale, times were turbulent in Bergen. He had formed a relationship with Wikan, to the astonishment and sometimes dismay of his colleagues. The only Norwegian anthropologists, apart from Barth, who participated at the scale symposium were Grønhaug and Blom. The latter did not present a paper, but was responsible for reporting from the event. Ahead of the symposium, Barth had circulated a few tentative pages about the relevance of the topic, along with the 1972 article on status repertoires.[5]

The conference was successful, and Blom wrote a detailed report which would eventually serve as a skeleton for *Scale and Social Organization*. In spite of this excellent starting point, six years would pass before the book left the printing press. Among the contributors were internationally respected anthropologists, such as Gerald Berreman, John Barnes, Ernest Gellner and Elizabeth Colson, and Barth did not have the same authority over them as he was used to with his Bergen colleagues. They failed to submit their chapters on time, and they did not share a common analytical platform either. They did not even use the concept of scale in the same way.

Barth wrote two chapters himself, 'Conclusions' and 'Scale and Network in Urban Western Society', in which he uses himself, for the first and last time, as his empirical data, as he maps out his interactions with other people over a two-week period, comparing his findings with the results of the same exercise carried out by a student.[6] The purpose is to show how complexity in a social system is embedded in personal networks. Compared to villagers anywhere in the world, Barth had many relations with the outside world, and many of them were single-stranded – he only knew the other person in one capacity, e.g. dentist or shop attendant. For an improved understanding of the changes that have taken place in the everyday life of an academic, and in general, it would be interesting to carry out a similar exercise today. Barth notes that some of his contact with the outside world took place via letters and telephone. In our time, it would have been necessary to include the many forms of electronic communication, from SMS to e-mail, Facebook and Twitter, that have transformed everyday communication in ways which are still not fully understood.

In the concluding chapter to the book, Barth raises a series of partly unanswered questions about scale and social organisation. Is it, for example, the case that conformity is at its greatest in systems of small scale? Not necessarily, he responds, with reference to the Baktaman, who are not mentioned elsewhere in the book. He also discusses his old schoolmate, the criminologist Nils Christie, and his argument about violence being most widespread in very loose and very dense societies, that is systems of small and enormous scale, respectively.[7] He also mentions the relationship between little and great traditions (Redfield's terms), where the little tradition is oral, local and based on personal acquaintance, while the great tradition is written, global and anonymous.

The book about scale is challenging and original, and it contains several excellent chapters, Grønhaug's arguably being the best, but it still comes across as unfinished and poorly integrated. The individual chapters scarcely speak directly to each other. Perhaps this is why the topic has been so rarely considered by anthropologists later. Yet, the book was noticed, sometimes in unexpected quarters. For example, *Scale and Social Organization* was used extensively by a group of French historians under the editorship of Jacques Revel.[8] Their project consisted in showing the interrelationship between micro-history and macro-history, that is the connections between the lives of individuals and larger, more encompassing processes. In this endeavour, the anthropological concept of scale was useful. It is also likely that the concept of scale might have contributed to a higher level of precision in the massive recent literature, mostly outside anthropology, about the global and the local. It points beyond the unhelpful contrast between micro and macro, person and system.

Only a couple of months after taking up the chair at the Ethnographic Museum, Barth would embark on a new piece of fieldwork, this time with his new wife. He had himself done extensive fieldwork in the Middle East and Pakistan, and Wikan had worked in Cairo and spoke fluent Arabic. It seemed expedient to draw on her language proficiency on the next trip, and the couple decided on the Arabian peninsula. The plan was to explore ethnicity and complexity in an urban society there, and subsequently do similar fieldwork in eastern Afghanistan, where they would benefit from Barth's knowledge of Pashto.

They wished to go to the southern part of the peninsula, preferably South Yemen. This short-lived country, seceding in 1967 and reuniting with Yemen in 1990, had an authoritarian communist government, and a research permit seemed out of the question. Barth's dream had been to do fieldwork in Hadramaut, the formerly autonomous sultanate, famous for its many-storied clay houses. Barth was also attracted to Socotra, an isolated island in the Indian Ocean, but it was administered from Hadramaut and thus also controlled by South Yemen. The decision to go to Oman was taken following a meeting with the Omani ambassador in London. The ambassador said that they would be welcome in Oman, but he was uncertain as to whether the country was suited to anthropological studies. 'You see, we've never had any anthropologists there before'.[9]

In Oman, the coastal town of Sohar recommended itself as a particularly interesting field location. The town had a long and fascinating history as a trade hub in the Indian Ocean, and still appeared to be something of a cultural crossroads. There were also interesting connections between the Omani coast and places where Barth had worked previously, thanks to long-term connections and migration from the nearby Persian coast and western Baluchistan.

The coastal cities of Oman, of which the largest and most famous is the capital, Muscat, have a long history as commercial centres and sites of intercultural encounters. For centuries, Oman's most important exports were frankincense and myrrh, two of the gifts that according to the myth were offered to the newborn Messiah 2000 years ago. But people in the Sohar region had been trading with Mesopotamia 6000 years ago, and the oldest copper mines were operating at least 4000 years ago. Later, the Omani coast was renowned for its trade in spices, silk and gold, and was until quite recently infamous for its slave trade. The marked Arabic cultural influence on the East African coast is Omani and Yemeni in origin, and probably extends back to the seventh century AD, when the first Arabs settled on the 'Swahili coast'. Later, regular trading connections were developed between the Arab peninsula and East Africa, eventually coming into competition with European colonial powers. Owing to seasonal variation in the prevailing winds, Omani sailors and traders spent months at a time in Kilwa, Zanzibar, Mombasa and elsewhere on the coast. In fact, Zanzibar was an integrated part of the Omani state from 1698 to 1856, and the Arab influence is very noticeable there even today. The influence went both ways, as witnessed in the spices used in Omani cooking, the passion for ivory and rhino horn and the rhythms in traditional Omani music. Moreover, there cannot be many areas in the world with a higher density of forts and watchtowers than the Omani coast, which indicates that the state was fragile and the wealth considerable.

At the time of Barth and Wikan's fieldwork, Sohar was a small city of about 20,000 inhabitants, halfway between Muscat and Dubai. The bumpy gravel road from the capital, 240 kilometres away, was only a couple of years old. For centuries, indeed millennia, all contact with the outside world had taken place by sea and, occasionally, by camel. In 2014, the city had 140,000 inhabitants, several hotels, shopping centres, a highway and an armada of white taxis with orange stripes. Wikan, who continues to visit Oman regularly, says that the changes have been so formidable that she can now only find her bearings by following the beach.

Sohar is said to have been the birthplace of the mythical Sinbad the Sailor. The whole region has more than a hint of *One Thousand and One Nights*, with its dense clumps of date palms growing in lush wadis (oases) surrounded by stony desert, its itinerant Bedouins, the smell of incense and spices, silk from the East and labyrinthine alleys. But Sohar was also a cosmopolitan city, an ethnically complex society of a different kind to those Barth had previously studied. The Arabs, the dominant group in the population, were divided into perhaps as many as 50 different tribes, defined by patrilineal descent. There were also Persians, Baluchis and Hindus from India in town. Moreover, some descendants of African slaves lived in the city (slavery was abolished only in the 1960s), and immigrant groups from various Gulf states. Arabic, Farsi (Persian), Baluchi, Zidgali, Kutchi and English were all languages spoken regularly in Sohar.

Until 1970, the conservative sultan Said bin Taimur ruled the country. During his reign, radios and sunglasses were banned. Anyone with a higher education from abroad was expelled, and only a handful of schools were left in the whole country. The son of the sultan, Qaboos, who had more liberal ideas and loved Western classical music, spent six years under house arrest in the palace in the southern city of Salalah, before he succeeded, with the help of the British, in deposing his father in a non-violent coup. Oil had recently been discovered in the country, and the young Sultan Qaboos embarked on an ambitious project of modernisation which has changed Oman enormously, some would say beyond recognition; the vast majority would add 'for the better'. This society was, in other words, only just beginning to open up to the modern world when Barth and Wikan arrived in Sohar in the spring of 1974.

The fieldwork had been planned, and took place, in a complementary fashion. The gender segregation of the city largely precluded contact between unrelated men and women, who did not naturally mix in any arena available to the anthropologists. Accordingly, Barth did his fieldwork among the men, while Wikan focused on the women. They naturally exchanged notes and impressions as they went along. However, as a married couple, they were eventually able to access arenas which had been closed to Barth in Swat and Kurdistan. By establishing 'quasi-kin relations' with other families, they were able to socialise with them. Barth says that 'some of our best friends invited us, and we sat there drinking green tea together, two couples, three couples … and it was a completely new experience for me'.[10]

There was one factor that the anthropologists had not reckoned with: the heat. Both enjoyed warm climates, and did not expect this to be an issue. They arrived in March, and people were talking about the coming heat in an anxious and concerned way. Barth and Wikan assumed that they would be able to deal easily with the rising temperatures. After all, people managed to live here, so they assumed that they would be fine. The fact is, however, that the summer months are considered an emergency period in Sohar. In July and August, the temperature often exceeds 40 degrees Celsius in the day, and rarely sinks below 27 degrees at night. The city lacked electricity, so there was no air-conditioning except for those who had their own generator. Wikan comments today that the greatest change for people in Sohar in the recent past may consist in their now having air-conditioning. All of a sudden, it was possible to lead normal lives even at the height of summer, and the locals, who had formerly had a reputation for being somewhat taciturn and apathetic, turned out to be just as lively as everybody else, she says.

After a while, Barth and Wikan came to know a group of development workers who were based in Sohar, and who lent them a diesel generator for a month while they were away, so that they could at least keep a fan running at night. When the aid workers subsequently went on holiday for a week, the couple borrowed their house, which contained both a generator and air-conditioning. They now encountered problems with adjusting to the contrast between the cool air inside and the sizzling air outside, and moved on, this time to an area where it was even hotter than in the city, but where the air was drier. They would soon move on anyway, to the desert town of Bahla on the border with 'the Empty Quarter', the desert on the frontier between Saudi Arabia and Oman. Barth studied the irrigation systems there, and managed to scrape together enough material for an article about productive factors and distribution in the area,[11] but when the thermometer reached 52 degrees on two successive days, Wikan suffered heatstroke, and they decided to call it a day for the time being.

At the beginning of August, the couple got onto a plane to Karachi, with a view to continuing to the Swat Valley for a week's convalescence. As it turned out, they only managed a few days in the fresh air (the temperature may have reached 25 degrees in the afternoon, comparable to summer temperatures in Oslo), before moving on, after having visited Kashmali and his family. Their internal thermostats might have gone awry, but their spirit of adventure had not, so instead of getting on the first flight home, they travelled westwards on local and regional buses, through Afghanistan and Iran, where they visited the Basseri, before ending up in Istanbul. When they finally returned to Oslo in September, the weather was unusually warm, but not warm enough for Unni Wikan, who had to wear an Afghan fur coat to keep warm. In fact, they indirectly suffered from the Omani heat for a long period after leaving Sohar. Both suffered from cold spells and had problems with their body temperatures for a couple of years after returning home. Still, they would return to Sohar from December 1975 to January 1976, the coolest time of the year, in order to complete their fieldwork.

Sohar has an exceptionally long and complex history, and written sources exist in several languages. One might perhaps expect a researcher to use past events and processes in their attempt to explain present complexity, and many would. Not Barth. As always, he endeavoured to come as close as possible to other people's life-worlds, and a historical account would distort the understanding of the present, he felt. In the monograph *Sohar*,[12] he only treats history as present-day people's understandings of their own past and their interpretation of the present seen through past events.

He also did not assume the existence of a tidy 'system' that might be mapped out in advance. As in his earlier fieldwork, he began the analysis through a study of social practice, in order to achieve, as far as possible, a naturalistic description. He got into contact with the different groups and found out about their structural position, their economic situation, their kinship system and marriage practices, and developed the analysis along the boundaries between groups.

In many ways, the project in Oman was a follow-up to Barth's earlier research on ethnicity. It is therefore worth noting that there are many parallels between his monograph and an older school in ethnicity research, namely that dealing with 'plural societies'.[13] In Oman, as in Burma as described by Furnivall, or in Jamaica as described by Smith, each group possesses its own cultural peculiarities, its tradition, its language, sometimes its religion. Apart from trade and other economic transactions, there is limited contact between groups, which are subjected to an authoritarian, centralised political power. To this I should add that when many societies, in recent history, have developed in a meritocratic direction, with shared educational institutions, shared mass media and a more or less liberal political system, inter-group contact has increased. They gradually develop broad cultural commonalities, although this does not necessarily entail the disappearance of ethnic boundaries, but rather a shift from complementarity to symmetrical competition.

An important difference between the plural-society school and Barth's analysis is that Barth does not presuppose the existence of a regulated system. He points out, referring to the prevailing cultural plurality in the city, that 'every person participates in several, though far from all, of these cultures'.[14] Besides, different statuses may be combined. Ethnic boundaries do not follow the division of labour in a strict sense, as would be the case in Furnivall's Burma. It is rather kinship, descent and marriage that produce boundary maintenance, with the result that cultural meaning, too, is largely reproduced within the group and not across boundaries. Barth describes Sohar society with a formulation borrowed from Anthony Wallace, who had argued that culture is not so much about the production of similarity as it is about the organisation of diversity.[15]

When he set to work in order to get a grip on the dynamics of complexity in Sohar, Barth was already a seasoned social anthropologist with a considerable amount of fieldwork experience and many succinct, lucid analyses behind him. Sohar may have turned out to be his most difficult challenge to date, and for the first time in his career as an innovator in social anthropology the limitations of his approach become evident.

There are chiefly two reasons that the analysis of Sohar is somewhat wanting. First, it is impossible to 'close' the system of interaction. The transnational groups living there have commitments and networks going in several directions and forms of belonging stretching across the Indian Ocean. Although transnational connections were of limited scope and frequency in the 1970s, and took place at a leisurely speed, and although most Baluchi in Sohar had never visited Baluchistan, the country of their ancestors was an important element of their existence. The Indians maintained a far closer contact with their homeland, and tended only to spend part of their lives in Sohar before returning. Traders and Bedouins also take part in networks on a large scale. The different groups did not live in a shared social reality, but in partly overlapping worlds; to some, the sea was the main focus, to others the desert, to yet others the bazaar. Barth's method of inquiry has always started with that which is close and observable, that is, social processes taking place here and now. But when it is necessary to develop a full overview of large-scale networks to understand local processes fully, the method is inadequate, since only a fraction of an individual's social network is accessible through participant observation.

This problem recalls Mauss's critical comments on Malinowski's analysis of the *kula* in the Trobriands and surrounding areas. Malinowski described and analysed this regional system of trade convincingly and well, taking his point of departure from *kula* expeditions in which he had participated. Mauss, who never did fieldwork but was very widely read and an excellent linguist, pointed out that similar systems of exchange existed in large parts of the Pacific, and that related practices might also be found along the north-western coast of North America as well.[16] Mauss's broader comparative perspective arguably adds a dimension to Malinowski's detailed ethnography. As regards the analysis in *Sohar*, it seems likely that a more systematic use of other kinds of data than local ethnography would have given a clearer demonstration of the functioning of the system and, arguably, a better understanding of people's lives.

The other limitation concerns the role of history. Barth explains his position in the introductory chapter to the book: 'Surely, it must be poor method to design one's argument so that the present, which one knows more about, is ... to be explained by a past about which one knows less'.[17] This is not really an argument. If the past is deemed to be important for an understanding of the present, it has to be incorporated into the analysis even if one does not have first-hand knowledge of it. Barth is interested in history in so far as it is *made relevant* for the present day, but not as an independent causal factor. He also points out that, 'knowledge of the past is so extensive (partly written, partly verbal tradition, partly personal recollection), and all of it so unequally known to different persons, often in contradictory versions'.[18]

This is not to say that Barth, as some have tended to believe, has not read and related to historical research in Sohar and other locations where he has done fieldwork. Both in the introductory chapters of *Sohar* and in other texts, such as the essay 'Swat Pathans Reconsidered', he demonstrates perfectly adequate knowledge about historical processes that have shaped present-day society. At the same time, he states that an anthropologist is normally not trained and competent to work with historical material, and that historical studies can therefore only be used as secondary sources. This view is debatable, but it is consistent with Barth's naturalist convictions, according to which the goal is to give the most truthful and accurate description as possible of something that can be observed directly.

Sohar is not a bad book, and it does what it sets out to do, but it lacks the degree of ethnographic detail and the analytical sharpness characteristic of his earlier work. The conclusion is credible, but not sensational. He there points out, among other things, that what holds the inhabitants of Sohar together is a set of common norms for dealing with difference and complexity; a kind of urban flexibility, one might say. The metaphor is not the mosaic, nor the melting-pot, but 'a kind of putty' that connects the parts.[19] The peculiarities of this pluralism, still characteristic of the Gulf states including Oman (strictly speaking not a Gulf country), become clear if one compares Oman briefly with the puritan version of Islam which predominates in Saudi Arabia. In the latter, conservative Wahhabism has, since the nineteenth century, purged the country of most of its diversity. In spite of the noticeable segregation between genders and between Muslims and Hindus, the Gulf states come across as oases of liberalism surrounded by strict religious uniformity.

In *Sohar*, Barth appears to be less confident and more tentative than before. After having analysed the differences between Baluchi and Arab marriage practices, he writes about ethnic communities and congregations. He then admits that his

> material offers no sound basis on which to identify the ideas, or cognitive and emotional structures, that lie behind distinctly Baluch behavior or preference (for example, Baluch men's more positive orientation to physical activity, danger, and martial occupations, or Baluch women's stronger involvement and creativity in design, color, and other esthetic expression).[20]

As he readily admits, his limited knowledge of Arabic was a practical problem, adding that Wikan's contributions in this and other domains during and after fieldwork were invaluable. He did not have access to the services of an Ali Dad or a Kashmali in Oman. Although the opposite has been claimed, there are indications that Barth's monograph from Oman is more strongly influenced by Wikan than her Omani monograph is by Barth. The relationship to Wikan did something to Barth, not only as a human being, but also as a researcher and anthropologist. He himself has spoken of an experience of rebirth and renewal, and this impression is by and large confirmed by a reading of his scientific production before and after the mid 1970s. The late Barth is less macho, more ambiguous than the early Barth, concerned to understand not only social complexity, but the complexity of human beings as well. From now on, he seems less concerned with the answers than with the questions and their ramifications.

9

Turbulent Times

The fieldwork in Sohar had not been completed, but interrupted when the couple returned to Oslo in September 1974. Oslo was basking in a sunny, unusually warm Indian summer, while the returning anthropologists were shivering. By now, Barth had started his work at the Ethnographic Museum in earnest as well, and this job would – like his writing – turn out to be not entirely devoid of friction and difficulties in the coming ten years or so.

Before Barth went to Bergen in 1961, he envisioned the possibility of taking the professorship at the Ethnographic Museum when Gjessing retired, and this opportunity was part of the equation when he bought the house in the western hills of Oslo. When Gjessing eventually did retire in 1973, it was no longer obvious that this was where Barth would end up. There were interesting opportunities abroad as well. Leach, who had recently been given a personal chair, wanted Barth to apply for the professorship after Fortes at Cambridge. In addition, there was a fully-fledged Department of Social Anthropology in Oslo, where the staff were free to concentrate on teaching and research, and did not have to spend time and energy on huge, dusty ethnographic collections and temporary exhibitions. Although the department in Oslo had to some extent languished in the shadow of Bergen, it was growing, quantitatively as well as qualitatively. The core staff consisting of Arne Martin Klausen, Harald Eidheim, Ingrid Rudie and Axel Sommerfelt tended to see themselves as undogmatic pluralists, in contrast to the 'Barthian' environment at Bergen. They all did their work well and competently. Eidheim was an internationally recognised ethnicity theorist and researcher on Norwegian–Sami relations. Rudie also published much of her work in English, and would go on to do fieldwork in Malaysia. Sommerfelt contributed to encyclopaedias and was known as an outstanding lecturer with a dry sense of humour and a hint of a stiff upper lip, while Klausen was about to become the public face of anthropology in Norway, although he lacked Barth's prestige as a researcher and theorist.

9.   With Unni Wikan at the Ethnographic Museum, Oslo (photo reproduced by permission of Museum of Cultural History, University of Oslo).

Around the same time that Barth began his work at the museum, the department at Oslo was further strengthened through the recruiting of Eduardo Archetti, an intellectually creative and playful Argentinean who had studied with Maurice Godelier and Sidney Mintz, and who would create a strong group of Latin Americanists around himself in the years and decades to come. There were others as well, and growing student numbers.

At the museum, there was a small handful of anthropologists, but no students. Alv Alver held a post as a lecturer, and was working on his ethnographic material from North Africa, which he would never publish. Instead, he had recently published an eloquent translation of Lévi-Strauss' *Tristes Tropiques*.[1] Alver was oriented towards French intellectual life, and he had little in common with Barth. There was a history of hostility between the two, and things did not improve when Barth arrived at the museum as a professor.

He got along better with the others. Barth had known Johannes Falkenberg since the days in the attic. Born in 1911, Falkenberg may have been the first Norwegian social anthropologist to have published exotic ethnographic material when he wrote about social organisation among Australian Aborigines just after the Second World War.[2] Tom Svensson, who had specialised in Sami culture and society, had studied with Barth in Bergen. Per Bjørn Rekdal, later the administrative leader of the museum, had done research on material culture in Zambia. Jan Brøgger was also at the museum, but soon left to become professor at Trondheim. The situation was in many ways different from that in Bergen. The scientific staff at the museum had not been handpicked by Barth, and he could not take it for granted that they would share his academic vision. In addition, the technical staff were a specialised and vocal group who did not always share the priorities of the academics. At the museum, Barth also had to take regional diversity into consideration to a greater extent than in a department. Even if the scale of the museum was modest, it aimed to cover the most important ethnographic regions in the world. So when a vacancy appeared, Barth managed to hire Harald Beyer Broch, who had done fieldwork among North American Indians. Unni Wikan was later hired, with special responsibility for South Asia, and soon after, the East Asianist Arne Røkkum was employed. The last new recruit was Arve Sørum, a young Melanesianist.

The irony of it all has often been commented upon. Arne Martin Klausen, who became professor at the Oslo department in 1973, was a full-blooded museum man. He was a good teacher and an excellent populariser, but he was not an intellectual leader. Klausen has always been passionate about material culture; his wife Liv is a handicraft artist. One of his best books is about the sociology of art, and he had written about basket weaving among the Dayak of Borneo in his magister dissertation of 1957.

With Barth, the situation was almost the exact opposite. He had always had an interest in material culture, but not viewed as museum objects. Quite the contrary; his passion for objects concerned the way in which they were seamlessly integrated into social processes, and arriving at the museum must have given him mixed feelings. Many a Norwegian anthropologist has over the years speculated about the possible outcome if Barth had ended up at the university and Klausen at the museum. Klausen actually did apply for the museum job, but was ranked second by a divided committee, a minority of which had placed him first. Barth was, for his part, not interested in the university department. As a matter of fact, the university director, sensing the situation, proposed a swap, which Barth rejected. It was Gjessing's chair he wanted.

Barth took his museum commitments seriously and got temporary exhibitions going, and he probably had a stronger affinity for museum work than many realised. Few knew that he had been a sculptor's apprentice, and he did retain an interest in art and material culture. His vision for his academic staff was nevertheless that they should organise one exhibition and 'thereafter do research for the rest of your life', as he put it to Beyer Broch upon his appointment. And it is doubtless true that the museum anthropologists had plenty of time for research. They had to teach at the department, but only two hours a week, and this might be done as postgraduate supervision. Barth himself supervised Sørum and others on their magister degrees. Falkenberg was still around, and with his wry sense of humour and witty turn of phrase he added some much needed light to this dark building with its mahogany furniture, shrunken skulls and old conflicts festering in the dimly lit corridors. Yet, Barth openly admits that he was incapable of recreating the kind of dynamic intellectual environment that he had enjoyed at Bergen.

This may have had something to do with the fact that the relationship between Barth and Blindern had already soured during the process that led to the appointment of Beyer Broch. Broch had been Barth's candidate, but the colleagues at the department argued that it would be more appropriate to give the job to Rekdal, who had a stronger record with museum work. It did not make the issue any simpler when the technical staff at the museum also went against Barth. A similar situation occurred later, when Barth wished to hire Røkkum, while the department wanted Lisbet Holtedahl, then (as now) at Tromsø in the far north. The case ended when Holtedahl withdrew her application, allegedly because her husband did not want to leave Tromsø, but the atmosphere was by now distinctly unpleasant, both between department and museum and internally at the museum. The hiring processes were somewhat untidy at the time, and encouraged informal lobbying. Barth also felt that Unni Wikan did not receive the professional recognition she deserved. Her first book, a popular account of life among the poor in Cairo, had been published in Norwegian in 1976, while she was busy at work on her doctoral dissertation. The book was well received and published in English in 1980,[3] with a preface by Nils Christie, who had a personal interest in Cairo since he had worked there as a criminologist. Cairo had many of the characteristics of 'the loose society', but very little violent crime. The book failed to establish Wikan's reputation as a respected scholar in Norwegian social anthropology. That would have to wait a few years yet.

With hindsight, but also with blurred vision of the passing of time, it would be risky and contentious to begin to distribute guilt and responsibility. By his opponents, Barth was depicted as an autocratic and tyrannical professor who privately hated the museum. He felt, for his part, that the department interfered in an untimely way with the internal affairs of the museum, and that the technical staff tried to trump academically sound decisions. It was not a good situation for anyone, and it did not make people look their best. Falkenberg would need all he could muster of easy conversational skill and ironic distance in the years before he left, just before his retirement, for a position at the Norwegian Folk Museum.

Partly because he had no functioning domestic professional community to play with, but also because it was considered a professorial duty, Barth joined the Council of Social Research at this time, one of the central committees of the Norwegian Research Council. He replaced Grønhaug, who had done an important job by placing social anthropology properly on the map of disciplines that needed funding. Fieldwork grants and funding for new research projects came into place during this period. Until the end of the 1980s, Barth had a direct influence on most of the new research projects in social anthropology, but he found no intellectual community in the research council.

Barth also had to face other issues in the mid 1970s, notably professional criticism, which was ultimately by far to be preferred to the intricate conflicts at the museum. Although still in his forties, Barth had become a senior figure in world anthropology by now, and the critical discourse concerning his theoretical positions, palpable since the publication of *Models*, increased in strength and became slightly less circumspect in the politicised 1970s. He was no longer a young and gifted iconoclast who poured out challenging monographs and articles, but an influential professor in mid career with a distinctive position that could easily lend itself to criticism.

That criticism of Barth came from several quarters, but gravitated around related questions. Among other things, he had to relate to a postcolonial and/or Marxist critique that raised questions about his approach, description and analysis of power relations in Swat, and an epistemological critique that raised fundamental questions concerning his processual, naturalist view of social life. Even some of the largely positive early reviews of his work on Swat were sceptical of some of his choices. In his review in *American Anthropologist*, Lawrence Krader had written that it was unfortunate that Barth did not place his analysis of the Swat Pathans in a broader regional context, taking in other enclaves of stateless peoples.[4] In Krader's view, the ethnographic myopia weakened the regional relevance of the book. It was fairly easy to live with this kind of objection. Barth's project was primarily analytical, although he also contributed to the ethnography of the region.

The Marxist critique was tougher. Talal Asad reinterpreted Barth's material from a class perspective, and argued that the vertical contradictions between landowners and labourers was far more important that the horizontal competition between landowners.[5] Asad also saw tendencies towards the greater centralisation of property and growing inequality, as smaller landowners were forced out of business. He thus claimed that a historical development towards a centralised feudal society was about to take place. Asad's article was well received in the radical 1970s, and his contribution was often placed on reading lists along with an original article by Barth. Barth would soon respond to Asad's criticism,[6] pointing out that when he described the organisation of the Pathans with concepts such as caste and lineage, it was not his invention but the concepts they used in order to explain who they were. By contrast, Asad's class concept was alien to Swat. A crucial difference between Barth and Asad is that while Asad employs allegedly universal concepts such as class – even if they do not form part of the local cultural repertoire – Barth would take as his point of departure local, or 'emic', understandings in order to account for local conditions. It should be mentioned that Barth had a good personal relationship to Asad, whom he knew from Khartoum, and who later became widely respected for his work on secularism and religion.

A more comprehensive work along the same lines as Asad's article was Akbar S. Ahmed's book *Millennium and Charisma Among Pathans*,[7] where the reinterpretation and reanalysis of Barth's work from Swat is a main topic. Ahmed argues that lack of historical depth made Barth unable to see irreversible processes of change, and criticises him for a methodological individualism which leads to ethnocentric interpretations, while a more holistic perspective would indicate that actors' strategies and actions cannot explain the maintenance of the system. Barth would respond to this critique as well, and would then give a detailed account of relevant historical processes in Swat; but his main response would consist in reminding the reader of the objectives of his research. He did not aim to describe 'an entire society', as earlier generations of anthropologists had done, but to identify a context for individual strategies that led to particular results and counter-strategies. The collection of articles where he answers his critics is not called *Person and Society in Swat*, but *Features of Person and Society in Swat*. In his response to his critics, Barth also expresses a certain irritation that they criticised his research without coming up with new empirical data.[8]

In 1967, the French anthropologist Louis Dumont published his main work about the Indian caste system, *Homo Hierarchicus*,[9] at the same time as he published a widely read article in English,[10] where he argues that caste is primarily an aspect of Indian culture, not of social structure. In both works, Dumont pays considerable attention to Barth's research on Swat, and takes exception to some of Barth's interpretations. Dumont based his analysis on the assumption that the concept of the person varies in fundamental ways, and that the Hindu concept of the person is socio-centric, in contrast to the Western, egocentric concept of the person. For this reason, Dumont argues, it makes little sense to use the Western theory of games to understand the actions of Pathans. For although Pathans are not Hindus, they are culturally encompassed (*englobés*) by Hinduism. At the same time, Dumont seems to contradict himself when he cautions against the use of the caste concept about professional categories in Swat, precisely because Pathans are not Hindus.[11]

Barth responded by arguing that Dumont exaggerated the differences, and that the same, individually based logic of action was just as valid in a society with a collectivist ideology, such as an India one, as it is in the West. One just had to be a little cleverer, look over one's shoulder a bit more and make a few more measured considerations before acting to maximise self-interest. In a crystal-clear formulation, he clearly shows the differences between himself and the Durkheimian Dumont:

> He seems to me to be speaking entirely in terms of a (highly selective and intellectualized) native *model of* a caste society, and to ignore the problematics of transforming this, if so can be done at all, into an actors' *model for* caste behaviour. My concern, as always, was primarily directed to this latter focus, seeking to identify factors which lay behind empirical patterns and generated them.[12]

The method he used to analyse the ritual life of the Baktaman was exactly the one recommended here: rather than assuming the existence of an underlying system, he begins with the actions and interpretations of persons, working backwards from these undisputable facts to find the underlying schemata and constraints, which are themselves generated by the relevant social process.

Much of the critique and discussion of Barth's theoretical perspectives followed similar lines, but he perceived some of the critiques to be more relevant than Dumont and Asad. Those critics were partly sceptical of his empirical focus on interaction to the exclusion of system and structure, partly frustrated by his tendency to see maximising strategies where symbolic and existential meaning was also essential. When people are enjoying themselves together, for example, it would be contrived to try to understand what they are doing as part of a strategy to maximise pleasure.

One of the first to produce a thorough, critical reading of Barth's 1966 essay *Models of Social Organization* was, as mentioned earlier, Robert Paine,[13] while the most comprehensive critical discussion of Barth's early work (up to and including *Models*) was in the large volume with the telling title *Transaction and Meaning*, edited by Bruce Kapferer.[14] Terry Evens, moreover, wrote a detailed critique in *American Anthropologist* in 1977, where he problematised what he saw as Barth's methodological individualism. Both Kapferer and Evens came from the Manchester School, and Kapferer later became a professor at Barth's old department in Bergen.

Grønhaug, for his part, wrote an essay entitled 'Transaction and Signification', which circulated for many years as a mimeograph, but which was never properly published.[15] Grønhaug tries to reconcile Barth and Lévi-Strauss, taking as a main example J.C. Mitchell's *Kalela Dance*,[16] a product of the Rhodes-Livingstone Institute. Like much of Grønhaug's theoretical work, this article deserved a far larger readership than it got.

Much of the criticism followed related lines, and most of the critics were largely sympathetic to Barth's project. They saw that his sharp criticism of structural-functionalism and other abstract social theory was a laudable effort to get rid of a clump of dead trees obstructing the view, and that there was something refreshing and enlightening about his insistent focus on actors, their motivations and the social processes that follow from people pursuing goals and trying to make the most of their situation. Barth here follows a tradition of actor-oriented social researchers which may be traced back to Weber and possibly even to David Hume and his empiricism, but which, while common in economics and political science, has always been poorly represented in anthropology, possibly because the insistence on ethnographic accountability makes it difficult to develop formal models of interaction without throwing the baby out with the bathwater, that is losing sight of context. Barth is nonetheless praised by his critics for having kept his credibility as an ethnographer in spite of his desire to use simple, generative models to explain observed behaviour.

Then, the caveats and objections come. Paine discusses *Models* systematically, chapter by chapter. His most significant objections are that Barth does not sufficiently take power, coercion and force into account, and that transactions are not sufficient for cultural integration to come about. As regards the last argument, Paine refers to *Ethnic Groups and Boundaries*, where it is shown that transactions *do* take place across boundaries, without the groups becoming similar or developing a shared identity. However, this is not his strongest argument; the transactions across ethnic boundaries tend to be sporadic and are often ritualised.

Regarding power, Paine also refers to others who have pointed out that even if a slave may theoretically declare themselves free, the price to pay is death. In such a situation, it seems insufficient to speak of power in terms of 'constraints and incentives'. Paine, moreover, has difficulties in accepting Barth's concept of value. Agreement over value standards does not necessarily emerge in spite of repeated negotiations and attempts at transactions, he says; brokers or entrepreneurs do not always succeed in bridging two separate spheres. On the contrary, they often contribute to cementing differences in valuation, and then function more as translators than as agents of integration.

Related arguments are also developed in the volume *Transaction and Meaning*, where most of the contributors are anthropologists born in the 1940s, like Kapferer himself: Don Handelman, Andrew Strathern, Michael Gilsenan, A.P. Cohen, John Comaroff and David Parkin; Paine is also a contributor. Several of the contributors experiment with the use of transactional models in unexpected areas, such as verbal communication, and some also try to develop Barth's transactionalism further. Most of them nevertheless see serious limitations with the models, and apart from objections that have been mentioned, Kapferer points out that people do not always know why they do what they do – or, that human interaction is less rational and goal-oriented than Barth seems to think. In addition, Kapferer and several others argue that social processes are not merely the products of strategic decisions and actions at the micro level, but also of structural conditions the actors cannot possibly be aware of, including unintended consequences of their own activity.

A few years would pass before Barth responded to his critics, in the essay 'Models Reconsidered'.[17] He takes the opportunity there to make some clarifications. Above all, he points out that he does not write about individuals, but about *roles* – that is, activities. (As Sartre said, 'existence precedes essence'.)[18] Persons do perform specific tasks, but they do not do so as whole human beings but as creative and strategic incumbents of a role, be it achieved or ascribed. Unlike the utilitarianists proper, he does not say that *people* are by definition strategic actors, but that strategic acts, performed by people in one capacity or other, generate regularities and social form. The premise is that status differentiation exists prior to the process under scrutiny, and that persons have particular tasks, or possibilities, by virtue of their statuses. It was on the basis of this premise that the Oxford anthropologist Edwin Ardener could describe, slightly tongue-in-cheek, transactionalism as a step towards 'the highest stage of functionalism'.[19] Barth would also dispute the claim that he did not care about power discrepancies, and that it is difficult to know which values people act upon. This can be studied ethnographically, he argued.

The debate went on. When I was a student in the 1980s, there was still a lively debate about Barth's models, the relationship between transactions and meaning, the significance of norms versus choice and improvisation in social interaction, and the dual concept value/values. People do not always maximise. Sometimes we just do as we are told, perhaps because we dare not refuse, or we may act in a value-rational rather than a goal-rational way (to use Weber's terminology). A defence of Barth's transactional model would, incidentally, come a few years later from an unexpected quarter when Eduardo Archetti, whose background was in French and Marxist anthropology, refuted the view that transactions needed to be maximising in a strict economic sense. Archetti argued that the choices people make in fact can be understood as moral choices, since they relate to culturally defined values.[20] This is a very important point. Barth did not reduce whole persons to 'rational actors'. First, he wrote about roles, not whole persons. Second, rationality was locally defined, so that what was reckoned to be valuable varied from place to place.

In the late 1970s, books and articles were published that refined and revised game theory as it had initially been formulated by Neumann and Morgenstern, defined new ways of studying networks, and problematised transactional models in social life. Barth's *Models* was a benchmark or a target, or both, in much of this literature, although it was clearly inadequate as a complete social theory. He taught the significance of showing how people tried to make the most of their situation when faced with several options, which resources they mobilise to achieve it and in which ways the systemic effects of these acts return through feedback as conditions of action. Anthony Giddens discussed Barth's transactional analysis in his widely read book *Central Problems in Social Theory*, where he concluded that all interaction may in principle be studied as strategic action.[21] At the same time, Giddens famously adds that the conditions for action, which are not chosen by the actors, must also be studied – what sociologists tend to speak of as social structure. Barth would instead be inclined to call it emergent form, and the difference is significant. To him, social life consists of movement and process, not fixed structures.

During this period, Barth also made a contribution to anthropological polemic by his own initiative. In 1972, the British anthropologist Colin Turnbull had published *The Mountain People*, a monograph, written in a popularising style, about the Ik people of the borderlands between

Uganda and Sudan.[22] Barth reacted very strongly to Turnbull's depiction of the Ik, which he perceived as offensive and unethical.

Turnbull's book, which sold well and was even dramatised successfully by Peter Brook, was meant to document a people falling apart – morally, economically, politically, socially. Barth read the book as a nasty ambush on a small tribe that had quite undeservedly become the victim of drought and political upheaval in their surroundings. In 1974, he published a short article, 'On Responsibility and Humanity: Calling a Colleague to Account', in *Current Anthropology*.[23]

The short critical piece about Turnbull is interesting, not merely because of its ethical considerations, but because Barth for once allows himself some normative perspectives on the objectives of anthropology. He begins by stating that anthropology must cease being a 'rich man's hobby' and become an 'engaged discipline'.[24] Anthropology must be sober and neutral, he continues, and it must transcend both slack tolerance and (cultural relativist) value freedom in its attempt to create a deeper understanding of the human condition. For that reason, anthropologists must be accountable to each other and to the people among whom they are guests during fieldwork. At this time, in the early 1970s, research ethics in anthropology was still a fairly unsystematic field, and there were few effective sanctions to be implemented against colleagues who transgressed common decency in the field. This would soon change, and today research ethics are formalised and comprehensive, with ethical codes having been adopted by the major anthropological societies.

Barth adds that anthropologists impose themselves uninvited; they use foreign peoples for the sake of their own careers, and they also depend on using themselves as research instruments, which means that they invest their own personality in their fieldwork. In Barth's harsh judgement, Turnbull abused the trust of the Ik, and his book was both methodologically inadequate, empirically flimsy and disparaging towards the group which was the subject of his descriptions. Turnbull appears to make no attempt to make his informants anonymous, and talks openly about cattle theft, illegal hunting and other activities that might create severe problems for the Ik were the book to become known to the authorities. He writes sarcastically about 'the splendid pastime of wifebeating' and paints, in journalistic language, a fundamentally grim picture of Ik society. As a matter of fact, the Ik were on the brink of starving to death, while Turnbull ate his tinned food alone in his car. Towards the end of the book, Turnbull philosophises about the lessons we may ourselves glean from the Ik about our own civilisation and growing egotism, broken families and so on. Barth is unable to contain his disgust with the sentimentality, ethnocentricity and fundamental lack of sensitivity Turnbull – in his view – expresses in the book.

Colin Turnbull was offended and refused to answer, but he must have brooded. A few months after the publication of the Norwegian edition of this book, I was approached by an elderly man in my regular coffee shop near the university campus. He introduced himself as a medical researcher who had read my biography, adding that he had spent a week with Turnbull at a conference in Senegal many years ago. Learning that he was accompanied by a Norwegian, Turnbull asked about Barth, and my new acquaintance confirmed that he knew Barth vaguely. 'Well, if you meet him, will you kill him for me?' Turnbull said, with a hint of a smile.

The sobriety of Barth's style and his naturalist ideals of knowledge may divert attention from his fundamental humanity, which is also a key to understanding his success as a fieldworker. He might doubtless appear to be a strong-minded alpha male in Bergen and at the museum, and he was doubtless a tall tree casting a long shadow. He has a personal charisma and a natural authority which entails that he fills every room he enters with his presence. But at the same time, Barth's profound and genuine empathy with his fellow human beings has been a necessary precondition for the quality of his research. In the preface to *Knowledge and Ritual among the Baktaman*, he writes that he has described religious secrets only after consulting the master of ceremonies, Kimebnok, who gave him permission to tell people in far away places about the rituals of the Baktaman. But the condition was that these truths, the secret names of things and the essence of the rituals, did not fall into the wrong hands. Towards the end of the preface, Barth implores his readers to be aware of this responsibility.

This kind of admonition is not foolish, if anyone should think so. Not everything is meant to be said directly, or to be shared with everyone. Secret knowledge imparted on the condition that it should not be shared has to remain secret. It was, after all, by virtue of his ability to keep secrets that Barth had been allowed to proceed directly to the sixth grade of initiation, and he would have been an inconsiderate anthropologist and human being if he had not understood the significance of this act of trust in return.

While Barth remained active internationally, in the 1970s he did not set the agenda in the way he had earlier. The two large theoretical edifices of Marxism and structuralism formed the framework for most of the major professional debates during the decade, and Barth's methodological preference for the life-worlds of individuals and their projects had little in common with these big theories. He cared little for them, and they cared little for him. He had also worked hard on the Baktaman book in the first half of the decade, in addition to having to deal with his personal life in new and challenging ways. As he says, 'While the productivity of the sixties had been plain sailing, in a way, and everything succeeded, the Baktaman were a pretty big intellectual and professional challenge. So I worked for quite some years on that monograph'.[25] This tendency continued with the Sohar monograph, which appeared eight years after fieldwork.

Life with Unni Wikan also entailed new priorities. Whereas Molly had taken care of all the domestic tasks, Barth and Wikan established another kind of division of labour, of a more equitable kind. As every academic who is also a spouse and parent knows, engaging seriously with your partner and children can divert attention away from research in very noticeable ways. Wikan was at the beginning of her academic career, and had not yet submitted her dissertation. The book on her Cairo research had not been presented as an academic work, and she needed a degree to be eligible in the academic job market. For this reason, more was at stake for Wikan than for Barth as regards the use of the field material from Sohar. Barth had to take this into account when making his own plans. Their initial idea to follow up the Omani work with fieldwork in Afghanistan was called off when they discovered that Wikan was pregnant. Instead, the couple travelled to India in 1976, where Barth lectured in Delhi and other cities. In the same year, both were invited as visiting professors at Johns Hopkins University by Sidney Mintz where they went in spring 1977. Along on this trip came their infant son, Kim Farhad Wikan Barth.

10

Cultural Complexity

But I do know that I want to do something in the sociology of knowledge. I think that a structuralist culture description about underlying patterns of deep structure points in the wrong direction, it leads us away from real life, to very abstract things. What I want is to study culture in a living context. It has to be a sociology of knowledge. What do they know, what is the knowledge foundation for their activities, what do they do and how does the experience they get through what they do, influence what they believed beforehand? That feedback effect; how does a cultural tradition emerge, in other words … Not how it came about through its origins, but how it changes marginally through its functioning.[1]

It was during a visit to Swat in 1977 that Barth suggested that Wali Miangul Jahanzeb should write his autobiography. The *wali* was born in 1908 and was visibly ageing. He was the last *wali* of Swat, since the valley was by now, formally at least, an integral part of the Pakistani republic.

The *wali* was attracted to the idea, but he made it a condition that Barth should write the book. This was naturally a great honour and a genuine act of trust, and in practice it was impossible to refuse the offer, even if the material from Sohar had not yet been fully analysed and written out. In April, Barth, Wikan and Kim, now three years old, went to Swat, where they spent two weeks together. Barth subsequently remained in the valley while the *wali* dictated his autobiography, interrupted only by a few questions and comments from Barth.

The *wali* had lived through major structural changes. The first Englishman ever to visit the valley had arrived there only 13 years before he was born. At the time, it was an unstable and politically turbulent area with frequent skirmishes between rich landowners. When the *wali* was nine years old, the state of Swat was founded under the leadership of his father. From 1917 to 1969, Swat had been officially recognised, first by the British, then by Pakistan, as a self-governing princely state. For a long time there were no schools, and only a handful of *mullah*s were literate. The

10.   At the Ethnographic Museum, early 1980s (photo reproduced
       by permission of the Museum of Cultural History, Oslo).

roads were few and poor. The present *wali*, who took the reins in 1949,
encouraged a slow and cautious modernisation. He abolished serfdom in
1950, and saw to it that schools were built and even a college, Jahanzeb
College. This was where Barth went soon after his arrival in Swat in March
1954. At the time of Barth's fieldwork, the society was slowly adjusting to
the age of global modernity, but traditional practices and notions were still
very much present.

    In the preface to the biography, Barth makes it clear that he does not
wish to alter the story of the *wali*, and that he considers himself chiefly
a secretary and a facilitator. Instead, he has equipped the book with a

lengthy postscript, which presents topics 'which are of importance to anthropologists and political scientists'.[2] In this way, he succeeds in remaining loyal to the *wali* and not abusing his trust by stabbing him in the back when he turns away, while at the same time he uses the postscript to supplement the main character's subjective reminiscences with a more balanced description of the facts on the ground.

In accordance with the intention of the biography, the postscript is written in a different style from Barth's purely academic publications from Swat. The prose is more narrative than analytical, at the same time as the goal is evidently to improve the analytical understanding of the reader. This text may be read as a potted political history of Swat in the twentieth century, and represents in its own way a version of generative processual analysis. Above all, Barth shows two things: First, it becomes apparent how leadership in the valley continuously had to relate to new parameters, largely as a result of increased contact with the outside world. Although neither the British nor the Pakistani state achieved political control of the valley until 1969, both the present *wali* and his father had to relate actively to the powerful political elites at the centre, and they knew about the risk of military invasion should they make a false or disrespectful move. The *wali*'s steps towards modernisation, from the professionalisation of the army to infrastructural improvements, must be seen in the light of this precarious relationship. Secondly, the postscript reveals the quality of statesmanship that was required to govern boisterous *khan*s and influential religious leaders, and to keep the peace within the extended family. For long periods in his youth, the *wali* was like a stranger to his father, and his relationship with his brothers was complicated and tense. In the final account, he could trust nobody. Surrounded by

> flatterers, opportunists, and enemies, and also many honest and competent associates … he would always find that he was entirely alone in his final judgements of what must be done, whom to trust and whom to fear, what was the portent of events, and where lay his best options.[3]

Several years after he had lost his formal position, the *wali* remained an important political force in Swat. Towards the end of his narrative, he confesses to a desire to withdraw from the power struggle and move into a smaller house, with just four or five bedrooms and five to six servants – an 'ordinary middle-class life'.[4] At the same time, he is aware that such a move would be socially impossible because of his many obligations towards family members and the many clients in the valley who depend

on him. Although Swat had been integrated into Pakistan by now, it was –
and still is today – a society where power can be a heavy burden, because
it carries with it so much uncertainty and responsibility. During the armed
resistance against the Soviet occupation in Afghanistan, which began
shortly after the *wali* had dictated his memoirs, Swat was one of the areas
where the American-supported Mujaheddin militia, later morphing into
the Taliban, received the strongest support. The tension between religious
and secular power had a long tradition in Swat, and it was now being
converted into a conflict between religious power and the state.

While Barth, Wikan and their son enjoyed the *wali*'s hospitality in Swat,
Barth also got to meet his old servant and friend Kashmali. It was as if
something had come full circle. He would never again do fieldwork in
Swat, but more than 20 years after the affair of the Curl Essay Prize,
he got his redress when the *wali* of Swat himself asked him to write his
biography.

He now had two books to write, the Sohar monograph and the
biography of the *wali*. In addition, he had a demanding situation to deal
with every day at the museum and new domestic challenges as well. With
Kim, Barth would become a father of a different kind to the one he had
been in his first marriage, present and actively participating in his son's
young life. In spite of the stack of projects piling up, when NRK, the
Norwegian state broadcasting corporation, contacted him with a view
to producing a series of TV programmes about cultural variation, he
accepted. The museum anthropologists had few teaching obligations, but
popularisation was all the more important. It accordingly seemed a natural
thing for Barth to explain anthropology to a larger audience through the
medium of television.

As a matter of fact, Barth has always enjoyed speaking and writing
about anthropology to broad, non-academic audiences, although he had
rarely found the opportunity to give high priority to this kind of activity
before. He had written several articles in Norwegian about development
issues and the importance of understanding other societies, and he now
wished to contribute to a widening of the horizon of the subject in the
Norwegian public sphere by giving talks on screen.

The programmes must have been low budget, even by 1970s standards.
If a television adept of our times, having grown up in a world of
multi-channel TV and remote controls, American serials, commercial
breaks, talk shows, *The Simpsons* and *The Sopranos*, watched these four
programmes, they would be historical curios: a glimpse into a TV

world where a recorded slide lecture could be captivating, enlightening, entertaining television.

The late 1970s were a markedly slower time than ours. Norway had just one TV channel, which broadcast from 5:55 PM to around midnight. Colour broadcasts had been introduced, to the protests of Christian conservatives, only five years earlier. There was a gravity and seriousness associated with being on TV which can be difficult to understand in today's multi-channel world, where most programmes have a hint of irony – the inverted commas of the postmodern condition – and where even politicians are expected to make the odd self-deprecating joke. In the present-day, very few single TV programmes endure in the popular imagination. It may take a season or more for a new series to establish itself, and you must appear on TV many times before people begin to notice you.

This was not the case then, and Barth recalls that in the autumn of 1979, for the first time in his life, he felt like a celebrity, approached on the street by strangers. He may have been a world-renowned anthropologist, but in the domestic public sphere he had been relatively unknown.

It was, in other words, not just me, but hundreds of thousands of others who came into contact for the first time with this now greying, moustached and charismatic professor at the Ethnographic Museum. As I recall the programmes,[5] Barth spent most of the time behind his large, dark brown office desk, with a globe to his right, speaking with an avuncular voice about the Basseri and their wanderings from semi-desert to mountain, the initiation rituals of the misty forests of New Guinea, gender segregation in Oman and power struggles in Swat. Occasionally, the camera shifted to show a slide, mostly in black and white, from one of his many ethnographic field trips.

A basic humanistic message implicitly underpinned the popularising narrative. What Barth tried to tell us was that many roads could lead to the good life, that we should not pass judgement before having properly understood other people's lives, and that the most important insight from other peoples does not ultimately concern them, but ourselves. He made the exotic familiar and the familiar exotic. I cannot remember if he said so explicitly, but having seen the four programmes, I was left with the conviction that everything could have been different here in the West as well. It was a liberating thought and one that stimulated the appetite for more. Two years later, I was studying sociology, intent on moving on to social anthropology after the first year. This is how it went, but Barth never taught my cohort formally. He was only a couple of kilometres away, but as first-year students we were given to understand, through comments made *sotto voce* by older students, that the relationship between the department and the professor at the museum left much to be desired.

The following year, the book *Andres liv – og vårt eget* ('Other people's lives – and our own') was published. The cover shows Barth with the Baktaman initiation leader Kimebnok; the anthropologist wearing shorts, Kimebnok wearing a penis sheath and ornamental decorations in his hair and face, with lush vegetation forming the backdrop. The book was distributed by Norway's largest book club, a major business at the time, and it must have been Barth's bestselling book of all time. An academic monograph in social anthropology is deemed to have done pretty well if it sells more than a thousand copies. Several of Barth's books have been reprinted time and again, but the print runs are small.

Barth had written popular texts before. In fact, he wrote half a dozen newspaper articles for the Oslo paper *Verdens Gang* (*VG*) from his fieldwork in Kurdistan and Swat, and he later showed his flair for popularisation through a further handful of short contributions intended for a general, Norwegian audience. His ability to identify telling events, and his interest in what concrete individuals do, is also an excellent qualification for a popularising anthropologist. *Andres liv* is a simple book about complex questions. The objective is not to convince the reader that Barth's analytical perspectives are superior, but to instil wonder, awe and respect for that teeming diversity of human ways of life that exist on the planet. Like Malinowski and Lévi-Strauss before him, Barth expresses anxious concern over the ruthless modernisation and one-dimensional ideas about development that were encroaching on the life-worlds of small peoples. After all, he had shown, 20 years earlier, that the quality of life was higher for the Basseri when they could live as nomads than if they were to become sedentary farmers, loyal citizens and obedient taxpayers.

When it is converted to normative public education, as in this context, social anthropology has to find the right side of the fine boundary between enlightened humanism and the reactionary romanticisation of pre-modern societies. Barth can scarcely be regarded as a reactionary romantic. However, he does notice how the road to hell is paved with excellent intentions in development projects, and how individuals and entire populations who have lived traditionally lose their self-esteem and belief in their own capabilities if they are being 'developed' without having been asked how they would prefer to be 'developed'. Their opportunity situation, to use one of his preferred concepts, changes for the worse. The practical knowledge they have drawn upon for generations is swiftly devalued, and ultimately loses value altogether. And the skills and wisdom they have inherited from their ancestors are rendered invalid overnight. This was the message in an article where Barth warned against designing development projects that failed to take local conditions into consideration, and the same message may be gleaned between the lines of *Andres liv.* Such a view, which is doubtless shared by most anthropologists, is not tantamount to saying that things should be left as they are, but rather that change should take place, as far as possible on local terms, such that people who are directly affected by processes of change may still feel that they are capable of making their own choices.

Around the same time as the TV series made waves in Norwegian society, the economic, cultural and social implications of immigration were on the agenda in West European societies, including the Scandinavian ones. Barth largely stayed away from this debate. Instead, both Grønhaug and Wikan contributed to it, each in their own way.

The secondary literature about Barth's research continued to grow. The articles from Swat were by now standard references and were placed on reading lists in political anthropology across the Western world. The book about the Basseri became obligatory reading for everyone who studied pastoral nomads. *Models of Social Organinzation* remained a common reference in theoretical and epistemological debates. The introduction to *Ethnic Groups and Boundaries* was by now cited by virtually everybody who studied ethnicity, regardless of their discipline. Even the book about the Baktaman started to attract readers outside of the smallish community of Melanesianists.

In Norway, Barth was increasingly discovered by non-anthropologists, and different readers saw completely different things in his work. The aforementioned Arne Næss (1912–2009), who had gone from being a positivist hardliner to a sceptic and eco-philosopher, wrote, in 1969, a small book called *Hvilken verden er den virkelige?* ('Which world is the real one?').[6] While at work on the book, he contacted Barth and read some of his central works. A full chapter is devoted to cultural relativism as a methodological device, and the anthropological gaze seems to have nudged Næss towards his sceptical philosophical position. For even if the physical world does exist independently of people's ideas, our experienced world is socially, to some extent even individually, constructed. When a mining engineer looks at a mountain, he sees something quite different to that which a mountaineer or skier sees when considering the same mountain. This kind of perspective, on which the comparative method of anthropology is based, gave Næss useful ammunition in his philosophical scepticism. What you see does not just depend on what you are looking at, but also what you are looking with. This insight forms, in a nutshell, the fundamental premise for Barth's anthropology of knowledge.

A very different reading of Barth came from Dag Østerberg (b. 1938). Østerberg, a precocious adolescent and young man like Barth, had produced a widely read and influential contribution to the Scandinavian positivism controversy in 1961, as a 23-year old influenced by Continental social philosophy and interpretive sociology. Østerberg argued against natural science models for the social sciences, showing that humans are ambiguous and unpredictable.

Østerberg would later work extensively with Sartre's philosophy. In the slim, beautifully written *Samfunnsteori og nytteteori* ('Social theory and utility theory'),[7] Østerberg critically discusses Barth's analysis of the fishing vessel off the Møre coast. His main objection is that Barth's analysis of the interaction aboard the vessel is an interpretation, not a naturalistic description of a factual series of events. He concludes that while generative processual analysis cannot possibly produce predictions, it may develop 'ingenious postdictions', interpretations of something that has already happened. From this analysis it also follows that other interpretations might be credible.

While Næss commends Barth for his cultural relativist approach to knowledge and life-worlds, Østerberg castigates him for being a reductionist, positivist and utilitarian. What makes Barth a genuinely original thinker is, perhaps, that both are right. Østerberg is perfectly right to point out that another, just as credible interpretation of interaction on the fishing boat would have given a different result. One might even imagine a generative processual analysis where the maximised outcome was not individual benefit, but solidarity. Barth does not reject this perspective, and he has often remarked that critics pounced on the concept of transaction, instead of seeing the generative and processual perspective as a method of inquiry with a broader application than mere economic gain and loss. Besides, what is maximised in any given setting is culturally determined. This is where Næss's interpretation of Barth comes into its own, since the philosopher recognises the cultural breadth in the choices humans make; after all, they act on the basis of widely different world-views and understandings of reality.

Barth was aware of the critical reception of his work in Norway, but he rarely responded to it. In 1985, the social anthropology students at Oslo organised a meeting between him and Østerberg. At the meeting,

Barth made an appeal to the concrete, that of which we are certain that it exists since it can be observed, and also spoke about the importance of finding out what was at stake for actors. Østerberg, never a great empirical researcher, argued on the basis of social philosophy that human agency is in principle unpredictable and multifaceted, and that the emphasis on maximisation was implicitly ideological. As I remember the meeting, many of those present were sympathetic to both sides. Interestingly, both Barth and Østerberg had an affinity for Weber's sociology, but whereas Barth spoke of Weber's interest in individual agency, Østerberg might point out that there are several types of action in Weber, notably value-rational and goal-rational action. Weber also conceded that value-free research was impossible since the researcher, whether consciously or not, carries their own values with them throughout the project, from the delineation of the topic to the final footnote.

His new family life, the complicated situation at the museum, the unproductive tensions regarding the Oslo social anthropology department at Blindern, administrative duties and committee work were taxing. Wikan gained her doctorate in 1980 based on the material from Oman, with Emrys Peters as her first opponent.[8] Two years later, her monograph from Sohar, *Behind the Veil in Arabia*, was published.[9] It would seem that she had got more out of their joint fieldwork than him. She also published several articles, among others a widely quoted article about the *xanith*, 'the third sex' in strongly gender-segregated Omani society, that is cross-dressing men who function as prostitutes in the absence of female incumbents of that status.[10] She has continued to visit Oman regularly ever since. Barth would for his part not publish much from Oman apart from the monograph, published the year after Wikan's volume.

His own projects nonetheless continued to proliferate and overlap. Barth never seemed to finish a project before he had started a new one. Ever since Braidwood got him to Kurdistan, he had practised the maxim that hunger comes while you are eating. In the autumn of 1981, while he was busy writing the monograph from Sohar and Wali Miangul Jahanzeb's autobiography, a letter came from Papua New Guinea. Gold had been found in the Ok Tedi area, near Baktaman territory, and Barth was asked to advise on possible cultural consequences of mining. He felt he should use this opportunity.

However, he might well have declined. Even if Barth has occasionally revisited people among whom he has once done fieldwork, including the Swat Pathans and the Basseri, he has not done fieldwork in the same location twice. There are a couple of reasons for this. First, Barth has always moved ahead in his thinking by seeking new fields, travelling to new places. Secondly, he says, there is something socially difficult about returning. Perhaps one has forgotten the language, perhaps one does not recognise people, and there are expectations associated with revisits that can be difficult to satisfy. In this area, Wikan took a different path. She has continued to revisit both Cairo and Oman, thereby gaining an ever deeper understanding of these societies. So by noticing how well his wife managed her revisits, and after the experience with the *wali* and renewed acquaintance with old allies such as Kashmali, his doubts were mitigated.

Before Christmas 1981, Barth, Wikan and Kim went to Papua New Guinea and travelled by helicopter into the largely road-less interior, where Barth had spent most of 1968. The encounter with the Baktaman was moving. For the first time, they saw a white child, thereby realising that Europeans were more like them than they had been aware of. They were also shown a Norway spruce the size of a Christmas tree, which had been sown by Barth at the time of his fieldwork. Barth and Wikan, for their part, encountered what may be described, with more than a hint of travel writing cliché, as a Stone Age tribe entering into the nuclear age overnight. The Baktaman had a traditional counting system where they used body parts to count up to 27. However, to them, counting was embodied and concrete, and abstract calculations like 5 plus 7 had no meaning for them. They knew nothing of clock time or the exotic notion that there was a boundary separating work from leisure. Yet, it transpired that the Baktaman, the Seltaman and other peoples of the Ok Tedi region had adjusted quickly to the new era. Shortly after the opening of the mine, they took up wage work, and they almost immediately began to negotiate about working hours and salaries. Like many other Melanesian peoples, they had a pragmatic and fairly relaxed attitude to change. Barth, however, found the transition problematic to grasp. He did not know exactly how to account for this incredibly fast change from subsistence horticulture in a closed, small-scale society to a life of modern wage work.

He did, however, write a report with Wikan, which was accepted and used.[11] In it, they warned against the potentially disastrous consequences of mining if it was not accompanied by change in other domains. The risk was that the population in the region might grow accustomed to a monetised way of life, but sooner or later the gold would be exhausted, and the Mountain Ok peoples would just be left with an enormous, toxic slag heap. The journey from the Stone Age to the industrial wasteland would in that case only take a few decades.

The Ok Tedi gold and copper mine was still operating in 2014, but with very tangible ecological side-effects owing to the contamination of land and water. It is often mentioned in the critical literature on mining and the environment as the realisation of a worst-case scenario. At the same time, its importance to the Papua New Guinea economy – to which it has at times contributed a full quarter of the country's export earnings – makes it difficult to close down in spite of local and environmentalists' protests.

Barth had known from the start that the real objective for his stay in Papua New Guinea was not to offer advice to a mining company, but to continue to work on the themes covered in the monograph on the Baktaman. He now had a good grasp of one cosmology and one set of initiation rituals, and was interested in comparing what he had found among the Baktaman with rituals and world-views among other small peoples in the region. Altogether, Barth and Wikan spent three months in the region, which is, of course, inadequate for doing a proper ethnographic job among a people whose language one does not know. And they were not just looking at one group, but seven, apart from the Baktaman!

This was, naturally, impossible, but neither had it been the intention to study all the groups ethnographically. In the years following Barth's Baktaman fieldwork, several anthropologists had been to the area and done research on peoples neighbouring the Baktaman. Of the eight Mountain Ok peoples gravitating towards the mine and living within walking distance of sorts to the Baktaman, only the Bolovip had not yet been described. Barth and family spent some time with them, with the assistance of an interpreter; they visited the other Mountain Ok groups for shorter periods, not to study them in detail, but to receive some first-hand sensory impressions that might enrich and complement the reading of other people's research.

Barth wanted to continue working in Melanesia. He had identified Malekula, one of the islands that make up Vanuatu, as a possible location. Wikan was less enthusiastic. In the Ok Tedi region, creature comforts were very basic. It rained almost continuously, and the smell of mould and decay hung in the air. Although the oceanic climate in Malekula would be more pleasant than that of the misty forest in the heart of New Guinea, she did not feel particularly attracted to fieldwork under such conditions, often longing for a dry bed at night. After two laborious fieldwork periods, in Cairo and Sohar, she now wanted them to produce ethnography in a location where it might be pleasant to stay. This wish would soon take the couple to Bali.

Projects in the making had to be completed first, however. They wrote the report itself quickly. The books about Oman and Barth's biography of the *wali* were also finished. He now only had to get a grip on the analysis of the material about cosmologies and initiation rituals among the Mountain Ok peoples. At this time, he was conveniently invited to give the annual James Frazer lecture in Cambridge in 1982, an occasion he used to develop a sketch of comparative analysis. He then began to systematise the material, both his own and that which he had found in other research, in order to develop a model. The result was *Cosmologies in the Making*,[12] a creative and unusual book which may well be regarded as volume two of *Models*. This time, he did not develop generative models of strategic action and social form, but of knowledge systems. He tried to show how modest variations in ritual symbolism and form propagated themselves further up in the system and led to relatively large differences in world-view. The basic assumption was that thought begins with practice, quite the opposite of Lévi-Strauss, who had gained world-wide fame and recognition for his own comparative work on symbolic systems.

Barth remained a committed fieldworker, and his large and varied amount of fieldwork is one of the main reasons for the respect he enjoys in the anthropological community. It is only through meticulous empirical work that anthropologists produce data that can be used analytically, by themselves and others. Since anthropology has comparative ambitions, the work of others is indispensable for one's own efforts. Other researchers thereby become both discussion partners and sources contributing to the enrichment of one's own material.

Barth had often provided this raw material for others. He was now in a situation where he was going to help himself to other researchers' ethnography. He had never done this before to any great extent. As mentioned earlier, he refers infrequently to and rarely discusses other people's contributions in his earlier monographs. In this way, *Cosmologies* represents something new in his career as a writer. He drew extensively upon doctoral dissertations, articles and unpublished manuscripts written largely by younger colleagues who had done fieldwork in the Ok Tedi region. He tried to single out the most important elements in those peoples' world-views and investigated how they were connected to practices and people's engagement with their environment. He then developed a generative model demonstrating diversity and variation within the eight cosmologies.

Like *Models*, *Cosmologies* had a polemic aspect as well, and it was not just directed towards the deductive logic of structuralism. French and British social anthropologists had tended to follow Durkheim in assuming that since society is projected onto the world, the external world is made to express social relationships and cultural categories. However, Barth wished to explore whether it could be the other way around. If you lived in a natural environment where pandanus trees grew, and where cassowaries and big-eyed marsupials roamed the forests, and where there was some rain nearly every day, then it might be the case that these physical, ecological facts influenced the cultural world-view in a fairly direct way.

The methodological challenge here was different to that in the societies where Barth had worked before, from Kurdistan and Sohar to Iran and Swat. These societies possessed a rich written tradition, and in academic centres such as Harvard and Oxford there were learned regional specialists who knew the languages and were familiar with the historical sources. The relationship between historical analyses and Barth's focus on the here and now could, as I have shown, be strained. Indeed, he himself contributed to this tension, or should I say estrangement, by stating that historical sources were thin when it came to the lived life, and had little to contribute to an understanding of the present. Regional specialists were for their part uncertain as to whether Barth's research was relevant to their work.

In New Guinea, the situation was different. There was no historical research on the New Guinea Highlands, and no local written tradition. The region had been unexplored by foreigners until the 1930s, in some cases decades later. This also implied that knowledge transmission between the generations necessarily became demanding. Without those crutches for thought that writing represents, the ritual leaders had to remember the main elements of their rites from year to year. None of the Mountain Ok peoples possessed the concept of a year, but the largest rituals were executed roughly every ten years. The leader then had to perform a powerful and compelling ritual which impressed and frightened the novices, and to which a handful of mature men might nod in recognition and acknowledgement. It goes without saying that the rituals would scarcely be identical from one performance to the next, yet there was a strong continuity. Most of the key symbols used to organise the rituals, such as the skull of the ancestor, the pandanus wigs, the pig's fat and animals such as the cassowary, had a physical shape and thus provided a rudimentary or symbolic skeleton for the ritual leader to work with.

It is reasonable to assume that initiation rites among the Mountain Ok peoples had a shared historical origin, and that this similarity may serve as a starting point for comparison. Change takes place through the actual implementation of the rituals, where the leader has to improvise, doubtless in concert with the other participants and spectators, roughly in the same way a jazz musician communicates both with their fellow musicians and with the audience during a long improvisation. Barth sees three kinds of transformations in Mountain Ok ritual, which can be substantiated by referring to variation between the groups: gradual changes in the connotations of sacred symbols; gradual changes in the meta-signification or metaphorical meanings of symbols; and gradual expansion or contraction of the validity of a particular logical schema or symbol in the world-view as a whole. For example, sexual symbolism is strongly foregrounded among the Bimin-Kuskumin, who, at the tenth and final grade of initiation, dramatise an ambiguous form of sexuality whereby the novices masturbate on a rod which is smeared with symbolic sperm at one end (actually white boar fat) and with symbolic menstrual blood (red sow fat) at the other. The Baktaman are less explicit in this area, and use animals and plants to symbolise the complementarity between the genders instead, while the Tifalmin ritually express sexuality by creating positive expectations without connecting them to a fertility mystery.

Moreover, water and dew are central symbols for many of the peoples, but they mean different things. Pandanus-leaf wigs are sometimes painted red (to signify death, virility or the feminine principle), sometimes not. In his attempt to make sense of these and many other variations, Barth consistently connects particular ritual practices to other elements in the same group's world-view and social organisation.

Throughout the book, Barth raises questions which are only partially answered, if at all. Why are the Baktaman so uninterested in the wild boar as a ritual symbol? Why did the Mafom leader refuse to explain to Barth what initiation meant, when he happily described all its elements? Why do the Faiwolmin hardly talk during initiation, while several other Mountain Ok peoples have a rich tradition of sacred discourse?

A reading of *Cosmologies* is different from a reading of *Models* in the sense that the author this time invites the reader into the book as a partner in dialogue, conversing with them as he goes along. In *Models*, the argument went in one direction, from author to reader; this time, it is as if you as a reader accompany the anthropologist on his journey, and in the end – if the result is as intended – you will be convinced that creativity in ritual practice is caused by interaction with people's surroundings, both man-made and natural. Ritual drama is an important part of these peoples' artistic repertoire, and contains a surplus of meaning which ensures that nobody, neither the ritual leader nor the anthropologist, can tell you exactly what they say or do. In *Cosmologies*, Barth comes closer to the boundary between art and science than ever before, both with respect to form and content, in spite of the fact that he invokes Darwin, who advises the naturalist to isolate a small segment of reality and study it in great detail in order to draw inferences about larger processes.[13] *Cosmologies* is as good an example of generative processual analysis as *Models* is, but what is generated here are neither political systems nor economic maximisation, but 'a forest of symbols', to use Victor Turner's evocative metaphor.[14] And what emanates from this forest is ultimately the sublime, the sacred and the ineffable. Barth's continued interest in art is more visible here than anywhere else in his writings.

Perhaps Barth himself sensed that he was moving away from a strictly scientific mode of reasoning while working with Mountain Ok symbolism. However, he returns to the fold in the last chapter, where he produces a list of recommendations for future comparative research on ritual practices.[15]

The manuscript of *Cosmologies* was completed in 1984, but it was another three years before Cambridge University Press published it, equipped with an interesting preface by Jack Goody, who begins by stating that 'Fredrik Barth needs no introduction from me'.[16] The preface is instructive and contributes to positioning Barth in the world of Anglophone anthropology. Goody, a comparatively and historically oriented anthropologist who has written a medium-sized library of books developing the contrast between Eurasian and African societies, has a professional identity far removed from Barth's. Yet they share several interests, such as the importance of kinship for politics, and – as in this book – the ways in which knowledge is transmitted. Goody has written about creativity in non-literate societies, and also draws a parallel to his own ethnographic home turf, northern Ghana. He had there worked with the LoDagaa, who organised their ritual life around the long, complex Bagre myth. Fortes, who had studied the nearby Tallensi, wondered if he himself might have missed something essential, as he had not found the faintest trace of a similar myth there. He probably had not, for as Goody says, myths of this kind are unevenly distributed in West Africa. Some have them while others do not, and this variation is neither wholly random nor wholly systematic, but has to be understood from concrete, local circumstances.

Towards the mid 1980s, Barth began to feel that he had spent too much of his time on administration and management at the museum and that it could be cumbersome and time-consuming to 'defend simple decisions' and exert leadership in a sometimes intransigent environment. He began to play with the idea that he might escape from all this if he could get a government grant, which he did in fact receive in 1985. These fellowships are for life, and are usually awarded to writers and artists of especial cultural significance. It is very rare that an academic receives one. In a certain sense, Norway lost Barth – paradoxically – by honouring him with a government grant. He was tired of conflicts, left the museum behind and became a transatlantic academic with few attachments to university life in his home country. As a free intellectual, he became noticeably less visible and active at home than he had been as a professor in Bergen or Oslo.

On the day that Barth left his professorship to take up the grant, Alver arrived early at work and saw to it that the name plate on Barth's office door was taken down and the furniture removed. By now, however, Barth and Wikan were already engaged in new fieldwork, this time in Bali. For reasons of family and other practicalities, this would not be a long, continuous period of fieldwork, but a long-term project which took place in fits and starts. They would commute to Bali, separately or together, between 1983 and 1988.

Kim usually accompanied his parents on their travels. His father had himself grown up in the leafy western suburbs of Oslo, and he did not approve of the idea that his son should go to the local school at Slemdal, which he dismissed as 'a posh school' (*en jåleskole*). For this reason, Kim started primary school at the Catholic St Sunniva's school in August 1982. On the first day of school, the teacher asked the children what they had been up to during the summer. Well, some had spent the summer in the family's cabin down on the coast, whereas others had been to Spain. Kim explained to the teacher that he had lived in the rainforest in Papua New Guinea and then travelled around the world. The teacher did not respond. On the first meeting with the parents, she informed Kim's mum and dad that their son was an inveterate liar. The teacher, evidently, did not know who Fredrik Barth and Unni Wikan were.

11

The Guru and the Conjurer

The task is endless and ever self-transforming. For most of my lifetime I have seen it as a social science version of the naturalist's old task, of watching and wondering.[1]

Bali was not an obvious next stop in Barth's life as an ethnographer. While he would have liked to go to Vanuatu, Bali had been Wikan's preference. One reason for Barth's initial doubt was the fact that Bali had been studied by good anthropologists previously. Margaret Mead and Gregory Bateson had been there in the 1940s, Clifford Geertz in the 1960s. The British anthropologist Mark Hobart was about to devote a lifetime of study to Bali. And there were others. Barth sensed that others had already been there and taken the prime cuts.

It is not difficult to understand why Bali has had a magnetic attraction on anthropologists. Not only was the island an aesthetic pleasure with its lush landscapes, well-tended rice terraces and beautiful temples, a pleasant climate, wholesome, tasty food and a population renowned for its friendliness; it also had its undisputable social and cultural specificities. Unlike most of South-East Asia, where Buddhism and Islam were the major religions, Hinduism has survived in Bali. Christian missionaries, who had been active on many other Indonesian islands in the seventeenth century, had made little impression there. Balinese Hinduism, moreover, had its own, unique characteristics, owing to long historical separation from the Indian subcontinent.

In addition, the 'Balinese character' was considered inscrutable and fascinating, especially to psychologically oriented anthropologists. Bateson and Mead argue, in their study *Balinese Character*, that Balinese culture 'lacks climax', trying to document this by means of photography. Balinese fear both anger and ecstasy, the couple argue, and they tend to avoid emotionally laden situations that might lead to tensions. For this reason, they smile even when they feel sad.[2]

11.   Bhutan, early 1990s (photo reproduced by permission of Fredrik Barth and
      Unni Wikan).

Barth and Wikan were especially interested in Geertz's work. He had
described the Balinese concept of the person, perception of time and
norms of politeness with insight and elegance, he had analysed the illegal
(but widespread) cockfight as a potent Balinese symbol, and given a
detailed account of their intricate system of naming. His articles were
well constructed and written, empirically founded and came across as
convincing. Wikan was initially attracted to the Geertzian perspective on
Balinese culture, while Barth was more critical. After all, the American had
little to say about everyday interaction and internal diversity, preferring
generalisations about Balinese culture as a patterned symbolic universe. It
was nevertheless a pressing question what they could achieve in Bali that
had not already been done by Geertz and others.

A tentative answer came when the couple visited the island on a
short tourist trip in 1982. They then discovered that there were Muslim
villages in Bali, and that internal cultural variation appeared to be far more
extensive than Geertz had let on. They soon developed a project each.
Wikan would study personhood, especially Balinese ways of dealing with
emotions. Barth meanwhile would work comparatively with a cluster of
villages which displayed interesting variations amongst themselves, and
would try to develop generative models which could account for both
similarities and differences between the villages. His ultimate ambitions

were nevertheless greater, and he would try to develop his anthropology of knowledge to show how different worlds of experience and of the imagination produced different kinds of people and societies, and he wanted to do this with a basis in local realities, not theoretical concepts from foreign countries.

Although Wikan would eventually learn Bahasa Indonesia, Barth never learned either of the local languages (Bahasa and Balinese) well enough to use them as a working language. However, he did, as so often, team up with skilful assistants cum interpreters who doubled as a conversational partner and informant. Getting hold of multilingual assistants in the global South does not have to be too expensive for a Western anthropologist. As he says, 'there is a lot of underemployment in Bali, so he [Ghazi Habibullah, Barth's field assistant in the Muslim villages] had a few things going on, but as soon as I arrived, he would let go of everything and come with me'.[3] Ghazi was the proud owner of a Vespa, making it easy to move from village to village during fieldwork. Subsequently, Barth worked with another assistant, Made Artja, who helped him out in the Hindu villages.

Bali was arguably a pleasant place to be, yet Barth has described fieldwork there as extremely tiring. The reason is, paradoxically, the very friendliness of the Balinese. He experienced it as intensely social and the hospitality as exhausting. Since an anthropologist depends on the goodwill of their informants and has to use themselves as a research instrument, it was difficult to get away; it was nearly impossible to be left alone. Besides, Balinese culture was ritualised in such a way that one always had to stay calm and in social settings. Gestures and displays of emotion were considered an indication that one was out of balance.

In the end, they wrote a monograph each. Wikan's was published in 1990, Barth's in 1993.[4] By now, Wikan's academic career was also taking off in earnest. With the Bali book, apart from several books of popularised anthropology and a clutch of well-published articles, she had three ethnographic monographs to her name. The significance of their close professional collaboration can scarcely be overestimated. Barth's increasingly multifaceted interpretations of social life from the mid 1970s onwards correspond exactly with his marriage to Unni Wikan. His influence on her is more difficult to gauge, since there is no basis for comparison, but it has doubtless been considerable. Kim says that there were always stacks of books lying around at home, and that the boundary between leisure and work was non-existent. At the same time, his father always found time for Kim if the son came knocking on his office door. But the three would never become an average Norwegian nuclear family with holidays in Tenerife and mum's gingerbread for Christmas. As compensation, Kim continues, there were quite a few earthen floors and trips into the jungle.

At the outset, Barth had a simple, clearly phrased hypothesis: given the essential uniformity of Balinese culture, in what ways do the Muslims distinguish themselves from the majority Hindus, and what are the forms of articulation between Muslims and Hindus? He soon got a grip on this level of analysis. However, he wished to grasp something more difficult, namely an understanding of the relationship between knowledge, social process and local organisation. As his work proceeded, the monograph and the conclusion became more and more remote. The complexity was greater than anything he had experienced previously. Bali is like an India in miniature, in the sense that the island has layers upon layers of history, living traditions and half-dead traditions that are sometimes brought alive, impulses from many quarters, not least from tourism, and a very considerable degree of internal variation from region to region, from village to village. For example, there are still a few Bali Aga villages in the eastern parts of the island where pre-Hindu traditions are kept alive and scary-looking roosters painted in strong colours sit in cages awaiting the next cockfight. And, by 2014, the growth in tourism and immigration from other Indonesian islands has led, among other things, to traffic jams that compare favourably with those in Bangkok or São Paulo, in persistence and intensity if not in size.

By showing internal variation, Barth had at least succeeded in showing that Geertz had not told the whole story. Reading Geertz, one could easily get the impression that Balinese culture was uniform and homogeneous. That was certainly not the case.

Bali is an island of a certain size (nearly 6,000 square kilometres), and with its nearly four million inhabitants (2014 figures; it was less than half that in 1983), it is more densely populated than the Netherlands. Less than 10 per cent of the population are Muslim, and many of them live in the Buleleng province in the north, far from the airport and the tourist areas. Barth found a village there where all residents were Muslim, and he also studied a purely Hindu village as well as a few other communities. Buleleng did not correspond to common assumptions about Bali. It had been politically separate from the rest of Bali for much of its history, and the largest town, Singaraja, is a cosmopolitan port with an illustrious history of piracy, which also did not fit with the standard anthropological views of Bali, which were based on research in southern Bali.

As fieldwork proceeded, with long gaps between each visit, complexity grew. It had long been clear that it was not possible to describe Bali, with or without its Muslim contingent, as a homogeneous culture, and Barth identifies no less than six cultural streams that had reached the island at different times, and which still characterise it today: the Malayo-Polynesian (dating back 4000 years), the Indonesian Megalithic, the Indian, the Chinese, the Islamic/Javanese and the Western. These streams did not just consist in easily identifiable elements such as religion, language, architecture and so on, but also contained moralities, kinship practices, property rules and so on, and all of this somehow had to be incorporated into the analysis. As the centuries and millennia have gone by, these cultural streams have created distinctive layers, mixed unevenly and incompletely, more like a lumpy gravy than a kneaded dough, and no 'natural law of society' implies that the mixture will one day become even and uniform. When the project in Bali gradually found its shape, it became clear that it represented a continuation of Barth's last project in New Guinea, in the sense that the question was which aspects of knowledge generated variation, but also which factors limited that variation. Unlike the Mountain Ok peoples, all Balinese participated in partial systems – political, legal, commercial etc. – which encompassed the whole island. In other words, they needed to have enough in common to interact meaningfully, at the same time as they maintained their mutual differences.

Barth found that internal variation had not been taken sufficiently seriously in research on the large Asiatic civilisations. He tried to develop a research method, a language and a model where variation was depicted as a premise and not an afterthought, where internal diversity was a matter of course and not an exception, and where the peculiarities of local world-views were not subsumed under the categories of Western social science.

Some of the differences between the Muslim and the Hindu villages, in the book given the pseudonyms of Pagatepan and Prabakula, might be attributed to religion, since the temple organised people differently from the mosque, and Muslim gurus taught different things, using different methods, than the Hindu gurus. But even the *subak*s, the irrigation cooperatives which are fundamental institutions in Balinese rice cultivation, were organised differently in the two villages. In Prabakula, *subak*s were more centralised and more productive than in Pagatepan, amongst other things.

The analysis continues with chapters about village politics in these and other, mixed, villages, about ritual life and conflict management, and how communism has periodically created alternative patterns of alliance and conflict. It eventually transpires that there are considerable commonalities across the religious boundaries, but that there is also a lot of internal variation and creativity within each community. Practice is, as so often, more flexible than the 'system' would lead one to presume. Generalisations about 'culture' are more difficult. Near the middle of the book, Barth presents a model where he sketches the opportunity situation of persons by distinguishing between premises (knowledge, values, experiences), intentions and actual behaviour (with consequences in the physical world).[5] It may be seen as a generative model which does not generate social form, but rather variation – since the actors are so differently positioned and act by improvising in a goal-oriented way from where they are in terms of knowledge and opportunity. This may sound trivial, but we should keep in mind that Barth is arguing against a tradition of studies of Bali where what is described is purportedly *the* 'system' or *the* 'culture'. Well, he would say, perhaps the system may be described in this or that way at a general level, but locally there are great variations which mean something to people in practice, and which may help in explaining how far their networks can take them, socially and spatially. The Balinese *subak*, as described by Geertz, is an abstraction and an ideal type, since real existing *subak*s may function in quite different ways.

Balinese Worlds is an ethnographically rich book. It is less technical, less condensed than Barth's earlier monographs. At 350 pages, it is his longest book, but it is thematically wide-ranging and holistic in the sense that it covers most central institutions and aspects of life, from property rights to marriage, from religion to language. It is also untypical in the sense that the book is to a great extent shaped as a critical response to much earlier anthropology on Bali, which may identify important aspects of Balinese society and Balinese ways of life, but without coming sufficiently close to the actual people, who are more diverse than general descriptions allow for. Again, Barth shows the strength of the ethnographic magnifying glass.

Although he had found his main narrative, Barth found it difficult to finish his work on Bali. He was no regional specialist, and even after repeated stints of fieldwork, he did not have the feeling that he 'knew' Balinese culture the way he knew that of the Baktaman, the Pathans or the Basseri. The complexity, the depth and the diversity of cultural traditions were so overwhelming that it would take years of fieldwork and literature studies to penetrate it fully. At the same time, he had an abundance of fieldnotes. He would later write about this situation, 'As so often in our discipline, my research plan collapsed under the weight of detailed ethnography'.[6]

On the other hand, he saw his contribution as being necessary and important, since it filled both historical and earlier anthropological studies with new stories, approaches, angles and details. The book may be seen to summarise the most important aspects of Barth's theoretical vision: the actor-oriented perspective, the generative models, internal diversity. It also points ahead in ways that reviewers of the book did not fully grasp. They read it as a contribution to the ethnography of Bali, while Barth's goal was to demonstrate the connection between knowledge, experience and social process without losing sight of locally produced reality.

In *Balinese Worlds*, but also in articles published before it appeared, notably 'The Analysis of Culture in Complex Societies',[7] Barth obliquely connects with a debate that had been going on in the USA for a few years, and which precisely concerned the concept of culture. This term is more important in American than in European anthropology, and culture had in general been considered something people in a given group or community had in common. That was mainly Geertz's view.[8] A group of younger anthropologists influenced by post-structuralist theory and postmodern philosophy, under the informal leadership of George Marcus and James Clifford, opposed this view, arguing not only that ideas of cultural homogeneity were fictional, but also that anthropologists actively 'wrote culture' through the creative act of producing ethnography.[9] Barth became an unexpected accomplice in this project. Early in his career, he had deconstructed structural-functionalist concepts of society, social structure and social systems, splitting them up into manageable social processes. Now that he increasingly wrote about meaning, symbols and world-views, following a similar procedure he necessarily became critical of Geertzian formulations, always elegant but not always sufficiently experience-near.

The young lions of American anthropology were keen to have Barth join their team. He saw the encouragement from the postmodernists as curious, but not uninteresting. He understood the connection between his project and theirs. Their view was that true descriptions do not exist, and that generalisations are futile, in accordance with philosophers like Lyotard and Derrida. Barth approached the issue from the diametrically opposite angle, since his naturalist project consisted in producing descriptions that were as true as possible. Yet they seemed to end in the same place: the postmodernists with their 'minor narratives', Barth with his strict empiricist naturalism. But this meeting place was probably a crossroads, and their paths would diverge. The postmodernists were at the time mostly interested in deconstructing discourses – Clifford was a historian of ideas, not an anthropologist – while the naturalist Barth preferred to study practice as realistically as possible.

The kinship between the French-inspired American postmodernists and Barth may not have been deep, although they had a common polemical project, but the parallel to British anthropologists inspired by postmodern philosophy was clearer. I have in mind Marilyn Strathern in particular, a Melanesianist who established herself, from the late 1980s, as a sharp critic of received wisdom about societies and persons, ideas that had been taken for granted on both sides of the Atlantic. The parallels, or convergence, were perhaps most clearly expressed at a conference in 1990 where both gave plenary lectures. The site was the beautiful Portuguese university city of Coimbra, and the occasion was the very first conference of the newly founded European Association of Social Anthropologists (EASA).

Like most sciences, anthropology was dominated by Americans or foreigners working in the USA. Since before the Second World War, there had been more anthropologists in the US than any other place, occasionally more than in the rest of the world put together. The largest annual conference in anthropology, the American Anthropological Association (AAA) meeting in late autumn, gathers thousands of anthropologists from around the world, keen to present their research and perhaps meet some of their heroes. Towards the end of the 1980s, Adam Kuper, a South African-born anthropologist who made his career in England, took an initiative to bring anthropologists from the various parts of Europe together. He was especially concerned to strengthen the dialogue between north and south, or the Germanic and the Romance if you prefer. The first conference was already being planned when history suddenly took a sharp turn, the Berlin Wall went down, and the Iron Curtain was rapidly on its way to oblivion. Kuper and his committee rapidly found funding enabling them to invite impecunious East and Central European colleagues to the conference as well. It became a great success. The colleagues from the communist countries had long been relatively isolated from theoretical developments in the West, and they had been raised on a nourishing, but somewhat monotonous diet of descriptive ethnography and Marxist theory. Many were keen to update their cognitive maps. Two years after the inaugural meeting, in 1992 the EASA conference took place in Prague.

The Coimbra event was nonetheless dominated by the most powerful traditions in European social anthropology: the Anglo-Saxon and the French. The first plenary lecture was given by Ernest Gellner, 'that most

European of anthropologists', as Kuper expressed it in his introduction. Gellner (1925–1995) was born in Paris and raised in Prague before he came to England as a Jewish refugee just before the Second World War. In his lecture, Gellner warned against the dual threats of postmodern irresponsibility and postcolonial expiation. Anthropology should neither play around with fuzzy concepts nor be driven by bad conscience towards formerly colonised peoples. The murmuring in the auditorium was audible. There were rolling eyes and dismissive shrugs. He had hit a couple of tender spots. Barth must have enjoyed himself. There had always been mutual respect between himself and Gellner.

The plenary sessions of the following days gave a good impression of the breadth and tensions in Western European anthropology at this time, and indicated where Barth stood in relation to some of his more prominent colleagues. Daniel de Coppet, from Paris, who had worked with Dumont, openly polemicised against an individualist anthropology of the kind customarily associated with people like Malinowski and Barth, arguing that human action springs out of socially sanctioned values, not the maximisation of utility. He regarded the projection of 'the Western individual' onto traditional peoples as an affront, since their actions were based on a collective logic and a sense of belonging in a value-based social community. In an important sense, de Coppet and Barth represented two extremes in their views on the logic of human agency. Barth held that people acted from similar motivations everywhere, while de Coppet, like Dumont, argued that there were considerable differences. Interestingly, they agreed that local realities were to be given primacy, but disagreed about the nature of this reality.

Maurice Bloch from the LSE spoke about making anthropology more scientific by connecting it more closely to cognitive science. Barth's anthropology of knowledge had something in common with this view, but derived theory from subjective human experience, while cognitive science – like structuralism – searched for mechanisms and categories located at a deeper level than pure subjectivity.

Philippe Descola from Paris then lectured about the relationship between humans and nature in Amazonia, arguing that they comprised a totality which could be understood if one acknowledged the underlying 'grammar' regulating human use, classification and understandings of nature. As in the case of Bloch, there are obvious similarities with Barth's anthropology of knowledge, especially his work on New Guinea. The most important difference is that Descola, who had studied with Lévi-Strauss, assumed that organising mental principles led to a socio-ecological universe that was integrated and uniform, with which people complied. In Barth's view, no systems are perfectly integrated, and rules are often made or adjusted as one goes along.

Ulf Hannerz from Stockholm was, and is, a leading anthropologist of globalisation. His lecture concerned the networks that connect and create streams of ideas, commodities and people across national and cultural boundaries. He showed that the idea of bounded societies is inadequate, certainly in our interconnected world, and that anthropology should instead focus on networks and flows. The intellectual kinship between Barth and Hannerz was, and is, obvious. Although Hannerz had taken cues both from macro-sociological theory about world systems and the Manchester School's research on networks, and worked with phenomena at a level of scale that often made direct observation impossible, he shared Barth's view of the nature of social life.

It was unsurprising that Hannerz and Barth were speaking from compatible positions. It was less expected that the last speaker, Marilyn Strathern of Manchester (later Cambridge) University, deconstructed the concept of society in ways resembling the young Barth's analyses of social process and interaction. She spoke of parts and wholes, and showed, using examples from Papua New Guinea and England, how both person and society were elastic, unstable entities. The acting entity was often smaller than a person (like Barth's statuses in *Models*), and Strathern used the term *dividual* (as opposed to *individual*) to illustrate a Melanesian concept of the person, where a person is not indivisible, but exists by virtue of their shifting relations to others. She also pointed out, like Hannerz, that societies may exist in certain respects and at given times, but that one cannot take it for granted that they are stable entities that can easily be studied at any time.

Strathern went further than Hannerz in arguing, like de Coppet, that the Melanesian person is constructed in a qualitatively different way from the Euro-American person, where notions about integrated individuals (and, similarly, integrated societies) are foundational. Still, one cannot but think, a quarter of a century after this memorable conference, that the convergences and similarities between the thinking of leading anthropologists were more striking than their differences.

Barth's lecture, published as the first chapter in the volume edited by Kuper and published after the conference,[10] returned to the themes in *Scale and Social Organization*, and used Grønhaug's material from Herat to show the existence of social fields there – social networks of interaction, obligations and transactions. But, he argued, one could not really talk of a bounded society, since the different fields overlapped only partially and were integrated at different levels of scale.

In this group of prominent European social anthropologists, Barth's position was clear. He had a substantial interest in understanding how people act on the basis of their available knowledge and within the given frame of constraints and incentives (or opportunities and limitations); he insisted, as always, on beginning the analysis with something observable and not an inferred entity like culture, normative system or society; and he wished to study ongoing processes and not fixed structures. One of the most striking things about Barth's lecture at this conference, at a time when he was about to become a grand old man in anthropology, was the continuity and consistency of his thinking from the early 1950s up to the present. Although with time he had developed a more narrative style in his writing, and even if his field of interest had shifted from economics and politics to knowledge and rituals, he still defended the same scientific ideals that he had internalised as a student. It was more difficult to study values and meaning than maximising behaviour, but he still stuck to his ethnographic method and the inductive principle that theory should emerge from observations, not the other way around. The starting point for research on humanly constructed universes had to be a 'particular constellation of experience, knowledge and orientation'.[11] The role of the anthropologist was *studying* reality, not *creating* it. On these grounds, the Coimbra lecture was entitled 'Toward a Greater Naturalism in the Conceptualization of Society'.[12]

Barth has often been accused of basing his research on a naively empiricist view of knowledge. A completely objective, neutral kind of social research is obviously impossible. As mentioned previously, Weber made this clear when he wrote about the impossibility of value-free research. The best a researcher can do, Weber wrote, was to make his own values explicit, in order for the reader to see where the researcher's gaze was coming from.[13] Yet, Barth has never claimed that his writings describe the truth, the whole truth and nothing but the truth, only that they shed light upon, and contribute to explaining, what it is that makes people do what they do, and how the result of these actions in turn influence the conditions for action.

In 1989, Barth had held his government grant for four years, and Wikan was now a professor at the Ethnographic Museum. He was free of professional commitments, but academically homeless. It was primarily the yearning for an academic community and a handful of good postgraduate students that prompted him to accept two offers of part-time chairs, which he received one shortly after the other, from Bergen and from Emory University in Atlanta, Georgia. He had come to understand that he needed some external stimuli, something that helped him to put pressure on himself, a framework around his professional life that was somewhat tighter than that which he had in his status as a free artist.

In Bergen, he once again became, after a 20 year absence, a part-time co-worker with old students and colleagues such as Jan Petter Blom, Georg Henriksen, Reidar Grønhaug, Sigurd Berentzen and Gunnar Haaland. Henning Siverts was still at the museum in Bergen, together with the Kenya specialist Frode Storås, and Gunnar Sørbø directed the Centre of Development Research. Most of his colleagues from the 1960s were still in the department. However, it had expanded, and there were signs of renewal. Younger anthropologists who worked in somewhat different traditions than Barth's had been added to the faculty. Anne Karen Bjelland studied ageing and gender in Norway; John Christian Knudsen did research on Vietnamese refugees from a psychodynamic perspective; and Robert Minnich studied political processes in Slovenia. Leif O. Manger continued the department's engagement in Sudan through his research on the Nuba, and the Ph.D. fellow Edvard Hviding had just returned from fieldwork in the Solomon Islands. And there were others. Still, Barth sensed that the intellectual development at the department had been somewhat sluggish, and Grønhaug once told me, with a guffaw, that when Barth took up his part-time chair, his first recommendation had been to 'get rid of those old articles of mine from the curricula'.

Some time before he began to travel to Atlanta and Bergen, Barth began to search for a new field site. Wikan's monograph on Bali was finished by 1989, while Barth chose to take his time. He would rather publish late than publish something unfinished, and in his position, the failure would be a noticeable one if he were to publish a bad book. Not publishing at all might even have been a better alternative. His stature was such that on the occasion of his sixtieth birthday in 1988, the sociology professor Gudmund Hernes, who would soon serve as a cabinet minister in Gro Harlem Brundtland's Labour government, wrote a witty, admiring op-ed in *Dagbladet*, at the time the most intellectual of the Oslo newspapers. Among other observations, Hernes pointed out that 'scarcely any other Norwegian has, in so many places and among so many tribes (*sic*), taken the anthropologist's fundamental position: the squat'.[14]

Barth had long been interested in Bhutan. A Buddhist country on the south-eastern slopes of the Himalayas, it was fairly closed and had remained unstudied by modern anthropologists. Back in the early part of the 1980s, he had sent a letter to the authorities inquiring about the possibilities of an anthropological project. They had then responded that this sounded interesting, but it was not convenient right now, so perhaps he could contact them again in a few years' time. Later, Haaland was engaged by the United Nations Development Programme (UNDP) on a project in Bhutan. Among his Bergen colleagues, it was Haaland who to the greatest extent shared Barth's fascination for exciting, remote, unexplored places. They had often spoken dreamily together about places like the isolated island of Socotra, the clay skyscrapers of Hadramaut, and of the isolated mountain country of Bhutan.

Thus Haaland knew that Barth was attracted to Bhutan, and made some inquiries among others who were engaged in development work there. This was how Barth and Wikan ended up being invited to a workshop in Thimphu in 1985. Wikan was less enthusiastic about this new adventure than her husband. Rather than opening up a new field site, she was intent on deepening her knowledge about the Middle East. She recalls being in Bali at the time while Barth was in Oslo. The two of them had planned a rare holiday together when she received a telegram saying 'Meet me in Calcutta. We are going to Bhutan'. She had mixed feelings about going to the mountain kingdom, but as she says, retrospectively, she was soon intrigued by the then relatively isolated country, and would soon enter the field with undiminished enthusiasm.

The topic of the workshop in Thimphu was sanitary conditions. Many Bhutanese now had access to clean water, but they tended not to keep the water sufficiently clean to avoid infections. It would seem that some anthropological advice might be useful.

More did not come out of this episode, but when Karl-Eric Knutsson, whom Barth in his time had helped to get a chair in social anthropology in Stockholm, became the regional representative for UNICEF in South Asia, he contacted Barth and brought the couple in as advisers. In this way they got a foothold in this closed country, where radio had been introduced only in 1973 and television in 1999. The school system had gradually been developed since the 1960s, with Indian teachers using English as a means of instruction, a language few Bhutanese could relate to. Barth and Wikan carried out extensive fieldwork in Bhutan between 1989 and 1994. Wikan spent altogether 20 months in the country, Barth much less owing to teaching obligations in the USA. Although some of this work was applied, they were given a free hand by the Bhutanese authorities and collected a considerable amount of basic ethnographic material about Bhutanese society. Their work in Bhutan was nevertheless cut short when, following an article by Wikan in *American Anthropologist*,[15] she was denied re-entry into the country. Although the circumstances remain dim, the article was controversial in so far as it discusses gender oppression and features a story about a Bhutanese woman who had been raped first by a monk, then by a nobleman.

Wikan oriented her work chiefly towards medical anthropology and concepts of personhood. Barth was chiefly interested, following his recent research elsewhere, on the relationship between knowledge systems and interaction in a situation of change. The anthropologists' interest in health and local organisation made their findings especially interesting for UNICEF. For example, many infants and toddlers died of diarrhoea, which was caused by unclean drinking water. When children were weakened by dehydration, the Bhutanese would address what they saw as the underlying cause instead of tackling the symptoms. Thus, they approached healers, shamans or monks who could identify for them which evil force or demon had caused the disease. A shaman might enter into a trance to communicate with the spirit in question, while a monk might feed the child holy butter. The fact was, however, that UNICEF were already running a successful project not too far away, in Bangladesh, where children suffering from diarrhoea were fed water containing nourishing salts and some sugar. They recovered quickly. What killed young children was not the amoeba or bacteria as such, but the dehydration. The anthropologists were in a position to explain the situation to the UNICEF people and give them some advice as to what kind of cooperation between UNICEF, families with sick children and ritual specialists that might lead to a positive result. Asking people not to go to their own specialists was not an option. Besides, it was unheard of, indeed illegal, to interfere with this ancient, scriptural tradition. The king at the time was conservative in matters of religion, and during the same period that Barth and Wikan were working in the country, he evicted nearly 20 per cent of the population, of Nepalese origin, ostensibly because they did not have a valid permit of residence. Some of them eventually ended up in European countries following years in Nepalese refugee camps.

As outsiders, Barth and Wikan could speak their minds more freely than others in this conservative, landlocked country of less than a million inhabitants. Eventually, a workshop was organised with the blessing of the king, with the participation of high lamas, Buddhist monks and astrologers, as well as people from UNICEF. Incense was burnt, long brass horns were blown, and the anthropologists were the main speakers. After three days of deliberations, there was an emerging consensus that local Bhutanese should take over the UNICEF project, but on the condition that sick children should now be fed water with nutrients instead of, or at least in addition to, holy butter. The local ritual leaders would remain in charge of administrating the cure. This story clearly shows the significance of knowing local conditions and taking local practices and knowledge seriously for change to be accepted by the community. Nobody, presumably, approves of being overrun by outsiders who tell them that their knowledge and traditions are worthless. The religious leaders were from now on in charge of the project and responsible for its success, which would if anything increase their standing in the community, were it to work out well.

The tradition of learning in Bhutan rests on the principle of reincarnation. A reincarnated lama in a Bhutanese monastery may not remember books he wrote in an earlier incarnation some three centuries ago, but it may be sufficient for him to cast a glance at a few pages to remember what it is about. Both the transmission of knowledge and the exegesis of profound religious wisdom rest on the belief in reincarnation.

Barth's analytical project in Bhutan did not only follow up his research in Bali, but there was a comparative dimension as well. Both knowledge traditions had their origins in the Indian subcontinent, but in very different ways. Bhutan was more hierarchical than Bali, with reincarnated lamas in ancient monasteries at the top. Although most Bhutanese families counted a monk among their members, most Bhutanese peasants did not possess a large amount of knowledge about religious tradition, which they used instrumentally whenever they had a problem. The objective was to identify some parameters where there was great variation, perhaps monasteries or traditions of learning that functioned very differently from each other, and then track down the cognitive and social factors which generated these variations.

Although the couple had chosen Bali because they were done with exhausting and unpleasant fieldwork, they ended up in Bhutan, which could also tax the stamina of visitors. I remember a chance meeting with Barth shortly after one of his visits to Bhutan, asking him in a conversational style what it had been like. He peered at me above his glasses and answered that it had been dreadfully tiring. 'It is the Middle Ages, you know, and the Middle Ages can be pretty uncomfortable'. Then he spoke in some detail about the Bhutanese passion for lukewarm tea with rancid butter in it.

The fieldwork in Bhutan was a long-term but intermittent affair, as in Bali, and it took place under far more difficult conditions, both practically and politically. It is therefore worth noticing that the report Barth and

Wikan wrote in 1989, *Bhutan Report: Results of a Fact-finding Mission*, was republished in 2011. The publisher is the Centre of Bhutanese Studies in Thimphu, and the small monograph is now entitled *Situation of Children in Bhutan: An Anthropological Perspective*. In the preface, the director of the centre writes that although 'much has changed since the advisers' field visits to the villages, most of their observations and descriptions of the underlying Bhutanese values, remain valid'.[16] He also expresses admiration for the amount of information the visitors had been able to gather in such a short period.

The willingness, and not least the ability, to be uncomfortable is a necessary, but rarely discussed, requirement for ethnographic fieldwork. Even fieldwork at home can be socially difficult, but further away it tends to be physically demanding as well. Not only do you speak the language poorly (if at all) and make many embarrassing mistakes in social settings to begin with, but the food can be unpalatable and the bed uncomfortable, the water filthy and the people pushy. Radcliffe-Brown could not bear it. He spent most of his time on the Andaman Islands not out in the jungle with the people he was meant to study, but in the town of Port Blair, where he interviewed defectors from tradition who were hanging around in the bars near the harbour. His ethnography, somewhat thin and anaemic, bore the marks of this unsatisfactory method.[17] Malinowski, for his part, endured the Trobrianders, but he never grew to like them.[18] Barth has voluntarily exposed himself to a lot of physical unpleasantness over the years, and he once remarked that Norwegians seem to have a couple of comparative advantages, compared to their British and French colleagues, in this respect. First of all, they have an egalitarian cultural ideology, making it possible to meet others as equals. Secondly, Norwegians, who live in harsh and shifting weather conditions themselves, are raised on the ideology that 'there is no such thing as bad weather, just bad clothes' (*det finnes ikke dårlig vær, bare dårlige klær*). They cultivate the simplicity of camping trips, and in spite of their considerable wealth, there is a cultural preference for simplicity in their leisure cabins as well. (In practice, it should be added, cabins these days tend to be fairly well equipped.) They go skiing in the mountains and are used to getting cold and wet. Traditionally, the food is simple. As Barth puts it, Norwegians tend to see nature as 'both a challenge and as something it is possible to handle with two empty hands. In connection with my fieldwork, I have always felt it as a great challenge and have derived great pleasure out of trying to adjust to new biotopes'.[19] His early emphasis on the way in which ecological conditions shape social differentiation may have been the fruit of a Norwegian cultural style where proximity to nature is valued very highly. About a French anthropologist who was working in New Guinea at the same time as Barth, it is said that he saw to it that regular supplies of red wine were brought to him up the river by canoe. This does not imply that he did a bad job, but he would have difficulties in sliding unnoticed into local society.

In spite of his considerable international recognition, Barth was still an outsider in Norwegian society. He had paid his dues through his years on the Norwegian Research Council committee, and he would later head the Council for Development Research (*Rådet for utviklingsforskning*). For many years, he had had an ongoing dialogue with NORAD, the state development agency, about the importance of anthropological knowledge, and had been able to assist many younger colleagues who were oriented towards development research. He was one of the country's most widely quoted social scientists internationally, and thousands of students worldwide had read his articles or books. His presence in the Norwegian public sphere was nevertheless almost unnoticeable, and his contact with sociologists and other social scientists remained scattered and rare. A couple of years after the success of the TV series, he was once again able to walk undisturbed on the street.

Given his standing in the social sciences, the decision by Universitetsforlaget (Norway's premier academic press) to publish some of Barth's most important articles in Norwegian translation came rather late, though considering his and the subject of social anthropology's outsider position in society it was quite important. The translator was Theo Barth (no relation), himself a social anthropologist, and the translations were excellent. The title may suggest that this is a book intended for the already initiated: *Manifestasjon og prosess* ('Manifestation and process').[20] As Barth makes clear in the newly written introduction:

> I consider life, as it appears somewhere in the world, as a manifestation of the thoughts, intentions and interpretations of a group of people, the way they are given shape through processes: interaction, exchange, conflict, learning, the transmission of tradition, community, dominance.[21]

The book was published in 1994, and the content overlaps somewhat with the two volumes of Barth's articles published by Routledge in 1981.[22]

One of the more recent articles is 'Are Values Real?', originally from 1993.[23] It clarifies the question of Barth's relationship to positivism and utilitarianism, and clearly enunciates the nuances in his own position. First, Barth holds that whatever has not been observed cannot constitute a datum. But in the second place, he argues that what has not been understood and interpreted has not really been observed either. Let us assume, he says, that we observe a man giving a spear to another man somewhere in Africa. What have we then really seen? 'Did it concern an exchange? Tax? Deference? The inauguration of a vassal? The transmission of bridewealth? Succession? Or an unknown number of other possibilities?'[24] The answer naturally depends on the broader context, which must be studied separately. An important part of this context consists in the deliberations of the actor themselves. Value may here refer to two things: norms regulating behaviour, or a scarce resource the actor wishes to obtain. Both are culturally defined, but there is no direct causal relationship between value and action. People simultaneously try to maximise value and to live their lives in accordance with certain values. Barth argues, not surprisingly, that the best way to study values is to do it as concretely as possible, through a close reading of individual evaluations, judgements and actions. That is something quite different from assuming that Christians and Jews do not kill just because one of the Ten Commandments says 'Thou shalt not kill'.

The other recent article deserving mention gives an excellent illustration of comparative thinking, which is bolder in the later Barth than it had been in the early Barth. The article, 'The Guru and the Conjurer', concerns knowledge transmission among Balinese and Baktaman.[25] Although they live fairly close geographically, they belong to widely different ethnographic regions, namely South-East Asia and Melanesia. Among the Balinese, knowledge is transmitted by a guru, among the Baktaman by a conjurer – a sorcerer or initiator. The contrast is striking. The guru verbalises, and tries to transmit as much knowledge as possible to the devotees. The knowledge is written down and may be verified by referring to sacred texts. The initiator, by contrast, keeps back knowledge which is secret and forbidden. His capital does not consist in his learning, but his possession of secret knowledge, which he can only share with the novices at particular times. One is abstract, the other concrete. The project in the article is, as so often with Barth, to develop generative models. Instead of proposing elaborate interpretations like Geertz, or postulating structural relationships like Lévi-Strauss, or for that matter celebrating the multiplicity of voices and meanings, as in postmodern or poststructuralist anthropology, Barth recommends strict observation, inferring the social implications of knowledge regimes directly from the processes being observed. In Barth's thought, there is no secret, hidden truth which is only made available when the novices reach the seventh grade of initiation. There is no shortcut to anthropological knowledge either. God is in the details, and reality is ultimately always concrete and tangible.

Barth was by the 1990s considered one of a handful of great men and women in contemporary anthropology. In his generation, they might perhaps be counted on two mutilated hands: Marshall Sahlins, Eric Wolf and Clifford Geertz in the USA; Mary Douglas and Jack Goody in the UK; Maurice Godelier and Claude Lévi-Strauss in France. They all represented clearly defined theoretical positions. They were widely quoted, mostly approvingly, but also critically. They had produced several weighty theoretical contributions over several decades. There seemed to be a real risk that Barth was about to receive the mixed blessings of a totemic ancestor, invited to prestigious occasions as a celebrity and a reminder of the continuity in anthropology's achievements, but not as an active contributor of new ideas. During the Nordic anthropology meeting in Reykjavik in 1990, where Barth gave the keynote lecture, I met an American student who had come to Iceland to do research on the Icelanders' exotic views of whales and whaling. I mentioned Barth's lecture, which she had missed, and where Barth had suggested a year's moratorium on the concept of culture, proposing to replace it with 'traditions of knowledge'. She exclaimed that of course she had read Barth, but she believed that he had been dead for years. It turned out that she had read his ecology article. At this point, 34 years after the publication of that article, the author was still a youthful and energetic man in his early sixties.

He was honoured by many signs of recognition at the time. In 1993, Dutch colleagues organised a major conference about the legacy of *Ethnic Groups and Boundaries*, where Barth spoke, in his keynote lecture, about the need to study migration in great detail.[26] In 1996, he received an honorary doctorate from the University of Edinburgh. In 1998, he received the first Lifetime Achievement Award of the Commission on Nomadic Peoples under the International Association of Anthropological and Ethnological Sciences. In 1998, the German film-maker Werner Sperschneider made a documentary film about Barth's life as an anthropologist.[27] The books about the Pathans and the Basseri were translated into Pashto and Persian, respectively.

Barth continued to receive invitations, and often accepted. In 2000, he gave the annual Sidney Mintz lecture at Johns Hopkins University, entitled 'An Anthropology of Knowledge', based on material from New

Guinea and subsequently published in *Current Anthropology*.[28] In 2003, I spent some prize money on a symposium about flexibility as an analytical concept, inspired by an article by Bateson. I was hoping that Barth would accept my invitation to participate, which he did, to everyone's great pleasure. Unfortunately, no joint publication came out of the symposium, but then again, that had also been the case with Barth's earlier workshops on tropical ecology and role theory.

From the mid 1990s onwards, Barth became less prolific. He would not write another major monograph after *Balinese Worlds*. He worked on the Bhutanese material for some time, but put it aside. A few scattered ethnographic vignettes from Bhutan turn up in his late articles, but apart from the UNICEF reports he has not published from this fieldwork. For some time, he talked about a new book he was working on, on the way in which theory in anthropology develops through its methodology. Although he gave the odd lecture on the theme, the book was not completed.

Yet, Barth was by no means retired. In the first half of the 1990s, he travelled regularly to China as a consultant for the World Bank in connection with a dam project which would provide electricity to millions of rural Chinese, but at a price. He enjoyed the contrast between the frugal Bhutanese fieldwork and the business class existence in China as a highly paid expert. In 1996, he resigned from Emory in order to take up a similar part-time chair at Boston University, a post he held until 2008. In the same period, Wikan had several lengthy stays as a visiting researcher at Harvard, which is in the same city, which was why Barth decided to relocate from Emory.

In 2008, Barth published the book which will in all likelihood be his last, *Afghanistan og Taliban*. Written in Norwegian, it builds on his long-term and intimate knowledge of the region, and gives a rare historical depth to the understanding of religious leadership among Pashto speakers. During the launch of the book, Barth took part in a radio debate and several public meetings, one of them with politicians who represented a state (Norway) which took part in the Afghanistan war. Barth pointed out that political loyalty in this part of the world had never followed state boundaries, and that it would be wishful thinking to believe that most Afghans would support a remote president about whom they knew little, especially if he were forced to establish a centralised state without the support of local chiefs and religious leaders. Besides, Afghanistan, like Pakistan, contained peoples which did not necessarily feel that they had a great deal in common with each other. Readers who were familiar with Barth's writings about segmentary oppositions, game theory, clan leaders and saints might nod in recognition at this analysis. He also explained in a simple way how the Saudi Osama bin Laden had become fast friends with Mullah Omar and the Taliban. The explanation was, he said, that bin Laden and his group did not participate in local power struggles, meaning that they were unlikely to shift to other allies in a strategic move. For the same reason, they relied completely on support from the Taliban, since they had nobody else to go to. Al-Qaida were strong, but vulnerable, and could therefore be trusted. Moreover, Barth explained the predominant concept of freedom in this part of the world. In Western societies, people may generally consider themselves free, but we are obliged to follow many rules, regulations and prohibitions, and we have limited possibilities to influence important decisions. In the tribal belt from Afghanistan to the Pakistani lowlands, it is common to distinguish between 'the land of freedom' and 'the land of the government'. In other words: when you are ruled by a government, you are no longer free.

Certain parts of culture may change fast – mobile telephones are now widespread from Swat to Afghanistan – but other parts of culture are more resilient to change. Since it is property and kinship that generate options for political allegiance, nobody should be led to assume that a new political structure, put in place by foreigners, would change local political loyalties overnight. Barth was a splendid performer in this situation, demonstrating what a formidable public intellectual he could have been, had he not chosen otherwise.

Everybody understood his message, politicians included, but it had no visible political consequences. It is not always the case that anthropological knowledge is useful for politicians, even if it is evidently true. They have their own games to play, and they do not necessarily worship truth and transparency any more fervently than someone like Kimebnok does.

Perhaps the most unexpected invitation in the 2000s came from Halle in Germany. The newly formed Max Planck Institute of Social Anthropology wished to mark its opening in the spring of 2002 with a lecture series about the great traditions in anthropology: the French, the American, the British and the German. Just as in 1965, when Barth had been invited to showcase social anthropology at the Royal Society, he was now approached by Chris Hann, one of the directors of the new institute, about giving the five lectures about the British tradition. He accepted, but with ambivalent feelings, knowing that this assignment would entail a considerable amount of work. At the same time, it would give him an opportunity to write out some of the notes for the book that would never be completed, about the relationship of theory and method in social anthropology. These five lectures may indeed be read, up to a point, as a demonstration of theoretical developments which resulted from increasingly sophisticated research methods, with Malinowski as the pivotal character.

The Halle lectures are excellent, and Barth did not succumb to the temptation of elaborating on his own intellectual biography and genealogy.[29] He refers very scantily to his own work, and devoted two of the five lectures to the period from 1870 to 1922 – starting with E.B. Tylor – that is, before social anthropology as a modern, systematic, field-based science saw the light of day. The lectures are nuanced and balanced, and Barth holds back his personal, subjective judgements until towards the end. He there speaks of British anthropology around the turn of the millennium, mentioning in particular Cambridge and the LSE, but also Manchester and Queen's University in Belfast, as especially promising and dynamic milieus. Of greater interest is what he has to say about professional authority. It is a fact, he argues, that social anthropology has gradually become more peripheral in general intellectual life since the 1960s. The lecture about the period 1945 to 1970 is titled 'The Golden Age', which is arguably an accurate description, and it may be added that it coincides with Barth's own 'golden age'.

The causes of the reduced visibility of social anthropology in Great Britain are, in Barth's view, weakened authority among academic leaders and increased diversity. It has become unclear to the surrounding world what social anthropology actually represents. Nobody can speak on behalf of the discipline any more; there are several competing discourses and few common themes. This diagnosis is partly correct, but at the same time it should be kept in mind that Barth himself opposed conformity and streamlining from the 1950s onwards. And although he himself was an unchallenged intellectual leader in Bergen and later in Oslo, he never wished to form a school. He demanded excellence from his colleagues and students, which must have inhibited colleagues with low self-esteem, but he had no desire to control them or give them detailed instructions as to what to do. When postmodernism came along with its critique of intellectual authority, he welcomed it as a breath of fresh air, although he soon concluded that much of what they were actually doing was scholastic and distant from reality.

At the beginning of the last lecture, Barth indeed presents a fairly scathing critique of a certain form of intellectual authority which can be stifling precisely because it does not allow for diversity and internal criticism. His old friend Emrys Peters, who worked with Evans-Pritchard at Oxford and later became professor at Manchester, had not published all his work about kinship and politics in Libya. Only after his death in 1987 were his collected articles, including four unpublished ones, collated under the editorship of Jack Goody and Emanuel Marx.[30] In some of these articles, it turns out that Peters sharply criticised Evans-Pritchard and his model of segmentary opposition, indicating that tribal organisation was more pragmatic and situationally driven than structural-functionalist models would suggest. This had been a common critique of structural-functionalism almost since the beginning, but it had rarely been voiced from within, and never on Evans-Pritchard's ethnographic and professional home turf. Barth argues that Peters may have failed to submit these articles to journals as a result of the hierarchical nature of British academic culture, which inhibited originality. The golden age had, in other words, come at a premium. British social anthropology represented, in the 1950s and 1960s, an intellectual community which was thorough, effective and cohesive. The price was that internal criticism was hushed up or strongly discouraged.

Perhaps Barth indirectly comments on his own experiences, and choices, when he complains that Peters did not get to vent his most critical objections. Barth himself had never been forced to pay the price, nor to build a close relationship with Evans-Pritchard, or with anyone else in the British Isles for that matter. He had money from Norway while he was at Cambridge, and would later take up a position in Bergen. Besides, he would be able to draw on friends and supporters in the USA if need be. Barth was in several ways an anthropological entrepreneur, and by positioning himself at the junction of two major anthropological traditions – the American and the British – while at the same time being physically located in the semi-periphery, he achieved a degree of freedom which would have been difficult to attain were he to go to the pub with the Oxford colleagues every week or to a football match with Gluckman and his men twice a month. In all probability, it was only retrospectively that Barth realised how important it had been to turn down the job offer from Columbia in 1960. Through his own professional practice, he showed why new cultural forms tend to develop among those Pathans who live in the marginal areas on the hilly outskirts of Swat Valley, while at the same time retaining their Pathan identity.

12

Between Art and Science

Anthropology [may] represent a unique expansion of our consciousness, and give us knowledge about alternative ways of being human, which do not merely extend what we ourselves are and have, but opens up a radically broader set of opportunities. For this reason, the discipline may also function in a critical and liberating way in relation to any other knowledge tradition, way of life or ideology.[1]

Trends and fashions come and go in the social sciences, but rarely without leaving something useful behind. From Foucault, we have kept concepts about discourse, power and regimes of knowledge; from Bourdieu, habitus, doxa and forms of capital; from Marxism, a sustained critical interest in power and economics; and from structuralism, the acknowledgement that the human mind functions in a particular way, frequently by way of contrasts. Nonetheless, structuralism, in its original form, is all but forgotten today. Few take up the cues left by 1960s and 1970s Marxism. Neither ethnoscience nor ethnomethodology are read as anything but intellectual history today. For this reason, if nothing else, it is worth noticing that Barth's work from the 1950s onwards remains relevant today, either as authoritative ethnographic descriptions or as contributions to theory.

There is a consistency between his early and late work which may be obscured by his willingness to travel to new fields and ask new questions. The English anthropologist Richard Jenkins, himself the author of important books about ethnicity and identity, recognised the broader significance of Barth's contribution when he wrote, in 1996:

Barth hasn't had the recognition he deserves. Compared to global stars such as Bourdieu or Geertz, outside anthropology his work remains little known. This may be a consequence of being based in Oslo, rather than in Princeton or Paris, it may be a consequence of intellectual fad and fashion. Whatever the reasons, however, Barth's body of work is one of the richest and most imaginative in anthropology, and in social science more widely.[2]

12. Lecturing, early 2000s (photo reproduced by permission of Holbergprisen, University of Bergen).

Barth has also left a rich legacy in Norway. Social anthropology in Norway has a special, almost unique position. Anthropological teaching and research takes place at the four most established universities and at several polytechnics and colleges. Norwegian anthropologists work in many domains, from journalism to development organisations, and people outside academia often have some notion about what a social anthropologist is and does. That is not the situation in countries such as Sweden, Denmark, the Netherlands or even Great Britain. Relative to the size of the population (5 million), Norway arguably has more anthropologists than any other country. The answer to this conundrum is simple: Fredrik Barth.

It is true that others have also made a considerable effort to make anthropology visible and relevant, both in the public sphere and in the academic world. In Barth's own generation, Arne Martin Klausen played an important part, and he was a more active op-ed writer and public speaker than Barth. Although Barth himself wrote a handful of newspaper articles from his early fieldwork in Kurdistan and Swat, it would thereafter be another 35 years before he signed a newspaper article again, this time a jointly written petition against the Soviet invasion of Afghanistan.[3] In a word, he never became an active contributor to the press. But when it comes to research, international visibility and a source of inspiration for prospective students of anthropology, Barth has played a decisive role. He might seem somewhat intimidating to some of his peers, but to the younger generations his example showed that it is perfectly possible to submit your work ambitiously, to publish in excellent journals, and that anthropology in a country in the semi-periphery is not necessarily inferior in quality to that produced in the great academic centres.

A good illustration of Barth's contemporary influence on Norwegian academic life may be offered by the two festschrifts published on the occasion of his 60th birthday in 1988. The first book, published in Norwegian, was *På norsk grunn* ('On Norwegian turf'), edited by Ottar Brox and Marianne Gullestad.[4] The contributors, 18 in number, were all social anthropologists, many trained by Barth, and they were all doing research in Norway. The themes range from the rhetoric of the AIDS debate (Brox) and the aesthetics of television (Anders Johansen), to the moral economy of the cake raffle (Tian Sørhaug), language and boundaries (Blom) and Sami-Norwegian ethnicity (Trond Thuen). The book is a reminder of Barth's view of anthropology at home, as he expressed it when he took up the chair in Bergen: anthropology has a duty to contribute to the understanding of its own society, and the research anthropologists do at home is no less valuable than the research they do abroad. This view has many supporters today, who believe that there should be a niche available for a morally neutral social science which is able to surprise and place the taken-for-granted world of everyday life in a critical perspective. Anthropology may regard Norway from the inside, but also from a vantage point in the Trobriand Islands or Swat Valley, and the subject is by default sufficiently disrespectful of common complacency to argue that all lives have the same value, even if they unfold under different conditions and are chosen in different opportunity situations.

A few years later, the English-language festschrift titled *The Ecology of Choice and Symbols*, edited by Reidar Grønhaug, Gunnar Haaland and Georg Henriksen was published.[5] This book had 23 contributors, of whom only three (Berentzen, Brøgger and Brox) had also contributed to the other volume. As with the other book, all contributors to this one were Norwegian or had, like Paine, a strong connection to the department in Bergen. The editors had made a conscious choice in delineating the field like this; the objective was to show Barth's significance for Norwegian anthropology. They might well have invited a handful or two of foreign anthropologists to contribute, but they chose otherwise. In this collection, as in the other, a great diversity is apparent, from Paine's, Haaland's and Henriksen's chapters about ethnicity to Sørum's chapter about garden magic in New Guinea and Gulbrandsen's about change and egalitarian ideology among Bushmen in the Kalahari. Not all contributors to this festschrift had studied or worked with Barth, but they all relate to his theoretical ideas.

If there exists a 'Barthianism' in social anthropology, it is arguably well depicted in the festschrifts, especially in the chapters written by colleagues with a Bergen background. Their problem formulations are clear, theory is used in a pragmatic, sober way, the structure of the argument is methodological and logically stringent. Regarded together, the two festschrifts can be seen as a representative shop window for Norwegian social anthropology in the early 1990s – a well-established, creative, diverse, professional scientific activity. Both books would have deserved a broader readership, especially the English-language one, which was so obscurely published, by a small Bergen publisher, that it is to this very day virtually unknown, even among Scandinavian anthropologists.

In 2005, Barth published his own reminiscences, entitled *Vi mennesker* ('Us humans'). That is to say, the book was presented both by publisher and author as an 'in-depth travelogue', where glimpses from the anthropologist's travels are developed into more complex interpretations of particular cultural environments and individual lives. During his fieldwork in the 1950s and 1960s, Barth sent wonderfully rich and evocative letters home to his family, and the renowned criminologist, and childhood friend, Nils Christie told Barth several times that he ought to publish them. In *Vi mennesker*, it is as if these letters have been edited, expanded and published, but this time directed at a wider readership than his closest family. The book nevertheless reads as a personal memoir since Barth to an unusual extent *is* his travels. He has often pointed out that it is chiefly his field experiences, not poring over other people's studies, that has brought him forward. This lifelong passion for other people's lives also has an existential dimension. Although Barth never 'went native', he seems to have learnt something, even at a personal level, from all the peoples he has lived with.

Put differently, Barth is a more complex and dialectical thinker than many claim. He continuously oscillates between interpretation and explanation, between the universally human and the locally particular, which can only be grasped through deep observation and participation. When he speaks about fieldwork, he emphasises the importance of living like the people under study. This is not just about doing a good job in the field and ensuring the trust of the locals. To him, living like the locals concerns, more than anything else, sharing their ways of experiencing their lives and the world. When they are cold, you should be cold. When they eat rancid butter, you should do it as well. And when they become wet, you would not understand properly how they are using water as a ritual symbol unless you had yourself had the experience of being drenched, with your local interlocutors, by a sudden downpour. There is a hidden poetry in Barth's writings, even in the dry, early articles, which are ultimately the result of his realisation that it is necessary to come close to other people's private sense of their being and the world.

Vi mennesker tells stories about events, persons and the anthropologist's experiences in China, Bhutan and New Guinea, and among the Basseri and the Kurds. For the Barth habitué, the stories from China and Bhutan are especially intriguing, since no academic work has been published from these visits. The chapter on Bhutan begins with an explanation of Bhutanese cosmology, with its reincarnated lamas and its millennium-old tradition of learning, which may profitably be compared with medieval monasteries in Europe. Barth then contrasts it with the daily toil of the peasants, and institutions such as polyandry, which is especially widespread in the Himalayas. The chapter on China deals with some of the consequences of modernisation in the country, with his point of departure the hydroelectric power project for which he was an adviser. With the characteristic ambivalence that had by now become one of his trademarks (about Afghans, he once quipped that 'they hate America, but everybody wants to go there'), he concludes that modernity comes at a price, but that the current changes may after all give the locals a better life, at least for the time being.

Barth's analytical travel stories may remind the reader of a few dimensions of the man that are easily forgotten when concentrating, as I have largely done in this book, on his academic achievements. He has an exceptional gift for establishing contact with people, and an endless curiosity about their lives – how they are living, but also what they are living for, what is at stake for them, and what kinds of future-directed projects they see. For this reason, the localities and human lives in the book are not unduly overshadowed by the visitor's own experiences. Like a good novelist, Barth skilfully shifts between foreground and background, the actual lives of people and the environment within which they necessarily unfold.

The book may also be read as a credo of sorts, an intellectual testament from a man then in his late seventies. As a human being, but also as a researcher, Barth stands for a moderate version of cultural relativism. He might have said, following Marx, that humans create history, but not under circumstances they have himself chosen, or rather that all humans have the same dreams and yearnings, but they may be fulfilled in a myriad of different ways. In the introduction to *Vi mennesker*, he raises the question, 'what is it like to be a human?' And he immediately rejects the response, 'that entails being like ourselves'.[6] For in that case, all the cultural variation of the world would have been without significance.

Since that which is unique and specific is at the centre of the project of anthropology, he continues, this discipline cannot succeed in formulating general laws without losing its identity. The theories he himself has developed, in *Models of Social Organization* and *Cosmologies in the Making*, are of the middle-range kind. They can usefully be applied to a number of facts, but do not provide a key which unlocks the secrets to all variation and diversity, making them fall quietly and tidily in place.

Yet, there may be a stronger universalist tendency in Barth than he is prepared to admit. He tacitly assumes that humans have some fundamental commonalities enabling him to penetrate, given time and effort, the subjective worlds of the Bhutanese or the Baktaman, however different their worlds are from ours.

Would it not therefore be feasible, on the basis of ethnographic research from across the world, to develop a theory about human nature? Implicitly, Barth may have done this – as many other good social and cultural anthropologists have as well, albeit usually implicitly – through his experience-near and individually focused ethnography, which, when successful, creates identification in the reader, making them think that 'under those conditions, I might have done the same thing myself'. He assumes that human emotions are the same everywhere, although they are expressed in different, culturally sanctioned ways. However, what fascinates Barth the most is not what we have in common, but our contrasts; between fragmented Kurdish and the centralised Pathan political organisation; between the Balinese tradition of learning and the Baktaman mystery cult; between the net-boss, the skipper and the fishermen aboard the same smallish vessel. He might have subscribed to Zygmunt Bauman's words when the famous social theorist recommends, not entirely without inspiration from Barth's work on ethnic boundaries, an identity project where the aim is to avoid fixation and keep the options open.[7] To Barth, it is primarily flexibility, pragmatism and the skill of improvisation that characterises the art of being human.

It is easy, against this background, to understand why he never fell for structural-functionalism, structuralism, Marxism or – more recently –

evolutionary psychology. They all offer explanatory schemes which are so comprehensive and so perfect in a formal sense that the messiness of real life and real people disappears.

Yet, it is not impossible to imagine a closer relationship between Barth's models and sociobiology after it had matured into evolutionary psychology. The latter departs from Darwin's theory of evolution, and tries to show that the main traits of the human way of being, as well as the main variations between individuals and cultures, may be explained with reference to human evolution. It is naturalistic and driven by clearly formulated hypotheses, and seems to offer little space for subjective opinions. Barth has occasionally expressed admiration for Darwin, not least the naturalist's ability to build a theory of universal validity from the tiny building blocks of direct observation, such as the variations of beak shapes among Galapagos finches. The motto 'watching and wondering', to which Barth frequently returns, is taken from that undogmatic, curious naturalist tradition of which Darwin was an early, brilliant representative. It is moreover not entirely without interest that the same game-theoretical models that Barth had used to analyse politics in the 1950s were applied with great success by the biologist John Maynard Smith in the 1970s to show the functioning of natural selection at the micro level.[8] In spite of this, Barth has remained adamant in his rejection of evolutionary explanations in social anthropology. Indeed, his first programmatic statement to that effect was formulated in an unpublished manuscript for a Wenner-Gren conference as early as 1965.[9]

There are two reasons for Barth's scepticism. First, as formulated in 1965, social and cultural complexity are of a different order to biological complexity, and cannot be studied using the same methods. Cultural change is not linear and cumulative, but can be quite unpredictable. Secondly, what is essential to the object of study evaporates, namely its substance. Evolutionary theory does not incorporate the study of people's subjective life-worlds, intentions and willed actions. The scientific aims of anthropology might survive, even be strengthened, by a portion of evolutionary theory, but what would be lost is that part of anthropology which approaches art, namely the intricate tapestries of experienced life and its reverberations that are essential for convincing ethnographic descriptions. If the point is that there are many ways to be a human being, why try to reduce them to just one?

In spite of these objections, it is not unthinkable that Barth's ethnographic and comparative life project might enrich, and be enriched by, a closer engagement with evolutionary theory. As in intercultural communication, a first commandment is mutual respect and the ability to listen to the opponent's best arguments and not just the worst – evolutionary perspectives are not necessarily tantamount to 'selfish gene biology' – and there are ways of reconciling evolutionary theory with the anthropological study of unique, local life-worlds without reducing one to the other.

But this project will have to be left to others. Barth's life project has been completed, and his autobiographical article 'Sixty Years in Anthropology', from 2007, was his last academic work, unless there are hidden treasures languishing on a hard drive somewhere. In the following year, he was awarded a belated but deserved honorary doctorate from the University of Bergen, and later in the same year he received the Order of St Olav from King Harald of Norway. In 2013, by which time Barth was too frail to travel, Peter Finke from the University of Zurich made the trip to Oslo, and at a simple ceremony in the presence of the dean and the vice-rector of the University of Oslo, Barth was awarded an honorary doctorate by the university.

In the summer of 2011, Barth moved away from home for the first time in his life, as he puts it, when he left the house in the hills he had bought in the late 1950s, moving into sheltered housing a few kilometres down the hill. He has had poor legs for a few years, and has reconciled himself to the fact that he will no longer travel. To Barth, this means that his life as a watching and wandering intellectual nomad has come to an end.

Fredrik Barth made anthropology a more exciting place to be. He enriched the discipline with new approaches, undogmatic thinking and sharp, often controversial analyses which lifted professional debate to a higher level. He was as demanding of his colleagues as of himself, taught methodological stringency and the ability to use one's eyes and ask relevant questions, and – not least – contributed to a perceptible reduction in the amount of bullshit, a phenomenon which has unfortunately always been present as a fact or as a threat in a discipline such as anthropology. As Haaland has pointed out, Barth could liberate his readers from the holistic trap, the belief that everything had to fit together like pieces in a jigsaw.[10] No system is perfectly integrated, and nobody does exactly as they are told. Life tentatively finds its shape, as an intermittent and makeshift project, as we go along.

In an overview of Barth's research, Edvard Hviding and Harald Tambs-Lyche describe this project in an accurate way:

He asks how we could best find an approach to social analysis that is general enough to encompass most types of human action, yet specific enough to accommodate the virtually endless variation resulting from the peculiarities of individuals and situations.[11]

At the same time, Barth's anthropology is not a doctrine about everything, something he became increasingly and acutely aware of as he began to study complex state societies with long scriptural traditions. He is a social scientist of the kind who prefers crawling on all fours with a magnifying glass. Helicopter trips above the planet, with or without a pair of binoculars, may have fascinated him, but in the last instance they become too remote from experience. Of course, helicopters, too, need to be manned by competent people. Statistics and general overviews are, in their way, as important as detailed studies of life-worlds. This is also the case with history and deep familiarity with ancient written traditions. Barth is not oblivious to this, and he has remarked, with a hint of irony, that he does not consider himself a particularly cultivated person.

Barth never desired creating a school and producing students who were like himself. He wished to move forward on his own intellectual journey, and did not wish for others to remain stuck in his own earlier work. When Kim Wikan Barth began to think about his future education and career prospects, his father advised him not to become a social anthropologist, reasoning that if the son does the same as his father did, he will either be better or worse at it. Neither of the two is recommendable.

In spite of the strict scientific ideals, especially in the early Barth, his life's work is fuelled not just by academic ambition and curiosity about the cultural richness of the world. There is a poetic sensibility there as well, and not least an element of humanism, which is especially clear in the monographs. He is genuinely interested in how people get on, and how they succeed in making the best of their situation. An American colleague who spent some time with Barth at a conference in Mexico City in the early 2000s tells me that he had confessed to Barth one evening that he was worried about his own father, who was in poor health, retired and lived alone. My friend now feared that he might drink himself to death. What can I do, he asked Barth, to make my father stop drinking? Barth answered that maybe he shouldn't. 'Perhaps it is the only choice he has left to make for himself'.

This attitude expresses an optimistic view of the human condition and a recognition of the right to autonomy. In the final analysis, this attitude to other people – and not his good exam results or even his adventurous spirit and curiosity – is what made Barth such a phenomenal fieldworker. His efficiency as an ethnographic fieldworker was, at the end of the day, caused by the conviction that other people, who live in a completely different place, who think differently from you and do other things than you would have done, have the same value as yourself. You might have done the same thing yourself, had you been in their situation, and you should try to find out how that can be the case. Such an open, tolerant and curious perspective is not a bad point of departure for an earthy humanism tailored to confront the challenges of the twenty-first century.

Notes

Preface

1. Edvard Hviding, *Barth om Barth* ['Barth on Barth'], (unpublished typescript, 1995). Professor Hviding has generously placed at my disposal a large body of interview transcripts, which has been invaluable during my work on this book. The interviews were conducted at Emory University in 1995.

Chapter 1

1. Fredrik Barth, *Sohar: Culture and Society in an Omani Town* (Baltimore, MD: Johns Hopkins University Press, 1983), p.8.
2. This was the largest engineering polytechnic college in the country until its merger with the University of Trondheim to form the Norwegian University of Science and Technology in 1996, a name which, incidentally, was none too popular among social scientists and humanists, including the anthropologists.
3. Fredrik Barth, 'Sixty Years in Anthropology', *Annual Review of Anthropology* 36 (2007), p.2.
4. Andre Gingrich: 'The German-speaking Countries', in Fredrik Barth, Andre Gingrich, Robert Parkin and Sydel Silverman, *One Discipline, Four Ways: British, German, French, and American Anthropology* (Chicago: University of Chicago Press, 2005), pp.61–156.
5. Thomas Hylland Eriksen and Finn Sivert Nielsen, *A History of Anthropology*, 2nd edn. (London: Pluto, 2013), pp.12–15.
6. Hermann Giliomee, *The Afrikaners: Biography of a People* (Charlottesville: University of Virginia Press, 2003).
7. Gingrich, 'The German-speaking Countries'.
8. English edition: Claude Lévi-Strauss, *The Elementary Structures of Kinship*, 2nd edn., trans. James Harle Bell, John Richard von Sturmer and Rodney Needham (London: Eyre and Spottiswoode, 1969).
9. See Ulf Hannerz, *Exploring the City: Inquiries toward an Urban Anthropology* (New York: Columbia University Press, 1980).
10. Incidentally, a sensitive ethnographic study of the American hobo had been carried out decades earlier by Nels Anderson, a Chicago sociologist, in *The Hobo: The Sociology of the Homeless Man* (Chicago: University of Chicago Press, 1923).

11. Fredrik Barth, *Vi mennesker: Fra en antropologs reiser* ['Us humans: From an anthropologist's journeys'] (Oslo: Gyldendal, 2005), p.14.

12. Thorgeir Kolshus, personal communication.

13. As pointed out by Gudmund Hernes ('Nomade med fotnoter', *Dagbladet*, 22 December 1988), Barth might also demonstrate, during a lecture, how the Melanesian lion frog attached itself below large leaves in the jungle. There was definitely a playfulness about him.

14. Barth, 'Sixty Years in Anthropology', p.2.

15. Fredrik Barth, *Principles of Social Organization in Southern Kurdistan* (Oslo: Universitetets Etnografiske Museum, 1953), p.9.

16. Raymond Firth, *Elements of Social Organization* (London: Watts, 1951).

17. *Principles of Social Organization in Southern Kurdistan*, p.139.

18. Fredrik Barth, 'The Guru and the Conjurer: Transactions in Knowledge and the Shaping of Culture in Southeast Asia and Melanesia', *Man* 25, 4 (1990): 640–653.

19. See Stanley J. Tambiah, *Edmund Leach: An Anthropological Life* (Cambridge: Cambridge University Press, 2002).

20. Edmund R. Leach, *Political Systems of Highland Burma* (London: Athlone, 1954).

21. Edmund R. Leach, 'The Structural Implications of Matrilateral Cross-cousin Marriage', *Journal of the Royal Anthropological Institute of Great Britain and Ireland* 81, 1/2 (1951): 23–55.

22. Edmund R. Leach, *Culture And Communication: The Logic By Which Symbols Are Connected* (Cambridge: Cambridge University Press, 1976).

23. Fredrik Barth, 'The Social Organization of a Pariah Group in Norway', *Norveg* 5 (1955): 125–144.

24. Hviding, *Barth om Barth*.

25. Fredrik Barth, *Models of Social Organization*, Royal Anthropological Institute Occasional Paper 23 (London: Royal Anthropological Institute, 1966).

Chapter 2

1. Fredrik Barth. 'Ecological Relationships of Ethnic Groups in Swat, North Pakistan', *American Anthropologist* 58, 6 (1956): 1079–1089; Barth, 'Segmentary Opposition and the Theory of Games: A Study of Pathan Organization'', *Journal of the Royal Anthropological Institute of Great Britain and Ireland* 89, 1 (1959): 5–21; Barth (ed.), *Ethnic Groups and Boundaries* (Bergen/Boston: Universitetsforlaget/Little Brown, 1969).

2. Hviding, *Barth om Barth*.

3. Fredrik Barth, *Political Leadership among Swat Pathans* (London: Athlone, 1959), p.v.

4. Meyer Fortes and E.E. Evans-Pritchard (eds), *African Political Systems* (London: Oxford University Press, 1940).

5. E.E. Evans-Pritchard, *The Nuer* (Oxford: Clarendon Press, 1940).

6. Hviding, *Barth om Barth*.

7. Karl Wittfogel, *Oriental Despotism: A Comparative Study of Total Power* (New Haven: Yale University Press, 1959).

8. Barth, *Political Leadership among Swat Pathans*, p.23.

9. Fredrik Barth with Miangul Jahanzeb, *The Last Wali of Swat: An Autobiography as told to Fredrik Barth* (Oslo: Universitetsforlaget, 1985).

10. Barth, *Political Leadership among Swat Pathans*, p.101.

11. Hviding, *Barth om Barth*.

12. Ibid.

13. Barth, 'Ecological Relationships', p.1089.

14. Commenting on the first draft of this book in its Norwegian version, Barth suggested that I delete a few anecdotes and contextual descriptions, which seemed to add some flavour and texture to the narrative. In his view, they were superfluous and digressive, diverting attention from the main story.

15. Fredrik Barth, *Afghanistan og Taliban* (Oslo: Pax, 2008).

16. Now obsolete, the magister degree was roughly equivalent to the Ph.D. Norwegian doctorates (*doctor philosophiae*) were, at the time, closer to the French *doctorat d'état*, and typically submitted in mid-career by academics with university jobs.

17. Arne Martin Klausen, *Kultur – variasjon og sammenheng* ['Culture – variations and connections'] (Oslo: Gyldendal, 1970).

18. Arne Martin Klausen, *Kerala Fishermen and the Indo-Norwegian Pilot Project* (Oslo: Universitetsforlaget, 1968).

19. Hviding, *Barth om Barth*.

20. Adam Kuper, *Anthropology and Anthropologists: The Modern British School*, 3rd edn. (London: Routledge, 1996), p.121.

21. James Frazer, *The Golden Bough: A Study in Magic and Religion*, abr. edn. (New York: Touchstone, 1995 [1922]).

22. James Frazer, *Totemism and Exogamy: A Treatise on Certain Early Forms of Superstition and Society*, 4 vols. (London: Macmillan, 1935).

23. Fredrik Barth, 'Britain and the Commonwealth', in Fredrik Barth, Andre Gingrich, Robert Parkin and Sydel Silverman, *One Discipline, Four Ways: British, German, French, and American Anthropology* (Chicago: University of Chicago Press, 2005), pp.1–57.

24. Gregory Bateson, *Naven*, rev. edn. (Stanford, CA: Stanford University Press 1958 [1936]).

25. Christoph von Fürer-Haimendorf, 'The Southern Mongoloid Migration', *Man* 52, 2 (1952), p.80.

26. Hviding, *Barth om Barth*.

27. Hviding, *Barth om Barth*.

28. Tambiah, *Edmund Leach*, p.64.

29. John von Neumann and Oskar Morgenstern, *Theory of Games and Economic Behavior* (Princeton: Princeton University Press, 1944).

30. Emile Durkheim, *The Division of Labour in Society*, trans. E.W. Halls (New York: Free Press, 1984 [1893]), e.g. pp.263, 265.

31. Barth, 'Segmentary Opposition and the Theory of Games', p.5.

32. Edmund R. Leach, *Rethinking Anthropology* (London: Athlone, 1961), p.6.

33. Fredrik Barth, 'The System of Social Stratification in Swat, North Pakistan', in Edmund Leach (ed.), *Aspects of Caste in South India, Ceylon and North-West Pakistan* (Cambridge: Cambridge University Press, 1960), pp.113–146.

34. Fredrik Barth, 'Economic Spheres in Darfur', in Raymond Firth (ed.), *Themes in Economic Anthropology* (London: Tavistock, 1967), pp.149–174.

35. Hviding, *Barth om Barth*.

36. E.E. Evans-Pritchard, *Social Anthropology* (London: Cohen & West, 1951).

37. Karl Popper, *The Logic of Scientific Discovery* (London: Hutchinson, 1959 [1936]).

Chapter 3

1. Hviding, *Barth om Barth*.

2. Ibid.

3. Ibid.

4. Marcel Mauss, *The Gift*, trans. Ian Cunnison (London: Cohen & West, 1954 [1923/24]).

5. Hviding, *Barth om Barth*.

6. Derrick J. Stenning, *Savannah Nomads: A Study of the Wodaabe Pastoral Fulani of Western Bornu Province, Northern Region, Nigeria* (London: Oxford University Press 1959).

7. Fredrik Barth, *Nomads of South Persia: The Basseri Tribe of the Khamseh Confederacy* (Oslo: Universitetets Etnografiske Museum, 1961), p.vi.

8. Fredrik Barth, personal communication, autumn 2012.

9. Gunnar Haaland, personal communication, summer 2012.

10. Derrick J. Stenning, 'Household Viability among the Pastoral Fulani', in Jack Goody (ed.), *The Developmental Cycle of Domestic Groups* (Cambridge: Cambridge University Press, 1962), pp.92–119.

11. Barth, *Nomads of South Persia*, p.102.

12. Carletoon Coon, review of *Nomads of South Persia*, *American Anthropologist*, 64, 3 (1962), pp.636–638.

13. Barth, *Nomads of South Persia*, p.135.

14. Fredrik Barth, 'Capital, Investment and the Social Structure of a Pastoral Nomad Group in South Persia', in Raymond Firth and B.S. Yamey (eds), *Capital, Saving and Credit in Peasant Societies: Studies from Asia, Oceania, the Caribbean, and Middle America* (Chicago: Aldine, 1964), pp.69–81.

15. Robert N. Pehrson, *The Social Organization of the Marri Baluch*, compiled and analysed from his notes by Fredrik Barth (Chicago: Aldine, 1966).

16. Louis Dupree, review of *The Social Organization of the Marri Baluch*, *American Anthropologist* 70, 1 (1968): 140–142.

17. Fredrik Barth, 'Competition and Symbiosis in North East Baluchistan', *Folk* 6, 1 (1964): 15–22.

18. Roy A. Rappaport, *Pigs for the Ancestors: Ritual in the Ecology of a New Guinea People* (New Haven: Yale University Press, 1968).

19. Barth, 'Sixty Years in Anthropology', p.7.

20. Iver B. Neumann, personal communication.

Chapter 4

1. Fredrik Barth, 'Introduction', in Fredrik Barth (ed.), *The Role of the Entrepreneur in Social Change in Northern Norway* (Bergen: Universitetsforlaget, 1963), pp.5–18.

2. Jan Petter Blom and Olaf Smedal, 'En paradoksal antropolog', *Norsk Antropologisk Tidsskrift* 3 (2007): 191–206.

3. Hviding, *Barth om Barth*.

4. Erving Goffman, *The Presentation of Self in Everyday Life* (Garden City, NY: Doubleday, 1959).

5. Barth, 'Introduction', in *The Role of the Entrepreneur*, p.7.

6. Karl Polanyi, *The Great Transformation: The Political and Economic Origins of our Time* (Boston: Beacon Press, 1957 [1944]).

7. Alessandro Monsutti and Boris-Mathieu Pétric, 'Des collines du Kurdistan aux hautes terres de Nouvelle-Guinée: Entretien avec Fredrik Barth', *ethnographiques.org* 8 November 2005. Retrieved 12 August 2013 from: www.ethnographiques.org/.

8. Barth, 'Introduction', in *The Role of the Entrepreneur*, p.15.

9. Ibid., p.14.

10. Ottar Brox, *Hva skjer i Nord-Norge? En studie i norsk utkantpolitikk* ['What's going on in Northern Norway? A study in Norwegian district politics'] (Oslo: Pax, 1966).

11. Hviding, *Barth om Barth*.

Chapter 5

1. See Chris Hann and Keith Hart, *Economic Anthropology: History, Ethnography, Critique* (Cambridge: Polity, 2011), pp.55–71.

2. Jean-Paul Sartre, *L'Existentialisme est un humanisme* (Paris: Nagel, 1946), p.26.

3. Harald Eidheim, personal communication.

4. Hviding, *Barth om Barth*.

5. Barth, 'Economic Spheres in Darfur'.

6. Paul Bohannan, 'The Impact of Money on an African Subsistence Economy', *Journal of Economic History* 19 (1959): 491–503.

7. Georg Henriksen, *Economic Growth and Ecological Balance: Problems of Development in Turkana* (Bergen: Bergen Studies in Social Anthropology, 1974).

8. Hernes, 'Nomade med fotnoter'.

9. Fredrik Barth, 'Anthropological Models and Social Reality: The Second Royal Society Nuffield Lecture', *Proceedings of the Royal Society of London: Series B, Biological Science* 165/998 (1966): 20–34.

10. Ibid., p.21.

11. Max Gluckman, *Custom and Conflict in Africa* (Oxford: Blackwell, 1956), pp.3–12.

12. Barth, *Models of Social Organization*, p.3.

13. Fredrik Barth, 'On the Study of Social Change', *American Anthropologist* 69, 6 (1967): 661–669.

14. Barth, 'Capital, Investment and the Social Structure of a Pastoral Nomad Group in South Persia'.

15. Fredrik Barth, 'Ethnic Processes on the Pathan Baluch Boundary', in G. Redard (ed.), *Indo-Iranica: mélanges présentés à Georg Morgenstierne à l'occasion de son soixante-dixième anniversaire* (Wiesbaden: Otto Harrassowitz, 1964), pp.13–20.

16. Hviding, *Barth om Barth*.

Chapter 6

1. Hviding, *Barth om Barth*.

2. Ibid.

3. Clifford Geertz, 'Religion as a Cultural System', reprinted in *The Interpretation of Cultures* (New York: Basic Books 1973), pp.87–125.

4. Kuper, *Anthropology and Anthropologists*, p.158.

5. Bryan Wilson (ed.), *Rationality* (Oxford: Blackwell, 1970).

6. See Thomas Hylland Eriksen, *Ethnicity and Nationalism: Anthropological Perspectives*, 3rd edn. (London: Pluto, 2010) for a fuller presentation of early research on ethnicity.

7. Jan Petter Blom: 'Ethnic and Cultural Differentiation', pp 75–85; Harald Eidheim: 'When Ethnic Identity Is a Social Stigma', pp 39–57; Gunnar Haaland: 'Economic Determinants in Ethnic Processes', pp. 58–74, all in Barth (ed.), *Ethnic Groups and Boundaries*.

8. Gregory Bateson, in Nora Bateson's film *An Ecology of Mind: A Daughter's Portrait of Gregory Bateson* (Bellingham, WA: Bullfrog Films, 2011).

9. Edmund R. Leach, 'An Anthropologist's Reflections on a Social Survey', in D.G. Jongmans and Peter Gutkind (eds), *Anthropologists in the Field* (Assen: van Gorcum, 1967), p.79.

10. Barth, 'Sixty Years in Anthropology', p.10.

11. See e.g. A.P. Cohen, *Self Consciousness* (London: Routledge, 1994), pp.121–122.

12. Mary Douglas, *Purity and Danger: An Analysis of Concepts of Pollution and Taboo* (London: Routledge & Kegan Paul, 1966).

13. Barth, Introduction, in *Ethnic Groups and Boundaries*, e.g. p.24.

Chapter 7

1. Hviding, *Barth om Barth*.
2. Ibid.
3. Fredrik Barth, *Ritual and Knowledge among the Baktaman of New Guinea* (Oslo: Universitetsforlaget, 1975), p.16.
4. Barth, 'Sixty Years in Anthropology', p.10.
5. Hviding, *Barth om Barth*.
6. Barth, *Ritual and Knowledge among the Baktaman*, p.83.
7. Leach, *Political Systems of Highland Burma*, pp.12–13.
8. Unni Wikan, *Resonance: Beyond the Words* (Chicago: University of Chicago Press, 2013).
9. Claude Lévi-Strauss, *The Savage Mind* (London: Weidenfeld & Nicolson, 1966), pp.1–34.
10. Fredrik Barth, *Andres liv – og vårt eget* ['Other people's lives – and our own'] (Oslo: Gyldendal, 1980), p.131–142.
11. Hviding, *Barth om Barth*.
12. Claude Lévi-Strauss, *Tristes Tropiques*, trans. John Russell (New York: Criterion, 1961), p.326.
13. Fredrik Barth, 'Analytical Dimensions in the Comparison of Social Organizations', *American Anthropologist* 74, 1/2 (1972): 207–220.
14. Fredrik Barth (ed.), *Mennesket som samfunnsborger: En uformell introduksjon til sosialantropologi* ['Man as a member of society: An informal introduction to social anthropology'] (Bergen: Universitetsforlaget, 1971).
15. Fredrik Barth, 'Et samfunn må forstås ut fra egne forutsetninger: U-landsforskning i sosialantropologisk perspektiv', *Forskningsnytt* 17, 4 (1972): 7–11.
16. Hviding, *Barth om Barth*.
17. Talal Asad, 'Market Model, Class Structure and Consent: A Reconsideration of Swat Political Organisation', *Man* 7 (1972): 74–94.
18. Gudmund Hernes, personal communication.
19. Robert Paine, *Second Thoughts about Barth's Models*. Royal Anthropological Institute Occasional Paper 32 (London: Royal Anthropological Institute, 1974).
20. Hviding, *Barth om Barth*.
21. Ibid.

Chapter 8

1. Fredrik Barth (ed.), *Scale and Social* Organization (Oslo: Universitetsforlaget, 1978).

2. An excellent, recent exception is Anna Tsing's article about non-scalability in production systems: Anna Lowenhaupt Tsing, 'On Nonscalability: The Living World Is Not Amenable to Precision-nested Scales', *Common Knowledge* 10, 3 (2012): 505–524.

3. Reidar Grønhaug, *Micro–Macro Relations: Social Organization in Antalya, Southern Turkey*, Bergen Occasional Papers in Social Anthropology 7 (Bergen: Institutt for sosialantropologi, 1974); Grønhaug, 'Scale as a Variable in Analysis. Fields in Social Organization in Herat, Northwest Afghanistan', in Barth (ed.), *Scale and Social Organization*, pp.78–121.

4. Pierre Bourdieu, *The Field of Cultural Production* (Cambridge: Polity Press 1993).

5. Fredrik Barth, 'Analytical Dimensions in the Comparison of Social Organizations', *American Anthropologist* 74, 1/2 (1972): 207–220.

6. Barth, 'Scale and Network in Urban Western Society' and 'Conclusions', both in Barth (ed.), *Scale and Social* Organization, pp.163–183 and 253–273.

7. Nils Christie, *Hvor tett et samfunn?* ['How tight a society?'] (Oslo: Universitetsforlaget, 1975). It is a minor scandal that this brilliant book has not been published in English.

8. Jacques Revel (ed.), *Jeux d'échelles: La micro-analyse à l'expérience* (Paris: Gallimard/ Seuil, 1996).

9. Hviding, *Barth om Barth*.

10. Monsutti and Pétric, 'Des collines du Kurdistan aux hautes terres de Nouvelle-Guinée'.

11. Fredrik Barth, 'Factors of Production, Economic Circulation, and Inequality in Inner Arabia', *Research in Economic Anthropology* 1: 53–72.

12. Barth, *Sohar*.

13. J.H. Furnivall, *Colonial Policy and Practice: A Comparative Study of Burma and the Netherlands India* (Cambridge: Cambridge University Press, 1947); M.G. Smith, *The Plural Society in the British West Indies* (Berkeley: University of California Press, 1965).

14. Barth, *Sohar*, p.85.

15. Anthony F.C. Wallace, *Culture and Personality* (New York: Random House, 1961).

16. Mauss, *The Gift*.

17. Barth, *Sohar*, p.10.

18. Ibid., p.10.

19. Ibid., p.21

20. Ibid., p.211.

Chapter 9

1. Claude Lévi-Strauss, *Tropisk elegi*, trans. Alv Alver (Oslo: Gyldendal, 1973 [1955]).

2. Johannes Falkenberg, *Et steinalderfolk i vår tid* ['A stone-age people in our time'] (Oslo: Gyldendal, 1948). Falkenberg would later achieve international recognition with *Kin and Totem: Group Relations of Australian Aborigines in the Port Keats District* (Oslo: Oslo University Press, 1962).

3. Unni Wikan, *Life among the Poor in Cairo* (London: Tavistock, 1980).

4. Lawrence Krader, Review of Barth, *Political Leadership among Swat Pathans*, *American Anthropologist* 63, 5 (1961): 1122–1123.

5. Asad, 'Market Model, Class Structure and Consent'.

6. Fredrik Barth, 'Swat Pathans Reconsidered', in Barth, *Features of Person and Society in Swat: Selected Essays of Fredrik Barth*, Vol. 2 (London: Routledge & Kegan Paul, 1981), pp.121–181.

7. Akhbar S. Ahmed, *Millennium and Charisma among Pathans: A Critical Essay in Social Anthropology* (London: Routledge & Kegan Paul, 1980).

8. 'Swat Pathans Reconsidered', p.122.

9. Louis Dumont, *Homo Hierarchicus: The Caste System and Its Implications*, 2nd edn., trans. Mark Sainsbury, Louis Dumont and Basia Gulati (Chicago: University of Chicago Press, 1980 [1967]).

10. Louis Dumont, 'Caste: A Phenomenon of Social Structure or an Aspect of Indian Culture?' in A. de Rueck and J. Knight (eds), *Caste and Race: Comparative Approaches* (London: Churchill, 1967), pp.28–38.

11. Dumont, *Homo Hierarchicus*, p.208.

12. 'Swat Pathans Reconsidered', p.152.

13. Paine, *Second Thoughts about Barth's Models*.

14. Bruce Kapferer (ed.), *Transaction and Meaning: Directions in the Anthropology of Exchange and Symbolic Behavior* (Philadelphia: Institute for the Study of Human Issues, 1976).

15. Reidar Grønhaug, 'Transaction and Signification: An Analytical Distinction in the Study of Interaction' (unpublished paper, 1975).

16. J. Clyde Mitchell, *The Kalela Dance*. Rhodes-Livingstone Papers 27 (Manchester: Manchester University Press, 1956).

17. Fredrik Barth, '"Models" Reconsidered', in Barth, *Process and Form in Social Life: Selected Essays of Fredrik Barth*, Vol. 1 (London: Routledge & Kegan Paul, 1981), pp.76–105.

18. Sartre, *L'Existentialisme est un humanisme*, p.26.

19. Edwin Ardener, *The Voice of Prophecy and Other Essays*, ed. Malcolm Chapman (Oxford: Blackwell, 1989), p.56.

20. Eduardo P. Archetti, 'Argentinean Tango: Male Sexual Ideology and Morality', in Reidar Grønhaug, Gunnar Haaland and Georg Henriksen (eds), *The Ecology of Choice and Symbol: Essays in Honour of Fredrik Barth* (Bergen: Alma Mater, 1991), p.283.

21. Anthony Giddens, *Central Problems in Social Theory* (London: Macmillan, 1979), p.95.

22. Colin Turnbull, *The Mountain People* (London: Jonathan Cape, 1973).

23. Fredrik Barth, 'On Responsibility and Humanity: Calling a Colleague to Account', *Current Anthropology* 15, 1 (1974): 99–103.
24. Ibid., p.99.
25. Hviding, *Barth om Barth*.

Chapter 10

1. Iver B. Neumann, 'Antroportrettet: Fredrik Barth', *Antropress* 4 (1982), p.7.
2. Fredrik Barth with Miangul Jahanzeb, *The Last Wali of Swat: An Autobiography as Told to Fredrik Barth* (Oslo: Universitetsforlaget, 1985), p.153.
3. Ibid., p.181.
4. Ibid., p.152.
5. Fredrik Barth and Ebbe Ording, *Andres liv – og vårt* ('The lives of others – and ours'), four-programme TV mini-series (Oslo: NRK, 1979).
6. Arne Næss, *Hvilken verden er den virkelige? – gir filosofi og kultur svar?* ['Which world is the real one? – do philosophy and culture provide the answer?'] (Oslo: Universitetsforlaget, 1969).
7. Dag Østerberg, *Samfunnsteori og nytteteori* ['Social theory and utilitarian theory'] (Oslo: Universitetsforlaget, 1980).
8. Doctoral defences in Norway, which are public events, involve two opponents who are given between one and two hours each to question the candidate.
9. Unni Wikan, *Behind the Veil in Arabia: Women in Oman* (Baltimore: Johns Hopkins University Press, 1982).
10. Unni Wikan, 'Man Becomes Woman: Transsexualism in Oman as a Key to Gender Roles', *Man* 12, 2 (1977): 304–319.
11. Fredrik Barth and Unni Wikan, 'Cultural Impact of the Ok Tedi Project: Final Report' (Boroko: Institute of Papua New Guinea Studies, 1982).
12. Fredrik Barth, *Cosmologies in the Making: A Generative Approach to Cultural Variation in Inner New Guinea* (Cambridge: Cambridge University Press, 1987).
13. Ibid., p.24.
14. Victor W. Turner, *The Forest of Symbols: Aspects of Ndembu Ritual* (Ithaca, NY: Cornell University Press, 1967).
15. Barth, *Cosmologies in the Making*, pp.83–88.
16. Jack Goody, 'Preface', in ibid., p.vii.

Chapter 11

1. Barth, 'Sixty Years in Anthropology', p.15.
2. Gregory Bateson and Margaret Mead, *Balinese Character: A Photographic Analysis* (New York: New York Academy of Sciences, 1942).
3. Hviding, *Barth om Barth*.

4. Unni Wikan: *Managing Turbulent Hearts: A Balinese Formula For Living* (Chicago: University of Chicago Press, 1990); Fredrik Barth, *Balinese Worlds* (Chicago: University of Chicago Press, 1993).

5. Barth, *Balinese Worlds*, p.159.

6. Barth, 'Sixty Years in Anthropology', p.15.

7. Fredrik Barth, 'The Analysis of Culture in Complex Societies', *Ethnos* 54, 3/4 (1989): 120–142.

8. See Adam Kuper, *Culture: The Anthropologist's Account* (Cambridge, MA: Harvard University Press, 1999) for a detailed analysis of the concept of culture in American anthropology.

9. James Clifford and George Marcus (eds), *Writing Culture: The Poetics and Politics of Ethnography* (Berkeley: University of California Press, 1986).

10. Adam Kuper (ed.), *Conceptualizing Society* (London: Routledge, 1992).

11. Barth, 'The Analysis of Culture in Complex Societies', p.134.

12. Fredrik Barth, 'Towards a Greater Naturalism in Conceptualizing Societies', in Kuper (ed.), *Conceptualizing Society*, pp.17–33.

13. Max Weber, 'Science as a Vocation', in *From Max Weber*, eds Hans Gerth and C. Wright Mills (Oxford: Oxford University Press, 1946), pp.129–156.

14. Hernes, 'Nomade med fotnoter'.

15. Unni Wikan, 'The Nun's Story: Reflections on an Age-Old, Postmodern Dilemma', *American Anthropologist*, 98 (1996): 279–89.

16. Fredrik Barth and Unni Wikan, *Situation of Children in Bhutan: An Anthropological Perspective* (Thimphu: Centre for Bhutan Studies, 2011), p.12.

17. See Thomas Hylland Eriksen, 'Radcliffe-Brown, A.R.', in R. McGee and R. Warms (eds), *Theory in Social and Cultural Anthropology: An Encyclopedia* (Thousand Oaks, CA: Sage, 2013), pp.678–682.

18. Bronislaw Malinowski, *A Diary in the Strict Sense of the Term* (London: Routledge & Kegan Paul, 1967).

19. In Ottar Brox and Marianne Gullestad (eds), *På norsk grunn: Sosialantropologiske studier av Norge, nordmenn og det norske* ['On Norwegian turf: Social anthropological studies of Norway, Norwegians and the Norwegian'] (Oslo: Ad Notam, 1989), p.209.

20. Fredrik Barth, *Manifestasjon og prosess*, trans. Theo Barth (Oslo: Universitetsforlaget, 1994).

21. Fredrik Barth: 'Innledning' ['Introduction'], in ibid., p.11.

22. *Process and Form in Social* and *Features of Person and Society in Swat*.

23. 'Er verdier virkelige?' in *Manifestasjon og prosess*, pp.128–144. Translated from, 'Are Values Real? The Enigma of Naturalism in the Anthropological Imputation of Values', in M. Hechter et al. (eds), *Origin of Values* (New York: Aldine de Gruyter, 1993), pp.31–46.

24. 'Er verdier virkelige?', p.129.

25. 'Opplysning eller mysterier', in *Manifestasjon og prosess*, pp.157–173. Translated from, 'The Guru and the Conjurer: Transactions in Knowledge and the

Shaping of Culture in South-East Asia and Melanesia', *Man* 25, 4 (1990): 640–653.

26. Fredrik Barth, 'Enduring and Emerging Issues in the Analysis of Ethnicity', in Hans Vermeulen and Cora Govers (eds), *The Anthropology of Ethnicity: Beyond Ethnic Groups and Boundaries* (Amsterdam: Het Spinhuis, 1994), pp.11–32.

27. Werner Sperschneider, *Fredrik Barth: From Fieldwork to Theory* (Göttingen: IWF Wissen und Medien, 2001).

28. Fredrik Barth, 'An Anthropology of Knowledge', *Current Anthropology* 43, 1 (2002): 1–18.

29. See Barth, 'Britain and the Commonwealth'.

30. Emrys Peters, *The Bedouin of Cyrenaica: Studies in Personal and Corporate Power*, ed. Jack Goody and Emanuel Marx (Cambridge: Cambridge University Press, 1991).

Chapter 12

1. Barth, *Manifestasjon og prosess*, p.11.

2. Richard Jenkins, *Social Identity*, 4th edn. (London: Routledge, 2014 [1996]), p.120.

3. See the newspaper articles in the List of Works of Fredrik Barth.

4. Brox and Gullestad (eds), *På norsk grunn*.

5. Reidar Grønhaug, Gunnar Haaland and Georg Henriksen (eds), *The Ecology of Choice and Symbol: Essays in Honour of Fredrik Barth* (Bergen: Alma Mater, 1991).

6. Barth, *Vi mennesker*, p.12.

7. Zygmunt Bauman, 'From Pilgrim to Tourist; or A Short History of Identity', in Stuart Hall and Paul Du Gay (eds), *Questions of Cultural Identity* (London: Sage, 1996), pp.18–36.

8. John Maynard Smith, *Evolution and the Theory of Games* (Cambridge: Cambridge University Press, 1982).

9. Fredrik Barth, 'On the Applicability of an Evolutionary Viewpoint to Cultural Change: Some Theoretical Points' (unpublished paper prepared in advance for participants in the Wenner-Gren symposium no. 30, 'The Evolutionist Interpretation of Culture', August 15–25, 1965).

10. Gunnar Haaland, 'Introduction', in Grønhaug, Haaland and Henriksen (eds), *The Ecology of Choice and Symbol*, p.21.

11. Edvard Hviding and Harald Tambs-Lyche, 'Curiosity and Understanding', *The Norseman*, 4/5 (1996): 21–28.

List of Works by Fredrik Barth

The following bibliography was prepared by the university librarians Astrid Anderson and Frøydis Haugane at the University of Oslo (Anderson and Haugane 2012), with contributions from Unni Wikan and Ørnulf Gulbrandsen.

Books

Author and Co-author

1953 *Principles of Social Organization in Southern Kurdistan*. Bulletin 7. Oslo: Universitetets Etnografiske Museum.

1956 *Indus and Swat Kohistan: An Ethnographic Survey*. Studies Honouring the Centennial of the Universitetets Etnografiske Museum, Oslo 1857–1957, 2. Oslo: Universitetets Etnografiske Museum.

1959 *Political Leadership among Swat Pathans*. Monographs on Social Anthropology, 19. London: Athlone Press.

1961 *Nomads of South Persia: The Basseri Tribe of the Khamseh Confederacy*. Bulletin, 8. Oslo: Universitetets Etnografiske Museum.

1966 *Models of Social Organization*. Royal Anthropological Institute Occasional Paper, 23. London: Royal Anthropological Institute. (Republished in: Fredrik Barth, *Process and Form in Social Life: Selected Essays*, Vol. 1, London: Routledge & Kegan Paul, 1981.)

1966 [in Robert N. Pehrson's name] *The Social Organization of the Marri Baluch*, compiled and analysed by Fredrik Barth from Pehrson's fieldnotes. Viking Fund Publications in Anthropology, 43. Chicago: Aldine.

1967 *Human Resources: Social and Cultural Features of The Jebel Marra Project Area*. Bergen Occasional Papers in Social Anthropology, 1. Bergen: University of Bergen.

1971 *Socialantropologiska problem*, trans. S. Hedman. Stockholm: Prisma.

1975 *Ritual and Knowledge among the Baktaman of New Guinea*. Oslo: Universitetsforlaget.

1980 *Andres liv – og vårt eget*. Oslo: Gyldendal.

1980 *Sosialantropologien som grunnvitenskap. Grundvidenskaben i dag, 21*. Copenhagen: Folkeuniversitetet.

1981 *Features of Person and Society in Swat: Collected Essays on Pathans, Selected Essays of Fredrik Barth*, Vol. 2. International Library of Anthropology. London: Routledge & Kegan Paul.

1981 *Process and Form in Social Life: Selected Essays of Fredrik Barth*, Vol. 1. International Library of Anthropology. London: Routledge & Kegan Paul.

1983 *Sohar: Culture and Society in an Omani Town.* Baltimore: Johns Hopkins University Press.

1985 [with Miangul Jahanzeb] *The Last Wali of Swat: An Autobiography as Told to Fredrik Barth.* Oslo: Universitetsforlaget.

1987 *Cosmologies in the Making: A Generative Approach to Cultural Variation in Inner New Guinea.* Cambridge Studies in Social Anthropology, 64. Cambridge: Cambridge University Press.

1993 *Balinese Worlds.* Chicago: University of Chicago Press.

1994 *Manifestasjon og prosess*, trans. Theo Barth. Det Blå bibliotek. Oslo: Universitetsforlaget.

2000 [with Tomko Lask] *O guru, o iniciador: e outras variações antropológicas*, trans. J.C. Comerford. Coleção Typographos. Rio de Jainero: Contra Capa.

2005 [with Andre Gingrich, Robert Parkin and Sydel Silverman] *One Discipline, Four Ways: British, German, French, and American Anthropology – the Halle Lectures.* Chicago: University of Chicago Press.

2005 *Vi mennesker: fra en antropologs reiser.* Oslo: Gyldendal.

2008 *Afghanistan og Taliban.* Oslo: Pax.

2011 [with Unni Wikan] *The Situation of Children in Bhutan: An Anthropological Perspective.* Thimphu: Centre for Bhutan Studies

Editor

1963 *The Role of the Entrepreneur in Social Change in Northern Norway*, Årbok for Universitetet i Bergen. Humanistisk Serie, 1963: 3. Bergen: Universitetsforlaget.

1969 *Ethnic Groups and Boundaries: The Social Organization of Culture Difference.* Results of a Symposium Held at the University of Bergen, 23 to 26 February 1967. Bergen: Universitetsforlaget.

1971 *Mennesket som samfunnsborger: en uformell introduksjon til sosialantropologi.* U-bøkene, 175. Bergen: Universitetsforlaget.

1978 *Scale and Social Organization.* Oslo: Universitetsforlaget.

Articles

Book Chapters

1960 'Family Life in a Central Norwegian Mountain Community', in T.D. Eliot and A. Hillman (eds), *Norway's Families: Trends – Problems – Programs.* Philadelphia: University of Pennsylvania Press, pp.81–107.

1960 'The System of Social Stratification in Swat, North Pakistan', in E.R. Leach (ed.), *Aspects of Caste in South India, Ceylon and North-West Pakistan.* Cambridge Papers in Social Anthropology. Cambridge: Cambridge University Press, pp.113–146. (Republished in: Fredrik Barth, *Features of Person and Society in Swat: Selected Essays*, Vol. 2, London: Routledge & Kegan Paul, 1981.)

1963 'Introduction', in Fredrik Barth (ed.), *The Role of the Entrepreneur in Social Change in Northern Norway*. Årbok for Universitetet i Bergen. Humanistisk serie, 1963: 3. Bergen: Universitetsforlaget, pp.5–18.

1964 'Capital, Investment and the Social Structure of a Pastoral Nomad Group in South Persia', in R. Firth and B.S. Yamey (eds), *Capital, Saving and Credit in Peasant Societies: Studies from Asia, Oceania, the Caribbean, and Middle America*. Chicago: Aldine, pp.69–81. (Republished in: Edward E. Leclair and Harold K. Schneider (eds), *Economic Anthropology*, New York: Holt, Rinehart and Winston, 1968; Walter Goldschmidt (ed.), *Exploring the Ways of Mankind: A Text-Casebook*, New York: Holt, Rinehart and Winston, 1971; David H. Spain (ed.), *Human Experience*, Illinois: Dorsey, 1975; Thomas Hylland Eriksen (ed), *Sosialantropologiske grunntekster*, Oslo: Ad Notam Gyldendal, 1996; Stephen Gudeman (ed.), *Economic Anthropology*, Cheltenham: Edward Elgar, 1998.)

1964 'Ethnic Processes on the Pathan Baluch Boundary', in G. Redard (ed.), *Indo-Iranica: mélanges présentés à Georg Morgenstierne à l'occasion de son soixante-dixième anniversaire*. Wiesbaden: Otto Harrassowitz, pp.13–20. (Republished in John J. Gumperz, and Dell Hymes (eds), *Directions in Sociolinguistics: The Ethnography of Communication*, New York: Holt, Rinehart and Winston, 1972, 2nd edn., Oxford: Blackwell, 1986.; Fredrik Barth, *Features of Person and Society in Swat: Selected Essays*, Vol. 2, London: Routledge & Kegan Paul, 1981.)

1967 'Economic Spheres in Darfur', in R. Firth (ed.), *Themes in Economic Anthropology*. ASA Monographs, 6. London: Tavistock, pp.149–174. (Republished in: Fredrik Barth, *Process and Form in Social Life: Selected Essays*, Vol. 1, London: Routledge & Kegan Paul, 1981.)

1968 'Forasien', in George J.N. Nicolaisen and Stephan Kehler (eds), *Verdens folkeslag i vor tid*. Politikens håndbøger. Copenhagen: Politikens Forlag, pp.220–240.

1968 'Ritual Life of the Basseri', in A. Shiloh (ed.), *Peoples and Cultures of the Middle East*. New York: Random House, pp.153–169. (Originally published in: Fredrik Barth, *Nomads of South Persia: The Basseri Tribe of the Khamseh Confederacy*. Oslo: Universitetets Etnografiske Museum, 1961.)

1969 'Introduction', in Fredrik Barth (ed.), *Ethnic Groups and Boundaries: The Social Organization of Culture Difference*. Bergen: Universitetsforlaget, pp.9–38. (Republished in: Fredrik Barth, *Process and Form in Social Life: Selected Essays*, Vol. 1, London: Routledge & Kegan Paul, 1981; Thomas Hylland Eriksen (ed.), *Sosialantropologiske grunntekster*, Oslo: Ad Notam Gyldendal, 1996.)

1969 'Pathan Identity and its Maintenance', in Fredrik Barth (ed.), *Ethnic Groups and Boundaries: The Social Organization of Culture Difference*. Oslo: Universitetsforlaget, pp.117–134. (Republished in: Fredrik Barth, *Features of Person and*

Society in Swat: Selected Essays, Vol. 2, London: Routledge & Kegan Paul, 1981.)

1971 'Forfedrekultus og fruktbarhet: livssynet i en primitiv religion på Ny-Guinea', in Fredrik Barth (ed.), *Mennesket som samfunnsborger*. Bergen: Universitetsforlaget, pp.10–21.

1971 'Minoritetsproblem från socialantropologisk synspunkt', in D. Schwarz (ed.), *Identitet och minoritet*. Stocholm: Almqvist & Wiksell, pp.59–78. (Republished in: Jacques Blum (ed.), *Minoritetsproblemer i Danmark*, Copenhagen: Gyldendal, 1975.)

1971 'Reaching Decisions in a Pastoral Community', in W. Goldschmidt (ed.), *Exploring the Ways of Mankind: A Text-Casebook*, New York: Holt, Rinehart & Winston, pp.451–457. (Originally published in: Fredrik Barth, *Nomads of Southern Persia*, Oslo: Universitetets Etnografiske Museum, 1961; republished in: Walter Goldschmidt (ed.), *Exploring the Ways of Mankind: A Text-Casebook*, 2nd edn, New York: Holt, Rinehart & Winston, 1977.)

1971 'Role Dilemmas and Father–Son Dominance in Middle-Eastern Kinship Systems', in F.L.K. Hsu (ed.), *Kinship and Culture*. Chicago: Aldine, pp.87–95. (Republished in: Fredrik Barth, *Process and Form in Social Life: Selected Essays*, Vol. 1, London: Routledge & Kegan Paul, 1981.)

1973 'Descent and Marriage Reconsidered', in J. Goody (ed.), *The Character of Kinship*. London: Cambridge University Press, pp.3–19. (Republished in Fredrik Barth, *Process and Form in Social Life: Selected Essays*, Vol. 1, London: Routledge & Kegan Paul, 1981.)

1973 'A General Perspective on Nomad–Sedentary Relations in the Middle East', in C. Nelson (ed.), *The Desert and the Sown: Nomads in the Wider Society*. Institute of International Studies Research Series, 21. Berkeley: University of California, pp.11–21. (Republished in: Fredrik Barth, *Process and Form in Social Life: Selected Essays*, Vol. 1, London: Routledge & Kegan Paul, 1981.)

1974 'Forord', in Erving Goffman, *Vårt rollespill til daglig: en studie i hverdagslivets dramatikk*, trans. Karianne Risvik. Oslo: Dreyer, pp.7–8.

1978 'Conclusions: Scale and Social Organization', in Fredrik Barth (ed.), *Scale and Social Organization*. Oslo: Universitetsforlaget, pp.253–273.

1978 'Introduction: Scale and Social Organization', in Fredrik Barth (ed.), *Scale and Social Organization*. Oslo: Universitetsforlaget, pp.9–12.

1978 'Scale and Network in Urban Western Society', in Fredrik Barth (ed.), *Scale and Social Organization*. Oslo: Universitetsforlaget, pp.163–183.

1980 [with Oddny Reitan] 'Baktamin (Faiwolmin) Kinship: A Preliminary Sketch', in E.A. Cook and D. O'Brien (eds), *Blood and Semen: Kinship Systems of Highland New Guinea*. Ann Arbor: University of Michigan Press, pp.283–298.

1980 'Betydningen av transaksjoner som analytiske begrep', in I.L. Høst and C. Wadel (eds), *Fiske og lokalsamfunn: en artikkelsamling*. Tromsø: Universitetsforlaget, pp.26–42. (Originally published as: Fredrik Barth, *Models of Social*

Organization, Chapter 1, London: Royal Anthropological Institute of Great Britain and Ireland, 1966.)

1981   "'Models" Reconsidered', in Fredrick Barth, *Process and Form in Social Life: Selected Essays of Fredrik Barth*, Vol. 1. London: Routledge & Kegan Paul, pp.76–105.

1981   'Swat Pathans Reconsidered', in Fredrik Barth, *Process and Form in Social Life: Selected Essays of Fredrik Barth*, Vol. 1. London: Routledge & Kegan Paul, pp.121–181.

1982   'Ottar Brox som elev i sosialantropologien', in R. Nilsen, E. Reiersen and N. Aarseter (eds), *Folkemakt og regional utvikling: festskrift til Ottar Brox' 50-årsdag*. Oslo: Pax Forlag, pp.23–30.

1987   'Complications of Geography, Ethnology and Tribalism', in B.R. Pridham (ed.), *Oman: Economic, Social, and Strategic Developments*. London: Croom Helm, pp.17–30.

1987   'Cultural Wellsprings of Resistance in Afghanistan', in R. Klass (ed.), *Afghanistan: The Great Game Revisited*. Focus on Issues, 3. New York: Freedom House, pp.187–202.

1987   'Preface', in A. Rao (ed.), *The Other Nomads: Peripatetic Minorities in Cross-cultural Perspective*. Kölner Ethnologische Mitteilungen, 8. Cologne: Böhlau Verlag, pp.vii–xi.

1989   'Om styring ved universitetene', in A. Graue and K. A. Sælen (eds), *Universitet og samfunn: Festskrift til Magne Lerheim på 60-årsdagen den 14. desember 1989*. Bergen: Alma Mater, pp.27–34.

1992   'Towards Greater Naturalism in Conceptualizing Societies', in Adam Kuper (ed.), *Conceptualizing Society*. London: Routledge, pp.17–33.

1993   'Are Values Real? The Enigma of Naturalism in the Anthropological Imputation of Values', in M. Hechter, L. Nadel and R.E. Michod (eds), *Origin of Values*. New York: Aldine de Gruyter, pp.31–46.

1993   'Nature as Object of Sacred Knowledge: The Case of Mountain Ok', in N. Witoszek and E. Gulbrandsen (eds), *Culture and Environment: Interdisciplinary Approaches*. Oslo: SUM, Universitetet i Oslo, pp.19–32.

1994   'Enduring and Emerging Issues in the Analysis of Ethnicity', in C. Govers and H. Vermeulen (eds), *The Anthropology of Ethnicity: Beyond 'Ethnic Groups and Boundaries'*. Amsterdam: Het Spinhuis, pp.11–32.

1994   'Innledning', in Fredrik Barth, *Manifestasjon og prosess*. Oslo: Universitetsforlaget, pp.9–15.

1994   'Nye og evige temaer i studiet av etnisitet', in Fredrik Barth, *Manifestasjon og prosess*. Oslo: Universitetsforlaget, pp.174–192.

1994   'A Personal View of Present Tasks and Priorities in Cultural and Social Anthropology', in R. Borofsky (ed.), *Assessing Cultural Anthropology*. New York: McGraw-Hill, pp.349–360.

1996   'Global Cultural Diversity in a "Full World Economy"', in L. Arizpe (ed.), *Cultural Dimensions of Global Change*. Paris: UNESCO, pp.19–29.

1997   'How is the Self Conceptualized? Variations among Cultures', in U. Neisser and D.A. Jopling (eds), *The Conceptual Self in Context: Culture, Experience, Self-Understanding*. Cambridge: Cambridge University Press, pp.75–91.

1998   [with Unni Wikan] 'The Role of People in Building Peace', in J. Ginat and O. Winckler (eds), *The Jordanian-Palestinian-Israeli Triangle: Smoothing the Way to Peace*. Brighton: Sussex Academic Press, pp.112–118.

1999   'Comparative Methodologies in the Analysis of Anthropological Data', in J. Bowen and R. Peterson (eds), *Critical Comparisons in Politics and Culture*. Cambridge: Cambridge University Press, pp.78–89.

2000   'Boundaries and Connections', in A.P. Cohen (ed.), *Signifying Identities*. London: Routledge, pp.17–36.

2002   'The Changing Structure of Public Opinion in the Middle East', in J. Ginat, E.J. Perkins and E.G. Corr (eds), *Middle East Peace Process: Vision Versus Reality*. Brighton: Sussex Academic Press, pp.51–55.

2002   'Toward a Richer Description and Analysis of Cultural Phenomena', in R.G. Fox and B.J. King (eds), *Anthropology beyond Culture*. Oxford: Berg, pp.23–36.

2003   'Epilogue', in I. Hoëm and S. Roalkvam (eds), *Oceanic Socialities and Cultural Forms: Ethnographies of Experience*. Oxford: Berghahn Books, pp.199–208.

Journal Articles

1947   'Nye muligheter for aldersbestemmelse av arkeologiske funn', *Viking* 11: 267–268.

1948   'Aktuelle antropologiske problem (Omkring American Anthropological Associations årsmøte i Chicago, 27.–31. desember 1946)', *Naturen* 1: 1–9.*

1948   'Cultural Development in Southern South America: Yaghan and Alakaluf versus Ona and Tehuelche', *Acta Americana* 6(3/4): 192–199.

1950   'Ecological Adaption and Cultural Change in Archaeology', *American Antiquity* 15(4): 338–339.

1950   'On the Relationships of Early Primates', *American Journal of Physical Anthropology* 8(2): 128–136. (Republished in: William W. Howells (ed.), *Ideas on Human Evolution*. Cambridge, MA: Harvard University Press, 1962.)

1951   'Førhistoriske datoer: De nye metodene til aldersbestemmelse av oldfunn', *Vi vet. Fra forskningens og vitenskapens verden* 13(1): 385–389.

1952   'A Preliminary Report on Studies of a Kurdish Community', *Sumer: A Journal of Archaeology in Iraq* 8(1): 87–89.

1952   'The Southern Mongoloid Migration', *Man* 52: 5–8.

1952   'The Southern Mongoloid Migration [commentary]', *Man* 52: 96.

1952   'Subsistence and Institutional System in a Norwegian Mountain Valley', *Rural Sociology* 17(1): 28–38.

---

*   This article, signed T.F.W. Barth, jr., was Barth's first, but its publication was delayed.

1954 'Father's Brother's Daughter Marriage in Kurdistan', Southwestern Journal of Anthropology 10(2): 164–171. (Republished in: Louise E. Sweet (ed.), *Peoples and Cultures of the Middle East: An Anthropological Reader*, Vol. 1: *Cultural Depth and Diversity*, New York: Natural History Press, 1970; *Journal of Anthropological Research*, 42(3): 389–396, 1986.)

1955 'The Social Organization of a Pariah Group in Norway', *Norveg* 5: 125–144. (Republished in: Farnham Rehfisch (ed.), *Gypsies, Tinkers and Other Travellers*, London: Academic Press, 1975.)

1956 'Ecological Relationships of Ethnic Groups in Swat, North Pakistan', *American Anthropologist* 58(6): 1079–1089. (Republished in: George A. Theodorsen (ed.), *Studies in Human Ecology*, Evanston, IL: Harper & Row, 1961; Charles C. Hughes (ed.), *Custom-made: Introductory Readings for Cultural Anthropology*, Chicago: Rand McNally, 1976; Robert F. Murphy (ed), *Selected Papers from the American Anthropologist: 1946–1970*, Washington: American Anthropological Association, 1976; Fredrik Barth, *Features of Person and Society in Swat: Selected Essays*, Vol. 2, London: Routledge & Kegan Paul, 1981; Michael Dove and Carol Carpenter (eds), *Environmental Anthropology: A Historical Reader*, Malden, MA: Blackwell, 2008.)

1958 [with George Morgenstierne] 'Vocabularies and Specimens of Some Southeast Dardic Dialects', *Norsk tidsskrift for sprogvidenskap* 18: 118–136.

1959 'The Land Use Pattern of Migratory Tribes of South Persia', *Norsk geografisk tidsskrift/Norwegian Journal of Geography* 17(1–4): 1–11.

1959 'Segmentary Opposition and the Theory of Games: A Study of Pathan Organization', *Journal of the Royal Anthropological Institute* 89(1): 5–21. (Republished in: Fredrik Barth, *Process and Form in Social Life: Selected Essays*, Vol. 1, London: Routledge & Kegan Paul, 1981.)

1964 'Competition and Symbiosis in North East Baluchistan', *Folk* 6(1): 15–22. (Republished in Fredrik Barth, *Process and Form in Social Life: Selected Essays*, Vol. 1, London: Routledge & Kegan Paul, 1981.)

1966 'Anthropological Models and Social Reality: The Second Royal Society Nuffield Lecture', *Proceedings of the Royal Society of London, Series B: Biological Science* 165 (998): 20–34. (Republished in: Fredrik Barth, *Process and Form in Social Life: Selected Essays*, Vol. 1, London: Routledge & Kegan Paul, 1981; Thomas Hylland Eriksen (ed.), *Sosialantropologiske grunntekster*, Oslo: Ad Notam Gyldendal, 1996.)

1967 'Game Theory and Pathan Society', *Man* 2(4): 629.

1967 'On the Study of Social Change', *American Anthropologist* 69 (6): 661–669. (Republished in: Morris Freilich (ed.), *The Meaning of Culture: A Reader in Cultural Anthropology*, Lexington, VA: Xerox College Publishing, 1971; Fredrik Barth, *Process and Form in Social Life: Selected Essays*, Vol. 1, London: Routledge & Kegan Paul, 1981.)

1968 'Forord', *Tidsskrift for samfunnsforskning* 9(2): 85–88.

1968 'Muligheter og begrensninger i anvendelsen av sosialantropologi på utviklingsproblemene', *Tidsskrift for samfunnsforskning* 9(2): 311–325. (Republished in: Vilhelm Aubert (ed.), *Sosiologien i samfunnet*, Oslo: Universitetsforlaget, 1973.)

1971 'Det som aldrig blir sagt och det som kunde ha sagts', *Antropologiska studier* 1: 9–11.

1971 'Tribes and Intertribal Relations in the Fly Headwaters', *Oceania* 41(3): 171–191.

1972 'Analytical Dimensions in the Comparison of Social Organizations', *American Anthropologist* 74(1/2): 207–220. (Republished in: Fredrik Barth, *Process and Form in Social Life: Selected Essays*, Vol. 1, London: Routledge & Kegan Paul, 1981.)

1972 'Et samfunn må forstås ut fra egne forutsetninger: U-landsforskning i sosialantropologisk perspektiv', *Forskningsnytt* 17(4): 7–11.

1972 'Synkron komparasjon: syntese, analyse, komparasjon', *Studier i historisk metode* 6: 19–35.

1974 'On Responsibility and Humanity: Calling a Colleague to Account', *Current Anthropology* 15(1): 99–103.

1975 'Møte med fremmede kulturer', *Over alle grenser (Norges Røde Kors)* 55(9): 10–13, 38.

1976 [with Unni Wikan] 'Cultural Pluralism in Oman', *Journal of Oman Studies* 4.

1976 'Forskning om barn i sosialantropologi', *Forskningsnytt* 21(5): 42–43.

1977 'Comment: On Two Views of the Swat Pushtun by Louis Dumont', *Current Anthropology* 18(3): 516.

1978 'Factors of Production, Economic Circulation, and Inequality in Inner Arabia', *Research in Economic Anthropology* 1: 53–72.

1981 'Hva skal vi med kamera i felten?' *Antropolognytt* 3(3): 51–61.

1983 'Sohar [Letter]', *Times Literary Supplement* 4208: 1321.

1984 'I stedet for myter: sosialantropologiske perspektiver på myter i andre samfunn, og våre alternativer', *Samtiden* 93(5): 2–5.

1984 'Letter to the Editor', *Journal of Peasant Studies* 11(3): 122–123.

1985 'Glimt fra et sosialantropologisk arbeid i Kurdistan', *Kurdistannytt* 1 (1985): 34–36.

1987 'Iran dyrker roser for duftens skyld', *Flyktning* 1: 40–41.

1989 'The Analysis of Culture in Complex Societies', *Ethnos* 54(3/4): 120–142.

1990 'Ethnic Processes on the Pathan–Baluchi Boundary', *Newsletter of Baluchistan Studies* 7: 71–77.

1990 'The Guru and the Conjurer: Transactions in Knowledge and the Shaping of Culture in South-East Asia and Melanesia', *Man* 25(4): 640–653.

1992 'Method in Our Critique of Anthropology', *Man* 27(1): 175–177.

1992 'Objectives and Modalities in South–North University Cooperation', *Forum for Development Studies* 1: 127–133.

1994 'Et flerkulturelt Norge?' *Kirke og kultur* 99(4): 297–302.

1995 'Other Knowledge and Other Ways of Knowing', *Journal of Anthropological Research* 51(1): 65–68.

1996 'Introductory Comment to O. Brox, My Life as an Anthropologist', *Ethnos* 61(1/2): 103–104.

1997 'Economy, Agency and Ordinary Lives', *Social Anthropology* 5(3): 233–242.

1999 'Comparing Lives', *Feminist Economics* 5(2): 95–98.

2000 'Reflections on Theory and Practice in Cultural Anthropology: Excerpts from Three Articles', *Napa Bulletin* 18(1): 147–163.

2001 [with Robert Borofsky, Richard A. Shweder, Lars Rodseth and Nomi Maya Stolzenberg] 'When: A Conversation about Culture', *American Anthropologist* 103(2): 432–446.

2002 'An Anthropology of Knowledge', Sidney W. Mintz Lecture for 2000, *Current Anthropology* 43(1): 1–18.

2007 'Overview: Sixty Years in Anthropology', *Annual Review of Anthropology* 36: 1–16.

Conference Papers, Dissertations, Reports and Working Papers

1957 *Political Organisation of Swat Pathans.* Ph.D. dissertation. Cambridge: University of Cambridge.

1959 'Tribal Structures of Iran', Social Science Seminar Working Paper. Tehran: Faculty of Arts University of Tehran/Paris: UNESCO.

1960 'Nomadism in the Mountain and Plateau Areas of South West Asia', paper read at General Symposium on Arid Zone Problems, Paris, 11–18 May 1960. Paris: UNESCO. (Published as: 'Herdsmen of Southwest Asia', in Peter B. Hammond (ed.), *Cultural and Social Anthropology*, New York: Macmillan, 1964; available online in French as 'Le nomadisme dans les montagnes et sur les hauts plateaux de l'Asie du Sud-Ouest', at: http://unesdoc.unesco.org/Ulis/cgi-bin/ulis.pl?catno=148735&set=4B8F9CF6_1_144&gp=0&lin=1&ll=1.)

1961 'Diffusjon – et tema i studiet av kulturelle prosesser', paper presented at 'Kultur og diffusjon', Nordic Ethnography Meeting, 1960, Oslo. *Bulletin, Universitetets etnografiske museum, 10.* Oslo. (Also published by Institutet för folklivsforskning, Stockholm, 1974.)

1964 'The Fur of Jebel Marra: An Outline of Society Paper'. Khartoum: Department of Anthropology, University of Khartoum.

1964 'The Settlement of Nomads as Development Policy', lecture given at Sudan Society II, Khartoum.

1965 [with Karl Evang] *Innstilling fra Norsk utviklingshjelps familieplanleggingsutvalg.* Report for Norwegian Foreign Aid's Family Planning Committee. Oslo: Utvalget.

1965 'On the Applicability of an Evolutionary Viewpoint to Cultural Change: Some Theoretical Points', unpublished paper presented at the Wenner-Gren

Symposium, 'The Evolutionist Interpretation of Culture', Burg Wartenstein, 15–25 August.

1965   'Utviklingslandene i vår tid', lecture given at the 28th West Norwegian Farmers' Meeting. *Vestlandske bondestemna. Skrift, 55.* Bergen: Vestlandske bondestemna.

1970   'Sociological Aspects of Integrated Surveys for River Basin Development', unpublished presentation to the 4th International Seminar, ITC-UNESCO Centre for Integrated Surveys.

1971   *Organisasjon og ledelse: innstilling fra Organisasjonskomitéen (oppnevnt av Det akademiske kollegium 8. og 15. november 1968).* Bergen: Universitetsforlaget.

1973   *Samfunn og kultur.* Oslo: NRK, Skoleradioen.

1976   'Socio-economic Changes and Social Problems in Pastoral Lands', in *Proceedings of an International Meeting on Ecological Guidelines for the Use of Natural Resources in the Middle East and South West Asia held at Persepolis, Iran 24–30 May 1975.* IUCN Publications New Series, 34. Morges, Switzerland: International Union for Conservation of Nature, pp.74–80.

1982   [with Unni Wikan] 'Cultural Impact of the Ok Tedi Project: Final Report'. Boroko: Institute of Papua New Guinea Studies.

1984   'Problems in Conceptualizing Cultural Pluralism, with Illustrations from Sohar, Oman', in Stuart Plattner and David Maybury-Lewis (eds), *The Prospects for Plural Societies: 1982 Proceedings of the American Ethnological Society.* Washington: American Ethnological Society, pp.77–87.

1985   'Complications of Geography, Ethnology and Tribalism', in *Aspects of Oman.* Exeter: Centre for Arab Gulf Studies, Exeter University, pp.17–30.

1987   'An Evaluation of a Nordic R & D Institute: The Case of the Scandinavian Institute of Asian Studies (CINA)', in Bertil Ståhle (ed.), *Evaluation of Research: Nordic Experiences.* Copenhagen: Nordisk ministerråd, pp.34–42.

1989   [with Unni Wikan] 'Bhutan Report: Results of Fact-finding Mission 1989'. Oslo: UNICEF/University of Oslo.

1989   'Beliefs and Decisions in Health Care', in *Workshop on Religion and Health 2nd–4th Oct. 1989.* Thimpu, Bhutan: Dratsang Lhentshog & Department of Health Services, pp.54–56.

1990   'Innledning. Presentasjon ved Fellesmøte, Det norske vitenskaps-akademi. *Årbok, Det norske vitenskaps-akademi, 1989*, pp.50–54.

1990–1991. 'Social/Cultural Anthropology', *Report of the Wenner-Gren Foundation for Anthropological Research*, 50th Anniversary Issue, pp.62–70.

1991   'Cultural Factors and User Orientation: The Transfer of Sanitation Technology to Bhutan', in *Technology Transfer to Developing Countries: Collection of Articles.* Oslo: Norwegian Research Council for Applied Social Science, pp.91–196.

1994   [with T.R. Williams] 'Initial Resettlement Planning and Activity (1992–1994) in a Large Scale Hydropower Process: The Ertan Dam in Southwest China'. (draft report).

1995 'Ethnicity and the Concept of Culture'. *Program on Nonviolent Sanctions and Cultural Survival Seminar Synopses*. Lecture at the conference 'Rethinking Culture', Harvard, 1995.

2006 'Minnetale over dr. philos Johannes Falkenberg', Holdt i Den historisk-filosofiske klasses møte den 10. februar 2005, *Årbok, Det norske videnskaps-akademi, 2005*, pp.128–131.

Book Reviews

1956 Herold J. Wiens, *China's March toward the Tropics* (Hamden, CT: Shoe Strings Press, 1954), *Man* 56: 13.

1958 Donald N. Wilber (ed.), *Afghanistan* (New Haven: HRAF Press, 1956) and *Annotated Bibliography of Afghanistan* (New Haven: HRAF Press, 1956), *Man* 58: 167–168.

1962 Sol Tax and Charles Callener (eds), *Issues in Evolution* (Chicago: University of Chicago Press, 1960), *American Anthropologist* 64(1): 166–169.

1962 Sachin Roy, *Aspects of Padam-Minyong Culture* (Shillong: North–East Frontier Agen, 1960), *American Anthropologist* 64(6): 1333–1334.

1964 Arnold J. Toynbee, *Between Oxus and Jumna* (London: Oxford University Press, 1961), *Oriens* 17: 246.

1965 A. Reza Arsateh, *Man and Society in Iran* (Leiden: Brill, 1964), *American Anthropologist* 67 (2): 561–562.

1980 Paula G. Rubel and Abraham Rosman (eds), *Your Own Pigs You May Not Eat: A Comparative Study of New Guinea Societies* (Chicago : University of Chicago Press, 1978), *Ethnos* 45(1/2): 114–115.

1990 John G. Kennedy, *The Flower of Paradise: The Institutionalized Use of the Drug Qat in North Yemen* (Dordrecht: Springer, 1987), *American Ethnologist* 17(2): 404–405.

1995 Hildred Geertz, *Images of Power: Balinese Paintings Made for Gregory Bateson and Margaret Mead* (Honolulu: University of Hawaii Press, 1995), *American Anthropologist* 97(4): 806–807.

1996 Emrys L. Peters, *The Bedouin of Cyrenaica: Studies in Personal and Corporate Power* (Cambridge: Cambridge University Press, 1990), *American Ethnologist* 23 (3):651–652.

1998 Richard Tapper, *Frontier Nomads of Iran: A Political and Social History of the Shahsevan* (Cambridge: Cambridge University Press, 1997), *Acta Orientalia* 59: 287–288.

2002 Marianne Gullestad, *Det norske sett med nye øyne: kritisk analyse av norsk innvandringsdebatt* (Oslo: Universitetsforlaget, 2002), *Norsk Antropologisk Tidsskrift* 13(3): 164–168.

2002 [with Pascal Boyer, Michael Houseman, Robert N. McCauley, Brian Malley, Luther H. Martin, Tom Sjoblom and Garry W. Trompf] Harvey Whitehouse,

Arguments and Icons: Divergent Modes of Religiosity (Oxford: Oxford University Press, 2000), *Journal of Ritual Studies* 16(2): 4–59.

2010 James C. Scott, *The Art of Not Being Governed: An Anarchist History of Upland Southeast Asia* (New Haven: Yale University Press, 2009), *Science* 328(5975): 175.

Newspaper Articles

1951 'Tilbake til kulturens kilder: på arkeologisk tokt i Kurdistan', *Verdens Gang*, 5 May, p.9.

1951 'Norsk etnograf i Suleimani', *Verdens Gang*, 14 July, p.9.

1951 'På besøk hos kongen i Kurdistan', *Verdens Gang*, 22 September, p.9.

1954 'Blant guvernører, høyheter og sekkepipere i Pakistan', *Verdens Gang*, 10 April, p.3.

1954 'Uro i Pakistan', *Verdens Gang*, 4 May, p.3.

1954 'Patanen og hvorfor: etnografiske betraktninger om: urene venstrehender – korte skjorteflak – effektive helgener – onde øyne – og slipsets fornedrelse. *Verdens Gang*, 5 July, p.3.

1954 'Skuddene smeller i patanenes land: Pakistanbrev om mord i retten – kvinners klagerop – sosialt tilpasset gråt – hallesbyske prester – og hevneren fra Bombay', *Verdens Gang*, 14 July, p.8.

1954 'Blant bortgjemte folkeslag i verdens høyeste fjell', *Verdens Gang*, 11 September, p.3.

1989 'Låt inte Afghanistan bli ett nytt Libanon', *Dagens Nyheter*, 3 September, p.3.

1993 'Obituary: Roger Keesing', *Anthropology Newsletter*, 34(6): 6.

1998 'Nekrolog: Marie Krekling Johannessen', *Aftenposten*, 7 December, p.11.

2001 'Afghanistan: historien om et hjemsøkt folk', *Aftenposten*, 2 December, p.11.

2001 'Universitetenes første oppgave', *Aftenposten*, 21 April, p.11.

2003 'Katastrofen rammer den siste uberørte øy', *Aftenposten*, 14 January.

2007 [with Petter Bauck, Finn Sjue and Eva Søvre] 'Nekrolog: Pål Hougen', *Aftenposten*, 21 November, p.16.

List of Other References

Ahmed, Akhbar S. (1980) *Millennium and Charisma among Pathans: A Critical Essay in Social Anthropology*. London: Routledge & Kegan Paul.

Anderson, Astrid, and Frøydis Haugane (2012) *Fredrik Barth: A Bibliography*. Oslo: Universitetsbiblioteket.

Anderson, Nels (1923) *The Hobo: The Sociology of the Homeless Man*. Chicago: University of Chicago Press.

Archetti, Eduardo P. (1991) 'Argentinian Tango: Male Sexual Ideology and Morality', in Reidar Grønhaug, Gunnar Haaland and Georg Henriksen (eds), *The Ecology of Choice and Symbol: Essays in Honour of Fredrik Barth*, Bergen: Alma Mater, pp.280–96.

Ardener, Edwin (1989) *The Voice of Prophecy and Other Essays*, ed. Malcolm Chapman. Oxford: Blackwell.

Asad, Talal (1972) 'Market Model, Class Structure and Consent: A Reconsideration of Swat Political Organisation', *Man* 7: 74–94.

Bateson, Gregory (1958 [1936]) *Naven*, rev. edn. Stanford, CA: Stanford University Press.

Bateson, Gregory, and Margaret Mead (1942) *Balinese Character: A Photographic Analysis*. New York: New York Academy of Sciences.

Bateson, Nora (2011) *An Ecology of Mind: A Daughter's Portrait of Gregory Bateson* (film). Bellingham, WA: Bullfrog Films.

Bauman, Zygmunt (1996) 'From Pilgrim to Tourist; or A Short History of Identity', in Stuart Hall and Paul Du Gay (eds), *Questions of Cultural Identity*. London: Sage, pp.18–36.

Blom, Jan-Petter (1969) 'Ethnic and Cultural Differentiation', in Fredrik Barth (ed.), *Ethnic Groups and Boundaries: The Social Organization of Culture Difference*. Oslo: Universitetsforlaget, pp.75–85.

Blom, Jan Petter, and Olaf Smedal (2007) 'En paradoksal antropolog', *Norsk Antropologisk Tidsskrift* 3: 191–206.

Bohannan, Paul (1959) 'The Impact of Money on an African Subsistence Economy', *Journal of Economic History* 19: 491–503.

Bourdieu, Pierre (1993) *The Field of Cultural Production*. Cambridge: Polity Press.

Brox, Ottar (1966) *Hva skjer i Nord-Norge? En studie i norsk utkantpolitikk*. ['What's going on in Northern Norway? A study in Norwegian district politics']. Oslo: Pax.

Brox, Ottar, and Marianne Gullestad, eds. (1989) *På norsk grunn: Sosialantropologiske studier av Norge, nordmenn og det norske* ['On Norwegian turf: Social anthropological studies of Norway, Norwegians and the Norwegian']. Oslo: Ad Notam.

Christie, Nils (1975) *Hvor tett et samfunn?* [How dense a society?']. Oslo: Universitetsforlaget 1975.

Clifford, James, and George Marcus, eds. (1986) *Writing Culture: The Poetics and Politics of Ethnography*. Berkeley: University of California Press.

Cohen, A.P. (1994) *Self Consciousness*. London: Routledge.

Coon, Carleton (1962) 'Review of *Nomads of South Persia*', *American Anthropologist* 64(3): 636–638.

Douglas, Mary (1966) *Purity and Danger: An Analysis of Concepts of Pollution and Taboo*. London: Routledge & Kegan Paul.

Dumont, Louis (1980 [1967]) *Homo Hierarchicus: The Caste System and its Implications*, 2nd edn., trans. Mark Sainsbury, Louis Dumont and Basia Gulati. Chicago: University of Chicago Press.

—— (1967) 'Caste: A Phenomenon of Social Structure or an Aspect of Indian Culture?', in A. de Rueck and J. Knight (eds), *Caste and Race: Comparative Approaches*. London: Churchill, pp.28–38.

Dupree, Louis (1968) 'Review of *The Social Organization of the Marri Baluch*', *American Anthropologist* 70(1): 140–142.

Durkheim, Emile (1984 [1893]) *The Division of Labour in Society*, trans. W.D. Halls. New York: Free Press.

Eidheim, Harald (1969) 'When Ethnic Identity is a Social Stigma', in Fredrik Barth (ed.), *Ethnic Groups and Boundaries: The Social Organization of Culture Difference*. Oslo: Universitetsforlaget, pp.39–57.

Eriksen, Thomas Hylland (2010) *Ethnicity and Nationalism: Anthropological Perspectives*, 3rd edn. London: Pluto.

—— (2013) 'Radcliffe-Brown, A. R.', in R. McGee and R. Warms (eds), *Theory in Social and Cultural Anthropology: An Encyclopedia*. Thousand Oaks, CA: Sage, pp.678–682.

Eriksen, Thomas Hylland, and Finn Sivert Nielsen (2013) *A History of Anthropology*, 2nd edn. London: Pluto.

Evans-Pritchard, E.E. (1940) *The Nuer*. Oxford: Clarendon Press.

—— (1951) *Social Anthropology*. London: Cohen & West.

Falkenberg, Johannes (1948) *Et steinalderfolk i vår tid* ['A Stone Age people in our time']. Oslo: Gyldendal.

—— (1962) *Kin and Totem: Group Relations of Australian Aborigines in the Port Keats District*. Oslo: Oslo University Press.

Firth, Raymond (1951) *Elements of Social Organization*. London: Watts.

Fortes, Meyer, and E.E. Evans-Pritchard, eds. (1940) *African Political Systems*. London: Oxford University Press.

Frazer, James G. (1935) *Totemism and Exogamy: A Treatise on Certain Early Forms of Superstition and Society*, 4 vols. London: Macmillan.

—— (1995 [1922]) *The Golden Bough: A Study in Magic and Religion*, abr. edn. New York: Touchstone.

Fürer-Haimendorf, Christoph von (1952) 'The Southern Mongoloid Migration', *Man* 52(2): 80.

Furnivall, J.H. (1947) *Colonial Policy and Practice: A Comparative Study of Burma and the Netherlands India*. Cambridge: Cambridge University Press.

Geertz, Clifford (1973) 'Religion as a Cultural System', in *The Interpretation of Cultures*. New York: Basic Books, pp.87–125.

Giddens, Anthony (1979) *Central Problems in Social Theory*. London: Macmillan.

Giliomee, Hermann (2003) *The Afrikaners: Biography of a People*. Charlottesville: University of Virginia Press.

Gingrich, Andre (2005) 'The German-speaking Countries', in Fredrik Barth, Andre Gingrich, Robert Parkin and Sydel Silverman, *One Discipline, Four Ways: British, German, French, and American Anthropology*. Chicago: University of Chicago Press, pp.61–156.

Gluckman, Max (1956) *Custom and Conflict in Africa*. Oxford: Blackwell.

Goffman, Erving (1959) *The Presentation of Self in Everyday Life*. Garden City, NY: Doubleday.

Grønhaug, Reidar (1974) *Micro–Macro Relations: Social Organization in Antalya, Southern Turkey*. Occasional Papers in Social Anthropology, 7. Bergen: Institutt for Sosialantropologi.

—— (1975) 'Transaction and Signification: An Analytical Distinction in the Study of Interaction', unpublished mimeograph. Bergen: Institutt for Sosialantropologi.

—— (1978) 'Scale as a Variable in Analysis: Fields in Social Organization in Herat, Northwest Afghanistan', in Fredrik Barth (ed.), *Scale and Social Organization*. Oslo: Universitetsforlaget, pp.78–121.

Grønhaug, Reidar, Gunnar Haaland and Georg Henriksen, eds. (1991) *The Ecology of Choice and Symbol: Essays in Honour of Fredrik Barth*. Bergen: Alma Mater.

Haaland, Gunnar (1969) 'Economic Determinants in Ethnic Processes', in Fredrik Barth (ed.), *Ethnic Groups and Boundaries: The Social Organization of Culture Difference*. Oslo: Universitetsforlaget, pp.58–74.

—— (1991) 'Introduction', in Reidar Grønhaug, Gunnar Haaland and Georg Henriksen (eds), *The Ecology of Choice and Symbol: Essays in Honour of Fredrik Barth*. Bergen: Alma Mater, pp.9–22.

Hann, Chris, and Keith Hart (2011) *Economic Anthropology: History, Ethnography, Critique*. Cambridge: Polity.

Hannerz, Ulf (1980) *Exploring the City: Inquiries toward an Urban Anthropology*. New York: Columbia University Press.

Harris, Marvin (1968) *The Rise of Anthropological Theory: A History of Theories of Culture*. New York: Crowell.

Henriksen, Georg (1974) *Economic Growth and Ecological Balance: Problems of Development in Turkana*. Bergen: Bergen Studies in Social Anthropology.

Hernes, Gudmund (1988) 'Nomade med fotnoter' ['Nomad with footnotes'], *Dagbladet*, 22 December.

Hviding, Edvard (1995) *Barth om Barth* ['Barth on Barth'], unpublished typescript.

Hviding, Edvard, and Harald Tambs-Lych (1996) 'Curiosity and Understanding', *The Norseman* 4/5: 21–28.

Jenkins, Richard (2014 [1996]) *Social Identity*, 4th edn. London: Routledge.

Kapferer, Bruce, ed. (1976) *Transaction and Meaning: Directions in the Anthropology of Exchange and Symbolic Behaviour*. Philadelphia: Institute for the Study of Human Issues.

Klausen, Arne Martin (1968) *Kerala Fishermen and the Indo-Norwegian Pilot Project*. Oslo: Universitetsforlaget.

—— (1970) *Kultur: variasjon og sammenheng* ['Culture: variations and connections']. Oslo: Gyldendal.

Krader, Lawrence (1961) 'Review of *Political Leadership among Swat Pathans*', *American Anthropologist* 63(5): 1122–1123.

Kuper, Adam (1996) *Anthropology and Anthropologists: The Modern British School*, 3rd edn. London: Routledge.

—— (1999) *Culture: The Anthropologist's Account*. Cambridge, MA: Harvard University Press.

Kuper, Adam, ed. (1992) *Conceptualizing Society*. London: Routledge.

Leach, Edmund R. (1951) 'The Structural Implications of Matrilateral Cross-cousin Marriage', *Journal of the Royal Anthropological Institute* 81(1/2): 23–55.

—— (1954) *Political Systems of Highland Burma*. London: Athlone.

—— (1961) *Rethinking Anthropology*. London: Athlone.

—— (1967) 'An Anthropologist's Reflections on a Social Survey', in D.G. Jongmans and Peter Gutkind (eds), *Anthropologists in the Field*. Assen: van Gorcum, pp.194–207.

—— (1976) *Culture and Communication: The Logic by which Symbols Are Connected*. Cambridge: Cambridge University Press.

Lévi-Strauss, Claude (1961 [1955]) *Tristes Tropiques*, trans. John Russell. New York: Criterion.

—— (1966) *The Savage Mind*. London: Weidenfeld & Nicolson.

—— (1969 [1949]) *The Elementary Structures of Kinship*, 2nd edn., trans. James Harle Bell, John Richard von Sturmer and Rodney Needham. London: Eyre & Spottiswoode.

—— (1973 [1955]) *Tropisk elegi*, trans. Alv Alver. Oslo: Gyldendal.

Malinowski, Bronislaw (1967) *A Diary in the Strict Sense of the Term*. London: Routledge & Kegan Paul.

Mauss, Marcel (1954 [1923/4]) *The Gift*, trans. Ian Cunnison. London: Cohen & West.

Mitchell, J. Clyde (1956) *The Kalela Dance*. Rhodes-Livingstone Papers, 27. Manchester: Manchester University Press.

Monsutti, Alessandro, and Boris-Mathieu Pétric (2005) 'Des collines du Kurdistan aux hautes terres de Nouvelle-Guinée: Entretien avec Fredrik Barth', *ethnographiques.org*, 8 November. Retrieved 12 August 2013 from: www.eth-nographiques.org/.

Neumann, Iver B. (1982) 'Antroportrettet: Fredrik Barth' ['The Anthropoportrait: Fredrik Barth'], *Antropress* 4: 5–13.

Næss, Arne (1969) *Hvilken verden er den virkelige? – gir filosofi og kultur svar?* ['Which world is the real one? Do philosophy and culture provide the answer?']. Oslo: Universitetsforlaget.

Neumann, John von, and Oskar Morgenstern (1944) *Theory of Games and Economic Behavior*. Princeton: Princeton University Press.

Østerberg, Dag (1980) *Samfunnsteori og nytteteori* ['Social theory and utility theory']. Oslo: Universitetsforlaget.

Paine, Robert (1974) *Second Thoughts about Barth's Models*. Royal Anthropological Institute Occasional Paper, 32. London: Royal Anthropological Institute.

Pehrson, Robert N. (1966) *The Social Organization of the Marri Baluch*, compiled and analyzed from his notes by Fredrik Barth. Chicago: Aldine.

Peters, Emrys (1991) *The Bedouin of Cyrenaica: Studies in Personal and Corporate Power*, eds. Jack Goody and Emanuel Marx. Cambridge: Cambridge University Press.

Polanyi, Karl (1957 [1944]) *The Great Transformation: The Political and Economic Origins of our Time*. Boston: Beacon Press.

Popper, Karl (1959 [1936]) *The Logic of Scientific Discovery*. London: Hutchinson.

Rappaport, Roy A. (1968) *Pigs for the Ancestors: Ritual in the Ecology of a New Guinea People*. New Haven: Yale University Press.

Revel, Jacques, ed. (1996) *Jeux d'échelles: La micro-analyse à l'expérience*. Paris: Gallimard/Seuil.

Sartre, Jean-Paul (1946) *L'Existentialisme est un humanisme*. Paris: Nagel.

Smith, John Maynard (1982) *Evolution and the Theory of Games*. Cambridge: Cambridge University Press.

Smith, M.G. (1965) *The Plural Society in the British West Indies*. Berkeley: University of California Press.

Sperschneider, Werner (2001) *Fredrik Barth: From Fieldwork to Theory* (film). Göttingen: IWF Wissen und Medien.

Stenning, Derrick J. (1959) *Savannah Nomads: A Study of the Wodaabe Pastoral Fulani of Western Bornu Province, Northern Region, Nigeria*. London: Oxford University Press.

—— (1962) 'Household Viability among the Pastoral Fulani', in Jack Goody (ed.), *The Developmental Cycle of Domestic Groups*. Cambridge: Cambridge University Press, pp.92–119.

Tambiah, Stanley J. (2002) *Edmund Leach: An Anthropological Life*. Cambridge: Cambridge University Press.

Tsing, Anna Lowenhaupt (2012) 'On Nonscalability: The Living World Is Not Amenable to Precision-nested Scales', *Common Knowledge* 10(3): 505–524.

Turnbull, Colin (1973) *The Mountain People*. London: Jonathan Cape.

Turner, Victor W. (1967) *The Forest of Symbols: Aspects of Ndembu Ritual*. Ithaca, NY: Cornell University Press.

Wallace, Anthony F.C. (1961) *Culture and Personality*. New York: Random House.

Weber, Max (1946) 'Science as a Vocation', in *From Max Weber*, eds Hans Gerth and C. Wright Mills. Oxford: Oxford University Press, pp.129–156.

Wikan, Unni (1977) 'Man Becomes Woman: Transsexualism in Oman as a Key to Gender Roles', *Man* 12(2): 304–319.

—— (1980) *Life Among the Poor in Cairo*. London: Tavistock.

—— (1982) *Behind the Veil in Arabia: Women in Oman*. Baltimore: Johns Hopkins University Press.

—— (1990) *Managing Turbulent Hearts: A Balinese Formula for Living*. Chicago: University of Chicago Press.

—— (1996) 'The Nun's Story: Reflections on an Age-Old, Postmodern Dilemma', *American Anthropologist*, 98: 279–89.

—— (2013) *Resonance: Beyond the Words*. Chicago: University of Chicago Press.

Wilson, Bryan, ed. (1970) *Rationality*. Oxford: Blackwell.

Wittfogel, Karl (1959) *Oriental Despotism: A Comparative Study of Total Power*. New Haven: Yale University Press.

Index

Compiled by Sue Carlton